Who Are You People?

Also by Shari Caudron

What Really Happened:
Unexpected Insights From Life's Uncomfortable Moments

Who Are You People?

A Personal Journey Into the Heart of Fanatical Passion in America

SHARI CAUDRON

For Pam —
Fanatically yours,
Shari Caudron

Published by Barricade Books Inc.
185 Bridge Plaza North
Suite 308-A
Fort Lee, NJ 07024

www.barricadebooks.com

ISBN 1-56980-304-8

Library of Congress Cataloging-in-Publication Data
A copy of this title's Library of Congress Cataloging-in-Publication
Data is available upon request from the Library of Congress.

First Printing
Manufactured in Canada

For Angela Ekker

"The formula for complete happiness is to be very busy with the unimportant."

- A. Edward Nelson

Contents

PART ONE : Approach

INTRODUCTION
Topless in the Woods

"I'm the chairman of the bored, I'm a lengthy monologue, I'm livin' like a dog, I'm bored."

—Iggy Pop

WHEN I WAS TWENTY-ONE YEARS OLD I DECIDED TO TAKE up black-and-white photography. I bought a Pentax single-lens reflex, rented darkroom space at the San Francisco Art Institute, and began to take long, watchful walks throughout the city. Pentax in hand, a scowl on my face, I scoured the streets for revealing city images. The crumpled newspaper in a grimy alley. The empty bottle under a park bench.

The weight of the camera felt good in my hands. I was a Photographer. I wore an oversized jacket, green fatigues with lots of pockets, and I smoked.

I was earnest, artistic, and totally consumed by photography.

For about five months.

Two years later, I hooked up with a group of pagan, Mother-Earth, goddess-worshipping feminists. I became a vegetarian. I bought Tarot Cards. I attended week-long festivals in Yosemite National Park with topless "womyn" who chanted, wore crystals, believed in past lives, and ate an alarming amount of tempeh.

As did I.

For about a year.

When my metaphysical musings came to an end, I became—what else?—a runner. I gave up smoking and began to carbo-load. I trained and entered a triathlon. I learned about shin splints, drafting, electrolytes, potassium, runner's high, lactic acid, pronation, and sand-bagging. I was a diligent convert to the world of the fit and entered races at least once a month.

The racing phase easily outdistanced the photography and metaphysical phases.

It lasted two whole years.

Months passed, seasons changed, and so did my roster of activities. For the next several years, I dabbled in backpacking, Buddhism, Scrabble, snowshoeing, bridge, belly dancing, golf, gardening, fencing, piano, and an abundant amount of non-professional, highly unstructured wine tasting. The operative word is dabbled. Through all these years, through all these hobbies, nothing ever took hold and swelled into a grand, all-consuming, get-a-load-of-this obsession. I once started a collection of antique Roseville pottery and actually managed to acquire six pieces before losing half to a lover when our relationship ended. Of the three pieces that remained, one was chipped and worth maybe twelve dollars. See, I was never good at this sort of thing. I got bored easily. Plus, I always thought zealots were a bit strange. I once attended a slide show given by an avid rock collector who described various pieces of her collection as "droolers" and "show-offs." After advancing to a slide of a rock with dazzling purple crystals, the collector slumped back in her chair. The light from the projector cast a warm glow on her thick glasses and curly hair.

"Oooohhh," she said, hand to her heart. "This baby could win a pageant."

Afterward, I invited friends to stone me to death if I ever got like that.

But truth be known, I admired the rock collector. She had something I didn't—passion. A passion so deep she was never at a loss for what to do with her weekends. A passion so consuming, she just *had* to share it with others. A passion so meaningful and enriching, she burned to excite in others her love of droolers, quartz, and feldspar.

Me, all I had were three pieces of chipped pottery and some memories of running topless in the woods with a crystal around my neck.

Given my history, I hadn't the faintest notion what it was like to love a single hobby or activity so much that I would plan all my spare time around it. And once I hit forty, once I was no longer obsessed with finding a job, snaring a mate or buying a house—I'd done all that, sometimes more than once—I began to want more.

I wanted to find something that I wouldn't, *couldn't*, get bored with. I wanted a grand, ferocious, larger-than-life fervor that knew no bounds. I wanted to love diamonds like Elizabeth Taylor or cooking like Julia Child. But I wasn't like these larger-than-life women with their over-the-top interests. I was more like MaryAnn on *Gilligan's Island*. You know. Nice. Temperate. Vanilla.

Because of this, I began to sense that something may have been holding me back. Sure, maybe I hadn't hit on the right activity. Nude volleyball had yet to be tested. But I started thinking there might be more to it. That something *else* had been preventing me from committing myself more thoroughly to an interest. But what? What had been standing in my way? I set out to learn the answer.

I began by asking friends about their deeply held delights.

"What hobbies do you have that you really, really love?" I asked my friend Lezah, who'd previously traveled with me into the worlds of Zen Buddhism and art appreciation.

"Well…I love golf," she said. "And horses. But I'm not

intense about either one. Well, I could be. Maybe not. I'm not sure."

I moved on to Dennis, my best friend since high school. "Dennis, what do you really, really love in life?"

"Duck liver pâté," he said.

Clearly, I needed to broaden my search.

Over the next few weeks, I conducted an informal straw poll among friends and acquaintances asking them what deeply held interests they possessed. Their responses surprised me. Not because they were so varied, but because they weren't. Few of the well-educated, middle-class professionals in my peer group could name a singular, all-consuming interest. With one notable exception—my partner, Angela.

Angela and I had been together ten years at that point, and every day of those ten years her list of interests had remained the same: our dog, other dogs, dog shows, dog books, and the Dallas Cowboys. Oh—and dog sledding. *Especially* dog sledding. She'd read Every Single Book Ever Written about dog sledding across arctic tundra, including one called *My Lead Dog Was a Lesbian,* a title I tried not to take personally. In her own way, Angela was not unlike the rock collector: she knew what she liked, liked what she knew, and felt no need to go searching for other ways to spend time.

But me, I was a searcher. I was searching for some kind of silly, shameless joy, something to give my life color and dimension, something I could go gaga over and not care that people actually used the word gaga when describing me. And based on my research, so were a lot of other people. Although relieved to know I wasn't alone, I was also alarmed. Why didn't more people I know engage their interests so thoroughly?

Years ago, Harvard professor Robert Putnam, in his book *Bowling Alone,* presented an abundance of evidence pointing to the steady decline in civic participation in American life. According to his research, Americans were increasingly less likely to volunteer for the school board, join the Rotary Club, attend church, or otherwise become engaged in civic life. But his book didn't say much about hobby groups. Were I and my lack of passion but small examples of a society that had become completely disinclined to participate in the world around it? Had we become nothing but a nation of glassy-eyed screen-gazers more attached to television and the Internet than we were to our friends, our families, ourselves? Surely, there were other corners of this country where interests bloomed and people shared those interests with one another. But where… and who?

On an overcast fall afternoon, I drove to the University of Denver library, parked myself in the reference area among dozens of students in baggy sweatshirts, and began my search. Problem was, I wasn't sure what I was looking for. A handbook for the habitually bored? A travel guide for trivial pursuits? I searched for several hours without much success.

Then, just when I was ready to call it a day, I overheard a student talking to a friend about his pet ferret. Bleary with research fatigue, I typed the words "ferret" and "Denver" into the search engine and landed on a site promoting the International Ferret Lovers Meetup Day, which was scheduled to take place at a Denver coffeehouse in three weeks. Already there were seven people signed up locally, and more than twelve hundred around the world. What I'd stumbled upon was Meetup.com, a website that helps people with specific interests find one another. This was not an Internet-based chat room. It was a site where people could connect in their own hometowns.

If seven ferret lovers were able to find each other in a metropolitan area with more than three million people, who else might be joining together in pursuit of shared interests? I checked Meetup's lists of topics and learned there were more than twenty-three hundred specific interests posted. There were scheduled meetups for people who loved aviation, beekeeping, cake-decorating, dumpster-diving, Elvis, flashlights, graffiti, juggling, magic, poi, pugs, robotics, roller coasters, scrapbooks, skyscrapers, yo-yos, Ukrainian eggs, and hundreds of other interests. If the list was accurate, not only was community alive and well in America, but so was passion, albeit in some pretty obscure ways. Try though I might, I failed to come up with a single illuminating reason why anyone would want to spend an evening chatting about flashlights.

I left the library and gradually began to notice things I hadn't before. I saw a sign advertising the sale of "collector" hockey pucks. I read an article about a whisker club that was having a beard-growing contest. I saw bumper stickers proclaiming love for all manner of things: bridge, the Denver Broncos, poker, the Denver Broncos, pugs, the Denver Broncos. It was the same feeling I got when I bought a Jeep Cherokee and suddenly realized there were thousands of other Jeep Cherokees on the road. Members of my immediate peer group may not have been able to name a single burning interest, but it seemed that millions of other Americans could.

All of which begged the question: Who were these people and what did they know about ardor and enthusiasm that I didn't?

There was only one way to find out.

Over the next several weeks, I devised a plan to spend time with some of these passionate fanatics. Perhaps they could teach me what they knew about passion and where it came from. Were passions connected to formative experiences? Culture? Class? Education? Were these people like me or different somehow? Maybe, if I could learn the answers to these questions, I might learn the secret to rapt engagement I'd been missing.

Now, I'll be the first to admit this was a peculiar approach to personal growth. People who feel as if they're missing something join churches, or go back to school, or volunteer. They don't get in touch with their inner Trekkie. But that's exactly why this idea was so appealing. Simply put, I'd reached a point in my life where I wanted to know what it would feel like to raise ferrets or collect rocks without a hint of shame or self-consciousness. Not that I would ever *do* these things, of course. But I wanted to know that I could, you know, should the need arise.

Four days after making this decision, I opened the local newspaper and spotted an article about a Barbie Doll convention. I immediately decided to go. Then I immediately changed my mind. I mean, come on. *Barbie?* That grinning she-wolf in designer clothing whose sole purpose was to brainwash girls into believing the only requirements for success were killer clothes, good looks, and appropriate fat distribution? No. Yes. *No!* I waged a little war with myself and ultimately decided that if I was serious about understanding passion, a hotel full of doll collectors was as good a place as any to begin.

CHAPTER ONE
Befriending Barbie

"If Barbie is so popular, why do you have to buy her friends?"
—*Anonymous*

DEBBIE BAKER HAS EXTRAORDINARY FINGERNAILS. THEY'RE long. Very long. And pink. Fantastically pink. So pink that if you weren't completely focused on your conversation with her, you'd be distracted by them. I'm trying not to be. I'm trying to learn why Debbie Baker has more than three thousand Barbie Dolls in her collection.

"So. Tell me," I ask, "What is it about Barbie that makes you so excited?"

Debbie straightens her right arm and gazes at her spread fingernails. "It's because Barbie is so beauuuutiful," she says. "She's hip. She keeps up with the trends. And she can do anything." Debbie falls silent for a moment as she thinks about all Barbie has accomplished. "I mean she can be a veterinarian. A stewardess. A secretary. *Anything.*"

I start to ask about Barbie's other careers, when we're interrupted by a stout older woman with dull gray hair. "I need to put up the decorations for tonight's dinner and I can't get into the ballroom," she says. Debbie tells her to use the same entrance that was used for the fashion show. The woman stares at her, mystified. "I'm with the design company," she says. "I didn't go to the fashion show."

"Oh!" Debbie apologizes. "You looked like a Barbie collector."

The woman widens her eyes and takes a step backward. She looks as if she's just been accused of being a racist or wearing a thong.

"I don't *think* so," she says, and huffs off.

Out of curiosity, I ask Debbie what a Barbie collector looks like.

"Those of us who love Barbie light up whenever we see anything to do with her. We love the dolls. We love the clothes. We love the Barbie 'B.' And pink," she says, waving her lacquered nails. "We really, really love pink."

• • •

Debbie Baker is the co-chair of the National Barbie Doll Collectors Convention being held this weekend in downtown Denver. She tells me that a thousand men and women from all over the world have converged here for four days of doll shopping, workshops, and social events. They range in age from twelve to one ninety-six-year-old woman who is attending the conference with her husband.

"They've come from Iowa in honor of their seventy-fifth wedding anniversary," Debbie explains.

According to people who study this sort of thing, doll collecting—especially Barbies—is second only to stamp collecting as the most popular collecting hobby in America. Debbie is doing her best to help me understand this world.

"There are two kinds of collectors," she explains. First, there are the people like her, who keep their Barbies in the original boxes. To be of any value, the boxes must be clean with no razor cuts or dents. Debbie boasts that all of the 3,000 Barbies arranged around her small apartment are indeed fully boxed. The other group of collectors is known, somewhat disparagingly, as the "de-boxers." These are people who experience no remorse in removing Barbie from her cardboard casing, even though the doll's value drops anywhere from 40 to 80 percent upon exit. Debbie doesn't get these people.

"I can't watch anyone take Barbie out of her box," she says. "It hurts too much."

When pressed, Debbie confesses that when she first started collecting Barbies at age eighteen, she too was indiscriminate in her choice of dolls. In the box, out of the box—it didn't much matter. But she soon realized this lack of discipline would overwhelm her.

"If I bought every doll out there, I'd have no place to store them all," she says.

So Debbie decided early on to pursue only the most perfect and pristine specimens. Today, her collection is so valuable she's had to purchase additional insurance on her home.

"Do you collect anything besides Barbie?" I ask.

"Oh, definitely. I collect, let's see, Depression glass, elephants, butterflies, antiques. Oh, and chickens. I love chickens. My whole kitchen is filled with chickens. My convention co-chair also collects chickens and whenever we buy one for ourselves, we have to buy one for each other."

"I see," I reply, although of course I don't see anything at all. I don't understand chickens. I don't understand Barbies. And while Debbie says she would really like to spend more time with me, she has, you know, a convention to run. She stands and shakes my hand.

"Feel free to walk around," she says. "Barbie people are really friendly."

Debbie leaves and I walk into the convention sales area, which won't open for another fifteen minutes. Behind a pink cord, about 150 people wearing psychedelic clothing are standing in line. The theme of this year's conference is "Rocky Mountain Mod," which commemorates the Barbie era from 1968 to 1972, a time when Barbie wore bell-bottoms, hip-huggers, and hot pants. To get into the spirit, conventioneers were encouraged to don their own mod-era clothing, and every last one of them seems to have complied. The people in line are wearing abstract geometric prints, Afro wigs, and lime-green fringed vests. Two men at the front are wearing matching, striped bell-bottoms, white belts and platform shoes. Any moment now, I expect them to burst into a rendition of "I Got You Babe."

Taking advantage of my privileged position inside the pink cord, I walk around to get a good look at the sales items before the crowd converges. In the sales area, vendors are putting the finishing touches on display booths and tables that are filled to overflowing with clothing, accessories, books, teeny-tiny jewelry, and more dolls than I've ever seen gathered in one place. The array of dolls is truly mind-boggling. There are *I Love Lucy* Barbies, Little Bo Peep Barbies, Erika Kane Barbies, and Olympic Athlete Barbies. There are Barbies equipped for college, Barbies outfitted as medics in Desert Storm, and a presidential candidate Barbie who ran in both the 1992 and 2000 elections on a platform of animal rights, educational excellence, and opportunity for girls. There's even a full military series of Barbies, whose costumes were approved by the Pentagon to ensure realism.

Turning a corner, I spot a boxed doll called the Big Boob Barbie. I stop to stare at it. Her. Whatever. How can there be a doll whose bust is bigger than the original Barbie, whose figure, were she a real woman, would measure 39-18-33? I sidle over to get a good look at Big Boob Barbie. She is lying on the sales table in a tight skirt and see-through blouse and appears identical to the standard-issue Barbie, except that her breasts cover her entire torso and swell out spectacularly on either side of her body. Plus, she has two large brown nipples. Something tells me this may not be an official issue from Mattel.

I stare at the doll with a kind of perverse fascination until Mattel's public relations representative, a thin young woman named Katie Caratelli, calls me from across the room.

"There you are!" she says.

I spin around in an effort to shield the well-endowed source of my enchantment. Either Katie hasn't noticed me staring at the doll or she's too polite to mention it.

Katie grabs my elbow and steers me into an adjoining sales room, stopping along the way to point out the new thirtieth anniversary Malibu Barbie. "This is the official convention doll," she says, pointing to the dime-sized convention logo embroidered onto Malibu Barbie's tiny yellow beach towel. This particular Barbie has a turquoise one-piece bathing suit, surfboard-straight blond hair, and pink sunglasses, just like the original Malibu Barbie of thirty years ago. The only difference between that doll and this one is that this one comes equipped with sunscreen.

"See!" Katie says. "It's SPF 30!"

She picks up the box and holds it toward me with two hands, as if presenting me with a bouquet of long-stemmed red roses. I peer inside.

"Nice," I say, although in reality, I fail to come up with anything that resembles a reaction to the doll. It's the same non-feeling I used to get when conducting séances with my friends as a kid. We'd be huddled in a circle on the floor of my darkened bedroom, holding hands and calling out to Abraham Lincoln or Lizzie Borden or whomever we were fascinated with at the time. After a while, everyone else in the room would claim to feel the cool, breezy presence of spirits. But not me.

Katie puts the doll back on the shelf and we walk over to a large, well-stocked display booth in the center of the sales room. The booth features dolls from a company named Doll Attic, which is owned by Sandi Holder, a middle-aged woman from California with short reddish-brown hair. I chat with Sandi and learn that she started collecting Barbies when her two daughters were little. Her girls are now in high school and her collection has grown from a part-time family hobby into a sixteen-hour-a-day Barbie empire that does close to a million dollars in annual sales. She tells me her favorite Barbies are the Bubble Cuts.

"Which ones are those?" I ask.

Sandi leads me to a display table where rows of boxed dolls are stacked five high and arranged chronologically by year of issue. She tells me the Bubble Cuts were produced between 1961 and 1967 and were so-named because of their lacquered bouffant-style hairdo. Picture Jackie Kennedy with reddish hair and you have some idea what a Bubble Cut is all about. As I admire the doll, my eyes catch sight of a vintage Barbie with a ponytail and black-and-white striped one-piece bathing suit.

Before I can stop myself, I tell Sandi, "That's the one my sisters played with!" Although I didn't play with Barbie, my older sisters had been fans and their old dolls—including the vintage Barbie on display here—were still around the house when I was a kid. Oddly, I find myself a little thrilled to recognize the doll. I confess this to Sandi.

She laughs. "That's what Barbie is all about," she says. "It's about reliving good memories and helping people get back a bit of their childhood." Sandi, who manages one of the largest Barbie auctions in the country, says the value of those childhood memories is going up each year. At her last auction, an in-the-box original Barbie issued in 1959 went for $15,750—a new auction record. The original price was three dollars. "But for me, money is secondary," she says. "What I like is bringing joy to people's lives."

I ask Sandi if she keeps her own dolls in their boxes. "No way!" she says. "It's like really anal to me to keep them in the box. Of course, I respect people who want to do that. I mean, they're my customers. But when I see a Barbie who's been boxed for decades, I feel like she's screaming, '*Take me out! Take me out!*'"

• • •

Sandi turns and introduces me to her assistant, George Marmolejo, a veterinarian from the San Francisco Bay Area who started collecting Barbies in the mid 1980s. He's short, and is wearing a tie-dyed T-shirt and a peace sign around his neck. At last count, George had over one thousand dolls in his collection, both in the box and out. Unlike other collectors, George swings both ways. But his affection is not solely reserved for Barbie. He also collects children's books, old toys, vinyl records, and doll accessories.

"Some people collect fishing lures and duck decoys," he says. "That's not my thing, but I can understand why they do it. I mean I'm here, right?" George spreads his arms and looks around the sales room. "Where else can I be surrounded by a thousand people who understand my passion and don't think I'm nuts when I spend a hundred dollars on doll clothes?"

I look around the room at zillions of dolls on display. Where else indeed?

George walks me through Barbie's various incarnations, while pointing to dolls on the display table. I learn that Barbie #1 had an exotic face with white irises. Barbie #3 was less exotic, smelled like crayons, and had a tendency to fade. Barbie #5 was a redhead with a hollow body.

We come to Sandi's favorite doll and in an effort to showcase my new knowledge, I tell George: "Those are the Bubble Heads, right?"

He corrects me. "They're called Bubble *Cuts*."

George continues his historical tour and I learn about Talker Barbies, the American Girls, Twist 'n' Turns—more commonly known as TNTs, and the Living Barbie, who was entirely posable and had flexible hands.

"Are there any other dolls still on your wish list?" I ask.

"Mostly, I'm satisfied with my collection."

"Really? There's nothing else you want?"

"Well," George admits, "I've been looking for a Glimmer Glamour Barbie, which was a Sears exclusive. She goes for between $1,700 and $1,800."

. . .

The twenty-second Annual National Barbie Doll Collectors Convention is an especially poignant one for collectors, because Ruth Handler, the Polish immigrant who created Barbie, recently passed away at the age of eighty-five. After talking with George, I walk into the center of the convention area and see that a memorial to Handler has been set up on a card table. A vase with pink roses sits next to a journal where conferencegoers can record their thoughts. I scan the entries.

"Without Ruth Handler, all our lives would be emptier."

"Thank you for creating the most beautiful doll in the world that I love so much!"

"I am 4-ever grateful."

Handler created Barbie, who was named after her daughter Barbara, to be a fashion show doll whose outfits could change with the season, and over the years Barbie's kept up her good fashion sense. According to a fact sheet by Mattel, the company Handler founded, Barbie has had more than a billion pairs of shoes. She receives over one hundred additions to her wardrobe annually, including designs by Givenchy, Versace, Vera Wang, and Gucci. Altogether, more than 105 million yards of fabric have gone into producing fashions for Barbie and her friends, making Mattel one of the largest apparel manufacturers in the world.

But to think Barbie is all about clothes would be to sell her short, for she is, in fact, quite accomplished, having dabbled in more than eighty careers over the years. She's also an animal lover who's cared for more than forty-three pets, including twenty-one dogs, fourteen horses, three ponies, a parrot and a panda. The unquenchable thirst for all things Barbie has swelled the Barbie line into a $2.5 billion-a-year industry. If placed head to toe, the number of Barbie Dolls and her family members sold since 1959 would circle the earth more than seven times.

• • •

My understanding of Barbie still far from complete, I drive downtown to subject myself to a second day at Rocky Mountain Mod. Upon arriving at the hotel, I look at the convention program and try to decide what activity to attend. Unfortunately, I've already missed the Shagadelic Catwalk fashion show, and the competition room—where conventioneers have entered treasured pieces of their collections for prizes—won't be open until this afternoon. Reading the program, I learn the rules of the competition are stiff. A doll dressed in "Sparkle Squares," for instance, will not be judged against "Jump into Lace."

Looking at the schedule, I notice that the Fashion Doll Stole Workshop has just started. Deciding it's time for an up-close experience of Barbie, I head to a small windowless conference room and sit down behind a long narrow table covered, naturally, in a pink tablecloth. Around me, about thirty people, mostly women, are hunched over their tables sewing and sticking straight pins into small rounds of fabric. There's a broad range of people here. Two older women in once-a-week beauty-parlor hairdos are reading the directions out loud to one another. A teenager with a black tattoo on her shoulder is breaking a strand of thread in her teeth. Next to me, two women who've just met are swapping stories about their doll clubs back home.

"We made pink, heart-shaped sandwiches at our last meeting."

"How *cute*. I'll have to remember that."

They stitch in silence for a few minutes until one asks, "Is your husband supportive of Barbie?"

"Oh, definitely. I have our club's Christmas party at my house, and he helps me clean and cook and set up tables, and ten minutes before the guests arrive he disappears for the night."

"Sounds like the perfect husband."

As the workshop continues, the participants snip and sew, the room starts to buzz with activity and conversation. In front of me, two women are taking photos of one another holding up their newly made origami stoles. I see smiling teeth and popping flashbulbs and waving Barbies, and for the first time since arriving, I'm feeling left out. Not that I want to sit down and make doll clothes, mind you, but it would be nice to have a hobby where friends are so easily made and smiles so easy to come by.

• • •

After the workshop ends, I ride the hotel escalator upstairs to meet a woman named Judy Stegner, a forty-three-year-old collector and single mother from Fort Worth, Texas. I've been told that Judy is a devoted collector and ardent advocate for all things Barbie. I notice a woman of medium build with straight-cut blond bangs looking around, as if expecting to meet someone. I walk toward her and introduce myself.

"Hi, Shari!" she says, thrusting her hand toward mine. "I'm Judy! It's so nice to meet you! Howsabout we sit right here?"

Judy and I proceed to sit down on a leather bench underneath an enormous stone sculpture of a horse. As we are getting settled, Judy talks nonstop about the convention, and Denver, and the wonderful people she's met in Denver, and the wonderful people she's met at the convention. Her hands and her mouth and her bangs are moving constantly, and her frenetic, fuel-burning activity makes me like her instantly. When at last we are seated across from one another, Judy pushes her glasses, which have slipped down her nose, back into place. She takes a deep breath and begins to tell me, her voice a deep Texas twang, how she met her Barbie friends.

"Well it was Thanksgivin' night in 1998 and my son Justin, who knew I loved Barbie, said to me, 'Mom, there's probably a chat room where you can talk with other Barbie people.' I looked at him like he was crazy. I mean, I didn't know anythin' about the Internet or chat rooms. Justin had to do everything. He found a site, logged me on, even gave me my screen name. I typed in some stupid sentence like, 'Hi! I'm Judy. I collect Barbies and I've never done this before.' I was online that night talking to Barbie people until two in the mornin'." Judy laughs and rolls her eyes, as if she still can't *believe* that she of all people was able to figure out the complexities of online communication.

"But you know," she says, "the Barbie collectors I've met on the Internet are great people. I mean, I never could have made it without 'em."

I put down the bottle of water I've been holding. "What do you mean," I ask, "that you couldn't have made it without them?"

Judy exhales. "Well," she says, "maybe you heard about this. In September 1999, there was a shooting at Wedgwood Baptist Church in Fort Worth in which several kids were killed."

I tell her I vaguely recall a story about a man who entered a church during a youth rally and randomly started shooting.

"That's the one," she says. "He murdered seven people that day, including my son, Justin." Judy's brown eyes grow pink with tears. "He was my only child."

I look at Judy, stunned by this information. The whir of noise and activity around us comes to an abrupt stop. I smell coffee from a nearby coffee cart. I notice the glossy deep-green leaves of a potted plant. Through the window behind Judy, I see silent business people, their bodies bent forward, hurrying to work or meetings or other very important places. How does this woman, how does anybody, go on with the routine of life after something like this?

Judy continues. "Well, my Texas friends gradually dropped out of sight after my son was killed. I mean, I don't blame 'em. They didn't know what to say. This kind of thing is hard for everybody. But my Barbie friends, you wouldn't believe what they did. They called or wrote to me every day. They sent me money. They sent care packages. They helped raise thousands of dollars for a tuition assistance fund in Justin's name. They also contacted Mattel. Can you believe that? They contacted Mattel, and the company sent me a special collectible Barbie and a handwritten note the first Christmas after Justin died. My Barbie friends even had a special Angel Doll made for me." Judy pauses to raise her glasses and wipe away tears. "I'm so blessed. This is the closest circle of friends I've ever had."

I swallow hard in an effort to hold back my own tears. I can't think of a single, comforting thing to say and feel deeply ashamed because of it.

Suddenly, Judy jumps to her feet. "Let me show you somethin'," she says.

I sense Judy Stegner is used to putting other people at ease over her grief. She grabs her convention tote bag, pulls out a quilt, and unfolds it on the cushioned bench in front of us. The quilt, made to honor her son's life, features eighteen hand-sewn panels created by her Internet Barbie friends in California, Texas, Oklahoma, Michigan, Virginia, New York, and Australia. The back of the quilt is covered in a white flannel swath of vintage fabric covered with Barbie silhouettes.

Judy bends over and runs her hand along the soft material. "I can't imagine how much that cost," she says. "That's practically antique." As we stand there, admiring the fabric, two women with convention tote bags walk up to Judy and give her hugs.

"I wondered where you were," one of the women says to Judy. "Are you still meeting us for lunch?"

"Absolutely," she replies. "I'll be there as soon as I can."

The women leave, and Judy returns her attention to the quilt. "You know, I used to have this hanging on a wall but then I thought that's silly. Quilts are meant to be *used*. Now I carry it with me everywhere—even here. At home, I curl up with it while watching television or reading a book. It makes me feel good. Makes me feel closer to Justin."

This finally pushes me over the edge, and my voice breaks. "That is so amazing," I say.

"Isn't it?" Judy asks, smiling. "You know, Barbie people everywhere are really giving. We're involved in lots of charities."

Judy then goes on to detail all the non-profit organizations she's been involved with, including Toys 4 Tots, doll auctions that raise money for children's charities, and an organization called Parents of Murdered Children. "Did you know this convention is also a fundraiser?" she asks. "The beneficiary is Angels Unaware, an organization that provides support for children living with HIV and AIDS. It was started in 1992 by a Barbie collector in Colorado."

"Why do you think Barbie collectors are so giving?" I ask.

"That's easy," she says. "It's because Barbie is about having fun, and when you're having fun you're not stressed and can naturally be more giving. We all have jobs and spouses and kids and things that make life hard. Anything that allows us to play is a good thing, and I don't know why people are so critical of Barbie sometimes. I mean, I can't believe it when people say Barbie is bad for a girl's self-image. That's ridiculous. It's a *doll*. Kids know that. It's adults that make Barbie a problem. In the 1960s, America was barely in space, and there was already an Astronaut Barbie. How can that be bad for kids?"

Feeling sheepish about my own past criticism of Barbie, I say nothing. Instead, I ask whether or not she plays with her dolls.

"It's total therapy for me to play," she says. "After my son died, I could lose myself for hours."

Across the lobby, another conventioneer calls to Judy and asks if she's ready for lunch.

Judy calls over to her. "I'll be there soon!"

I've never wanted to make sure someone meets up with her friends more than I want to make sure that Judy Stegner meets up with hers. I stand to thank Judy for her time, and she grabs my hand and shakes it vigorously, both of her hands encircling one of mine. It's the kind of handshake you might expect from someone who's just met you at the door and discovered she's won the Publishers Clearinghouse Sweepstakes. It's not the handshake of a single mother whose only son was murdered in a church.

I leave Judy and walk back through the lobby to the main convention area. Along the way, I see three women seated at a table talking with similar sweepstakes-like enthusiasm. One of them has a blond Bubble Cut Barbie sticking out of the top of her purse. One of Barbie's arms is raised as if she's eager to answer a question. I look at the doll and its owner with something that feels, oddly enough, like admiration.

• • •

The afternoon workshop on limb reattachment is just starting, and several conventioneers are waiting at the door to see if they'll be admitted despite the fact they failed to pre-register. A young, slim man with dark hair turns to four women nearby.

"Do you think we'll get in?" he asks.

"I hope so," one of the women replies. "I've got two dolls I want to display, but I can't get their legs to stay on."

"That's me too," he says, his eyes silently pleading with the door monitor to take pity.

After an anxious, ten-minute wait, the group is admitted and the workshop begins. There are about thirty-five people here and they're sporting an amazing array of pink. I see pink T-shirts, pink Barbie ball caps, pink hair bands, pink earrings, and pink jeweled pins that spell out the name Barbie in fake gemstones. The attendees have laid out an assortment of naked and limbless Barbies on the pink tablecloths.

An instruction sheet listing a seven-step limb reattachment process is handed out. The first step reads: "Heat limb by dropping it into freshly boiled water for 2-3 minutes." To give people a hands-on reattachment experience, so to speak, there is a portable burner with a pot of boiling water set up at the front of the room. Starting with the first row and working backward, everyone will have a chance to dip their limbs and make their Barbies whole again.

While waiting for her turn, a large woman named Brenda Blanchard from Carson, California, begins speaking to me. Brenda is one of the few black people I've seen in this white-bread Barbie world, and I'm curious how her interest in the doll began.

"I bought my first Barbie, a Holiday Barbie, for my daughter's high school graduation present," she explains.

Brenda speaks wistfully, like a war refugee describing her first taste of ice cream in the free world. "I liked that Holiday Barbie so much I took it back from my daughter. I now have 523 dolls. No, wait! Let's see, I've bought twelve dolls at the conference so far, add that to…" Brenda looks into her forehead and counts silently. "Yep! I've now got 523 dolls."

"Are you an in-the-box collector or a de-boxer?" I ask.

"I do both," she confesses. "I buy duplicates of every doll so that I can play with one."

When I ask Brenda what she likes about Barbie, she has no trouble finding an answer. "I used to be a schoolteacher. I like Barbie because she doesn't talk back." Brenda also grew up in a poor family that couldn't afford toys. "I'm making up for lost time." And like Judy Stegner, one of the things Brenda Blanchard loves most about Barbie is that she can lose herself for hours each night dressing and redressing her dolls. "My kids just moved out, and it gets kinda lonely," she says. "Oh! And one other thing. I like making clothes and creating dioramas that show dolls involved in different events. In fact, I won an award for a diorama earlier today. It was of the Black Panther Party."

Prior to coming to the workshop, I'd stopped in the competition room and noticed Brenda's diorama. It was a small box with an open front, about the size of a toaster oven. Inside was a miniature kitchen, complete with seventies-era macramé curtains and a gold refrigerator. Three black male dolls stood talking to one another, while two black female dolls sat nearby, one trimming the other's hair. There were small, curled hair cuttings on the floor around them. The caption read: "Black Panther Party leaders Eldrige Cleaver, Huey P. Newton and Stokely Carmichael prepare for a rally at Lake Merritt while the girls take a break from cooking to make sure they will look good."

Clearly, Brenda has found a way to creatively transform the white Barbie culture into something more directly meaningful for her own life. Instead of rebelling and rejecting the doll entirely—as I would have done—Brenda has made it her own.

I tell Brenda that I saw the diorama and was impressed by its level of detail. She smiles and drops her eyes.

"Thank you," she says.

• • •

There's no way to neatly categorize Barbie collectors. When I arrived at the convention yesterday, I had narrowly typecast the group as nothing more than middle-aged Midwestern women. Since then, I've talked to a broad range of people, including Jim Faraone, who designs one-of-a-kind fashion dolls and is the author of five books on the topic. Jim grew up in the Bronx and speaks like he's straight off the set of a Mafia movie. "I brought toity-seven dawls wit me," he says.

I've talked to men in flannel shirts who accompanied their wives to the convention and confess that they, too, enjoy the thrill of the hunt.

Since arriving, I've also learned that Barbie collectors tend to speak in exclamation points. I just witnessed a group of women in matching, pink engineer caps approach one of their friends.

"You won!" they squealed.

"*I won?!*" she squealed back.

"Yes! Your Barbie! She won second place!"

Originally, cynically, I attributed the happy glaze on the conventioneers' faces to some mysterious narcotic effect resulting from prolonged exposure to molded plastic. Now I'm smiling like the rest of them. And I'm not entirely sure what this means.

On my way out of the convention, I stop to thank Katie Caratelli, the Mattel representative, for her assistance, and she gives me a thirtieth anniversary Malibu Barbie as a memento. She presents it to me gently, like a missionary presenting a Bible to an aborigine.

I leave, place Malibu Barbie on the passenger seat of my car, and drive toward the exit of the parking garage. The cashier sees the doll riding shotgun.

"Oh! You have a Barbie!" she says, standing on her tiptoes to get a better look at the doll. "Which one is it?"

"It's the new Malibu Barbie," I say. And as I pick up the doll to show her, I'm astonished to find I'm a teensy bit proud of my new acquisition.

"See!" I add. "She even has sunscreen."

• • •

A week later, I'm in the backyard talking with friends about my experience at the Barbie convention. Without stopping to question the wisdom of my actions, I rush upstairs, grab my brand-new, in-the-box, convention-issue Malibu Barbie and return to the table. One friend, a veteran court reporter who's spent years listening to true-life cases of murder, dismemberment, and sexual assault, takes one look at the doll and recoils.

"Get that thing out of here," she says.

It's as if I've just displayed a rusty set of medieval dental pliers and told her to open wide. No amount of talking on my part can convince her that Barbie collectors are indeed a happy, harmless bunch.

"Why do you care so much?" she asks.

Which is an excellent question. Why *do* I care?

I don't like the doll any more than I ever did, and I'm fairly certain I'll never willingly attend another doll convention. But since spending time with the Barbie collectors, I've begun to realize that I'm, well, um, *envious* of the Barbie collectors. I envy their enthusiasm. Their deep connection with one another. Their ability to shriek with delight over a pair of Patio Party earrings just marked down 20 percent. I want what they have, what the rock collector has, what Angela has, and am willing to go to extraordinary lengths to get it. Or at least understand it.

Which is why I've just signed up for an ice-fishing contest.

CHAPTER TWO

Ice Whine

"If today was a fish, I'd throw it back in."

—*Anonymous*

IF YOU'VE NEVER BEEN ICE FISHING BEFORE AND YOU HAPPEN to mention that fact to people in the know, you have to be prepared to accept their advice. Not about lures. Or bait. Or how many layers of clothing to wear. The advice will inevitably revolve around what to drink.

"Budweiser," suggests one friend. "If you're going ice fishing, you're going to have to like Bud. Not just a little, either. You're going to have to like it a lot."

"Peppermint schnapps," instructs another. "That's what we always drank in Minnesota."

In the weeks leading up to my first ice-fishing adventure—the second stop on my passion quest—I'm told to bring tequila, coffee with brandy, a case of Coors, peach schnapps, apple schnapps, blackberry schnapps, Jim Beam, Jack Daniel's and Jägermeister. And Bud. Always Bud. Lots of Bud.

"But I'm going ice fishing," I protest. "Not ice *drinking*."

Then, a week before my first ice-fishing trip, I call Jeff Oliver, the fisherman who has agreed to be my guide during the Three Lakes Ice Fishing Contest in Granby, Colorado. We spend a few minutes talking about our plans for the weekend, and just when I assume the conversation is over, Jeff clears his throat.

"Um, can I ask you a question?" he asks. "You're not offended by a bit of social drinking are you?"

• • •

The Three Lakes Ice Fishing Contest has been one of the most popular winter events in Grand County, Colorado, since 1988. It's advertised as the largest ice-fishing derby west of the Mississippi, although organizers at the Granby Chamber of Commerce confess no one has actually gone to the trouble of verifying this claim. They just figure that when 1,600 people from as far away as Florida plunk down thirty-five dollars each to fish for three days and $50,000 worth of prizes, the competition must be bigger than most.

Margaret Crager, owner of the Budget Tackle Shop, tells me over the phone that her shop's busier during the ice-derby weekend than any other time of the year, including Memorial Day, the Fourth of July, and Labor Day weekend. It's so busy during the ice-fishing contest that she and her husband keep their tackle shop open around the clock.

"It gets real crazy in here around two or three o'clock in the morning when the guys from out of state start rollin' in," she says. "Because we're open, they can get their licenses, register for the contest, pick up bait, set up camp, and be on the ice by 6 a.m. when the contest starts."

I'm not like the guys from out of state. It's the first day of the three-day contest and I'm perfectly content to spend the day getting accustomed to the idea that I will, in fact, be going ice fishing tomorrow. I have to let the idea take hold. This is not the kind of thing someone like me, who thinks Percale sheets are too rough, wants to plunge into. So to speak.

So why go at all? Because I've decided that my sojourn into the world of fanatical passion has to involve activities in which I have no inherent personal interest. Hence, ice fishing—which, to me, looks like nothing more than the temporary refuge of tired men in bitter marriages. Studying people whose interests are far from my own will, I believe, allow me to more clearly see the roots of all passion.

. . .

It's early Friday afternoon, and Angela, who's come along for moral support, and I decide to drive along the lakeshore for a little terrain reconnaissance. One of the reasons the Three Lakes Ice Fishing Contest is so popular is that you can, indeed, fish on one of three lakes, all of which are located in a picturesque mountain valley on the edge of Rocky Mountain National Park. Lake Granby is the largest of the three lakes and from the road its flat frozen surface looks like an enormous white dinner plate. Pine trees crowd the banks to the water's edge. Thin, white clouds ripple across the sky. Any other time I'd really be enjoying this scenery, but at the moment, I'm thinking about all the other things I could be doing this weekend. Like not fishing.

We drive along a high dam road on the eastern shore of the lake. The road is lined with muddy, oversized pickup trucks, many of which have door signs indicating the owner's trade: plumber; electrician; dry-waller; HVAC specialist. The truck beds are filled with all manner of gear, including black rubber boots, empty whisky bottles, and Styrofoam ice chests. The bumper sticker on a red Dodge pickup informs me that it's not how deep you fish, it's how you wiggle your worm. I feel the first throbs of a headache coming on.

We stop the car, and I get out to look down at the groups of fishermen clustered on the flat white ice. I assume they're men, but from this high vantage point, it's hard to tell. The people on the ice seem miniaturized, like tiny fishermen figurines clustered around a mirror on a Christmas mantel display. They stand together in clumps of two or three or four. A few single ones are sitting on overturned buckets and staring into dark round holes in the ice. Their faces are shielded by oversized hoods. Although it's mild for late January—about forty degrees or so—it appears much colder on the lake itself. My throat is starting to feel scratchy. Maybe I *am* coming down with something.

Earlier today, I was worried about having to get up at some godforsaken hour tomorrow in order to be on the ice by daybreak. But looking at the fishermen dotting the ice, I now realize there are more serious issues to contend with. What if the ice breaks? Should I wear blow-up floaties on my upper arms, just in case? Where am I going to pee? What will I think about while on the ice for nine, ten hours? What if it snows? What will I talk to the guys about? I'm not used to guys. What do guys talk about anyway?

On the way back to our rented cabin, we stop at a small gas station/grocery store in a small muddy town called Grand Lake. One side of the crowded three-room store sells liquor, and according to the thin blond clerk it's been busy on that side of the enterprise. "The guys have been coming in here all day and buying twelve-packs of beer and pints of Pucker Schnapps," she says.

The other side of the store sells cellophane-wrapped pastries, motor oil, toilet paper, processed cheese, flashlights, fishing lures, and other small-town emergency provisions. After a bit of searching, I locate a bottle of Vitamin C, because I'm now certain I've got the makings of a thoroughly disabling head cold. I then proceed to select my lunch for tomorrow. I ultimately decide, for no particular reason other than ice fishing seems to provide a good excuse for junk food, to buy a small bag of Fritos, a cheddar cheese stick, Corn Nuts, a can of Red Bull, chocolate-covered espresso beans, apricot jam, extra chunky peanut butter, wheat bread, and a Fuji apple. I resist the urge to buy a hat that boasts, "Women Love Me, Fish Fear Me." But I do buy a fishing license.

• • •

It's six thirty in the morning, and Angela is still sleeping when I back my car out of the snow-packed driveway of the cabin. The first light of day is just starting to drain the blackness from the sky, and my headlights are the only ones on the two-lane high-way leading to Jeff Oliver's house.

Jeff is a forty-five-year-old Denver escapee who works for a homeowner's association, plowing the roads in winter, fixing the pool in summer. But when he's not working, he's fishing.

"I fish pretty much a lot," he told me, "about three hundred days a year."

Jeff's wife, Carol Sue, still lives in Denver, although she's driven up this weekend to participate in the derby. Their relationship pricks holes in my theory that ice fishing is a way to escape bad marriages. For them, fishing is a unifying force.

I pull into the gravel driveway of Jeff's house at 6:45 a.m., and he walks up to greet me. He is tall, with a salt-and-pepper beard, killer smile, and Santa Claus cheeks. He's appealing in that central-casting, mountain-man sort of way. "This is Carol," he says, introducing me to his wife. She's wearing a padded brown hunting jacket and oversized boots. Carol smiles at me and exhales a white plume of cigarette smoke. "And this here's Doug Harris," Jeff says, pointing his upturned thumb toward a large man with white hair, ruddy cheeks, and a canary yellow sweatshirt. "Don't believe anything Doug tells you."

Doug stiffens his neck and looks down at me. "So, you want to learn about ice fishing, huh?" He doesn't wait for an answer. He looks left and then right and then back at me. He lowers his voice.

"Well, you're going with the right guy," he says. "See, Jeff here is the president of the Dickhead Club. He knows the science and secrets of fishing better than anyone around here. He'll be standing there, pullin' out one fish after another, and the guys near him just look at him and say, 'If that dickhead can catch fish, so can we.' Jeff's been called a dickhead so many times by people who can't catch a damn thing that we made him president of his own club." Doug throws his head back and laughs at his story.

"So… if Jeff's a Dickhead," I ask, fully aware that Doug has lured me in and I must now accept the bait, "what are the other guys called?"

"They're the Oh-Shitters."

"The Oh-Shitters?"

"Yeah. That's 'cause every time Jeff pulls out another fish, he can hear the other guys muttering, 'Oh, shit. There he goes again'."

Next to Jeff's house sits a small, two-room log cabin with a hand-carved sign by the front door that reads, "Fish Tremble When They Hear My Name." One by one, Doug, Jeff and Carol Sue enter the cabin through its low-slung doorway and emerge carrying poles, tackle boxes, white buckets, padded seats, and ice chests. They load all of this into the back of Jeff's small blue pickup. When they're fully packed, I add my own contribution: a twelve-pack of Budweiser.

"Cool!" Jeff says. "We'll need that." Encouraged, he pulls a plastic pint bottle of what looks like brandy out of his pocket, takes a swig, and hands it to me. "You ready to get started?" he asks. I look at my watch and politely decline.

Carol Sue and I squeeze into the cramped back seat of the pickup and face each other, knees touching. Doug and Jeff heft themselves into the front seats, and the truck sinks a good six inches. The inside of the cab smells like a neglected tuna sandwich. I feel the return of my scratchy throat.

• • •

When I planned this trip, I assumed, based on everything I'd been told about fanatical ice fishermen, that we'd be on the ice at the crack of dawn. What I didn't realize, however, is that ice fishermen are also tragically, perhaps chemically, inclined to let time drift by. These are not the latte-loving red-light runners I'm used to back in the city. These are people you can rush as easily as a pan of rising bread dough. Ice fishermen are quite simply content to live in the moment, and at this particular moment we are standing outside Beacon's Landing, a small supply store on the edge of Lake Granby. We've been waiting here more than an hour for some friends of Jeff's to show up with the snowmobiles that will take us onto the lake.

I've already had a cup of coffee and allowed myself to be talked into entering the contest. I've learned about the difference between canal poles and lake poles: (canal poles are long; lake poles are short), I've applied Chapstick once, gone to the restroom twice, and now that the sun is up, I'm simultaneously starting to overheat in all my layers of clothing and worry that my socks won't be warm enough once we get onto the frozen lake. Searching for ways to pass the time, I read the list of contest regulations and learn that the first-place winners in each category will be subject to a polygraph test. I point this out to Doug.

"That's cause we're lyin' sons a bitches," he explains. "Some guys'll take a fish and shove lead weights up their aaaaa, um, rectum." Doug stops talking and smiles, plainly tickled by his ability to retrieve such a polite word for ass on such short notice. "You can't trust any one of us, that's for sure."

His comment sparks a spirited debate among several nearby fishermen as to who, exactly, is the biggest bullshitter in the group. It sounds like a conversation that's been underway for years.

At 8:30, the long-awaited snowmobiles finally arrive and we load our gear. I get onto a snowmobile behind Doug, and since I don't think I can get my arms around his canary-colored girth, I grip the handles by my side. The snowmobile roars to life. Doug throttles it, and we careen over the bumpy snow-covered bank toward the lake.

After several minutes, Jeff finds the place he believes will render multitudes of fish. He slows his snowmobile and dismounts before it comes to a complete stop, like he's part of some reality television show where every second counts. He unhooks his gas-powered auger from the sled and grinds several eight-inch diameter holes into various spots on the ice, while gassy fumes cloud around him. He then takes an oversized plastic slotted spoon and removes ice bits from each of the holes.

I walk over to one of the holes, stand about three feet away from its edge, bend at the waist, and peer down trying to gauge the depth of the ice. "So…" I ask. "How thick is the ice cap?"

"It's about fifteen inches," Jeff says. "The Army Corps of Engineers says you can walk on ice that is two inches thick, drive a car on ice that's seven inches thick, and drive a train across ice eleven inches thick."

"Have you ever fallen in?"

"Oh, yeah. Everybody does at some point."

Once the holes have been drilled and cleared of ice, Jeff drops a thin, stiff wire into one of them. The wire is attached to a small computer monitor the size of a paperback book that he sets into the snow next to the hole. Jeff explains the device is called a Hummingbird, which is a gadget that tracks fish by using sonar.

"Isn't that cheating?" I ask.

"Nah. All it tells you is that fish are down there. It doesn't tell you how to make 'em bite."

He turns on the Hummingbird, and it immediately starts to beep, indicating the presence of fish underneath. Dozens of digitized fish travel across the gray-and-black display screen. I stare at the Hummingbird, listen to its insistent beep-beep-beep, and am shocked to find that I am suddenly and quite oddly interested in ice fishing. If the Hummingbird is to be believed, there's a treasure trove of fish down there. It's as if you could plunge your fist through the ice, retrieve your dinner, and be on your merry way in a few brief minutes.

I haul a seat over to one of the holes, while Jeff—bless his heart—baits the hook for me. He puts a pale pink slab of something called sucker meat onto the hook and follows that with a neon orange ball of Power Bait which, according to the label, provides "eye-catching underwater visibility." I sit down in front of the freshly drilled hole with the early morning sunshine in my face. The glare off the white ice is blinding.

"You want the sun in your face as opposed to your back," Jeff says. "If the sun is at your back, you'll shade your hole, and ice will form." I nod. I may be new at this, but I can certainly comprehend the difficulties caused by an icy hole.

I drop my line into the water, and Jeff instructs me in the art of jigging, which is the continual up-and-down come-hither movement necessary to attract fish to the bait. Doug, who's been uncharacteristically quiet for the last ten minutes, pipes up. "You shoulda been out here last year when it was minus twenty-eight degrees with thirty-five-mile-an-hour winds. You didn't have to think about jigging, because your hands were trembling so much from the cold."

"Is that right?" I ask.

"Oh, yeah. Tell her Jeff. Wasn't it cold?"

"It was cold," Jeff agrees. He then reaches into his jacket pocket and retrieves a bottle of Buttershots. "You ready now?" he asks.

Eager to fit in, I grab the cool bottle, tilt back my head, and take a swig of the thick, sweet, butterscotch liqueur. And as I do, I realize it was exactly this same peer-pressure mentality that got me into trouble in high school. Next thing you know, I'll be agreeing to steal some Schlitz Malt Liquor from 7-Eleven just for the fun of it.

• • •

I sit and begin to jig my pole. A few yards away, Doug is sitting on an upturned white bucket looking like every photo of an ice fisherman I've ever seen. He's surrounded by white ice and blue sky, and the only sounds are the intermittent beep-beeps of the Hummingbird, the grind of far-off snowmobiles, and the murmurs of distant conversation. It's ten minutes after nine, and our day of ice fishing has finally begun.

"It should be a good day," Doug calls over to me. When I ask him why, he tells me that fish like change, and there is allegedly a lot of change on tap today. There's a low-pressure front coming in, it's the fourth day after a full moon, and it's fairly warm out. "Fish have less energy when it's colder," he says. Plus, there are a lot of people and snowmobiles on the ice, both of which get the fish excited. "Yep," he says, "should be real good all right."

Just then, the Hummingbird next to me starts to beep. I look down at the screen, and dozens of computerized fish appear. Excited, I start to jig. Slowly at first, as if biding my time for… hell, I'm not sure what. Abandoning a strategy of cool indifference, I begin to jig with more enthusiasm and feel something tug the line. I think. No… maybe not. Yes. *Yes.* Something is down there. The tip of my pole bows toward the ice. The muscles in my arm tighten. Suddenly I'm Hemingway, gritting my teeth, luring the monster beneath the deep with my steady, assured skill. But I say nothing. At least not at first. I pull on the line wanting to make sure I've actually grabbed hold of something. Something alive. Having never ice-fished before, however, I'm not sure what I'm looking for. When the pull on my line becomes even more insistent, I begin to reel it in, and my pole bends like the letter C.

"Um," I call to Jeff. "I think I have something."

He jumps up to help me. "Yell, 'Fish on the Line!'" he says.

"Fish on the line," I mutter, my fists tight on my pole.

"No!" he says. "Really yell it! That way, other people can come see what you've got."

"Fishontheline," I say again, at a level much faster than the first time, but still significantly below a shout.

Jeff yells at me to keep reeling in, and as I do, my chest thump-thumps, the short pole bends in half, and within seconds a flapping, splashing fish appears in the center of the black hole. Jeff reaches in and grabs it. I've been jigging in the sun less than five minutes and I've already caught a fourteen-inch Mackinaw.

He presents the glistening green-brown fish to me with both hands outstretched. It arcs its spine, first to the left and then to the right. "You want to keep it?" he asks. "It's not in the money for the contest, but you can still have it."

"Nah," I say, all cocky-like, as if catching a fourteen-inch Mackinaw is something I've done dozens of times before. "I'll wait to catch a bigger one."

Jeff unhooks the fish, tosses it back into the hole, and re-baits my hook. I settle back onto my seat. Suddenly, it's no longer enough for me to participate in the Three Lakes Ice Fishing Contest. I now want to *win*.

• • •

When I think sports, I think activity. Physical exercise. Power Bars. I don't think billiards. I don't think checkers. And as I sit here in the sun, smelling the faint coconut smell of my SPF 30 sunscreen (Malibu Barbie would be proud), I most definitely don't believe ice fishing qualifies for the designation. Except for the jigging of my wrists—which begs the question: can wrists jig?—I'm scarcely moving. I am, however, listening.

For the last hour, Doug Harris has been unspooling the variegated threads of his life story. I've learned that he's ridden bulls in rodeos, sold advertising for the radio, and once put a Korean tackle company out of business, leaving it with five million dollars worth of unsaleable inventory. Exactly why this happened is unclear, but Doug is exceedingly proud of the accomplishment. Doug also tells me he's a gourmet cook who grows his own herbs.

"There's nothing like fresh basil," he says. "*Nothin'.*"

If Jeff Oliver is the president of the Dickhead Club, Doug Harris is its first lady. He's the one who welcomes guests, puts them at ease with casual conversation, and can, in a pinch, whip up a little lemon-curry trout for supper.

"You know, I was once fishing on a lake in Minnesota with my son," he says.

"Really?"

"Yeah, and my son lost his pole in the water. Well, you won't believe this, but a year later I was back on the same lake. I dropped my line and—wouldn't you know it—I pulled up the *exact* same pole my son lost a year earlier. Even the lure was still attached!" I watch Doug from my seat a few yards away and wonder what his wife is like.

As I ponder this, he jumps to his feet. "Whoa! Whoa!" he says, his pole straining downward. Doug struggles against the tension in his line. His large frame teeters from left to right. The pole continues to bend. Then, almost as quickly as it started, the tension is released. "Shoot!" he says. "Just a snag. But man, what a rush!"

Doug settles back onto his white bucket and begins to tell me about the time he got spinal meningitis from drinking too much blackberry brandy. It's eleven thirty, the sun is high, and I wonder why I'd been worried about making conversation.

Several minutes later two snowmobiles pull up next to us. I recognize the drivers as two of the men who were hanging out by the tackle shop earlier this morning. "You ready to go?" one of them asks. He's wearing mirrored sunglasses, and I can't tell if he's speaking to me or not. I look behind me. I look back to him and point my index finger toward my chest.

"Yes *you*," he says. "Want to meet some other fishermen?"

I'm learning there are two kinds of fishermen in the world: the talkers like Doug who want you to know everything about them, and the non-talkers who assume you already do.

"Well, yeah. I'd love to meet some other people," I say, still not sure what he's getting at.

"Well then, let's go." He points to a dark green snowmobile nearby and motions for me to get on. "You take that one."

For five hours now, I've vacillated inside between two wildly different personality types. When the day began, I wanted to prove to my hosts—and no doubt myself—how self-sufficient I was. I wanted to prove that I could fish, dammit, and do so with-out being a bother. Then came time to bait the hook and retrieve a writhing fish from the line. When presented with smells and goo, my inner femme proved more resolute than my inner butch, and girliness won out. But now I'm being offered my very own snowmobile and butch-girl is startin' to hike up her Levi's and swagger across the ice. How cool is this?! I straddle the black leather seat, pull the starter cord as instructed, and am both thor-oughly thrilled and greatly relieved that the engine catches on the first try.

The three of us head out to the middle of the lake, rolling noisily over the flat ice at a good clip. We pass people barbecu-ing on little grills. Colorful nylon huts whiz by. The sun is shin-ing in our faces. We be bad.

Five minutes later, my two hosts—whose names I still don't know—stop and dismount to chat with a group of fishermen. I follow them, and a short, stout woman in a pink snowsuit waves me over. She's sitting sideways on a snowmobile and holding her rod over the ice.

"Hi," she says, in that friendly, mountain-town way. Her name is Mary, and she's been ice fishing for ten years. Not regu-lar fishing. *Ice* fishing. "It's kinda boring fishing in the summer when it's warm out," she says.

Mary is one of the few women I've seen on the ice, and I ask her how the guys treat her. "The guys don't really mind when yer out here with 'em as long as you don't say 'ew' when you put on bait or take off a hook," she explains. "You can think 'ew' but you can't say 'ew.' Actually, I don't mind being one of the few women. I keep trying to get my single girlfriends to come with me. I mean, the ratio is like, what? Twenty to one? But no, they won't. They think I'm weird. I have gotten my four-year-old granddaughter into ice fishing though. She caught a fish yester-day and named it Jessica."

Mary tells me that the first time she went ice fishing was

with her husband, when they were still dating. "He set up a nylon shelter, put in a propane heater, dug the hole, sat me down in a chair, and handed me a beer. Two years later we got married, and he didn't do that anymore."

I leave Mary staring at the ice and on the way back to my snowmobile, I catch sight of a brown fish lying sideways on a small pile of snow. I assume it's dead until I see it arc its spine and toss a bit of snow from its tail over its head. It's not dead yet, but its Maker is rapidly approaching.

"Ew," I think. But I don't say it.

I follow the two unnamed snowmobilers around the lake, where they introduce me to more of their friends. I meet a family of four that's been entering the Three Lakes contest for years. The thirteen-year-old daughter, her hair in braids, tells me she could have gone snowboarding this weekend, but chose ice fishing instead.

I asked her why.

"Well, it was really hard to pick," she says. "But my dad likes it when I come here." Her father, a burly man with a blond beard, smiles proudly. He turns to me and explains that people of all ages and occupations like ice fishing, even lawyers and CEOs.

"You can always tell the CEO types," he says. "They're the ones with the stuck snowmobiles."

We travel on, and I meet a small, slim man from Denver who drives to the mountains to fish every weekend with his sons. "If I wasn't here, I'd be in Denver-town cleaning up the crab apples in my yard or fixing something around the house," he says. "Why in the hell would I want to do that when I can be here?" He spreads his arms, palms upward, and looks around at the green trees, blue sky, and craggy mountains that surround the lake. "The guys at work think I'm nuts for wanting to come up and stand on ice all weekend, but who cares? They're the ones who're nuts for missing this."

The man's smile is so broad, and he is so genuinely delighted, that I find myself agreeing with him. He's right: who wouldn't want to be here? It's sunny, the air is fresh, and my snowmobile has been starting with just one authoritative pull of the starter cord every time.

. . .

It's 2:04 when I return to my fishing hole. The snow around it has grown slushy in the sun, and according to Doug, the Hummingbird has been silent for hours. I sit down, pick up my pole, and drop my line into the chill water once again. I jig. I look at the other fishermen. I jig again. I contemplate having a beer, then decide against it because I'm still not sure where to pee. I look at my watch. Still 2:04.

Ten minutes pass... then twenty... twenty-five... thirty. I look over at Doug. I look behind me at Jeff and Carol Sue. How come no one else looks bored? All around me people are staring silently at their holes and jigging, up and down, up and down, like battery-operated bears. This is exactly how I imagined ice fishing to be. Quiet. Catatonic. Up until now, I've been riding snowmobiles, visiting with people, sipping Buttershots—in short, doing everything I could *not* to fish. But the time has come. Fish I must. I jig slightly and look down, once again, at my hole.

Fifteen minutes pass.

I once read somewhere that the average American has approximately ten thoughts per second. This particular fact has always caused me to wonder how, exactly, scientists capture such data. Do research subjects make little hatch marks on a piece of paper whenever a new thought comes into their minds? And do they count thinking about the thought as a new thought or merely as an extension of the first one? And what about the need to record the thought on paper? That would surely require some forethought of its own. Does that constitute thought number three or not? And how does the average American's thought count compare to, say, the average European's?

I've been sitting by my hole for an hour without conversation, fish, food, or music to engage me. I haven't had much to think about and I'm worried I may be dragging down the national thought average. Worse yet, the thoughts I do have are starting to turn on me. Two hours ago, I felt happy and expansive and was convinced ice fishermen knew the secret to true contentment. But I now believe I may have given my new ice-fishing friends too much credit.

• • •

Dear God: Thankyou-thankyou-thankyou-thankyou. It's three thirty and Jeff and Carol Sue have decided they've had enough lake fishing for the day. I leap off my chair onto stiff legs. "Really?" I ask. "Do we have to go so *soon*?"

"Yeah," Jeff says. "If we don't get going now we won't have time to get any fishing in on the canal."

"The *canal*?" I ask. My mouth remains open.

"I need to catch my brownie," Carol Sue says. "I think I'll have better luck over there." And then I remember the story she told me this morning. Yesterday, on the first day of the Three Lakes Ice Fishing Contest, Carol Sue caught two of the three kinds of fish eligible for prizes in the tournament. If she can catch a brown trout today, she'll be in the money for the Grand Slam category.

"Okay," I say, zipping up my coat. "Great."

We load our gear onto the sleds, attach them to the snowmobiles, and drive to shore. We then load the sleds into Jeff's pickup and get in. The tuna-sandwich smell has intensified in our absence. Or maybe it's accompanying us. It's hard to tell. We stop at Jeff's house, replace the short lake poles with the much longer canal poles, and jump back into the truck. Within the span of thirty-five minutes tops, we're standing high on the snowy bank of a canal where the water has not frozen over. The canal channels water from Lake Granby into two smaller mountain lakes, through a tunnel underneath Rocky Mountain National Park to a river where it flows down the slopes of the Rockies toward the Great Plains. The water moves at such a continuous pace, it doesn't have time to freeze.

The sky above us has turned gray, and the pine trees are starting to blacken as night looms. The temperature is falling, but Carol Sue is oblivious. She's a retriever searching for a bone, a horse heading for the barn, a woman desperately needing a brown trout. Within minutes, she's fishing.

Jeff hands me a canal pole and I begin, as instructed, to walk slowly along the bank, dragging the clear white fishing line in the water alongside me. A small vee ripples on the water's surface behind the line. Snow crunches under my boots. I hear the gentle lapping of water along the bank.

The four of us—Doug, Carol Sue, Jeff and me—as well as four or five other people, are marching, single-file, along the bank with our poles. When the person at the head of the line reaches a certain point, he or she reels in the fishing line, turns around and walks back to the place where we began. One by one, we reach the end of the line, turn, and start over. A casual observer might think we're Tibetan monks on a walking meditation. Or demented, which is what I'm beginning to think. Twice when I go to cast, my line tangles in the bushes behind me. Three times, my bait flings off to points unknown.

"You know, experienced fishermen can tell whether they've got a carp or a salmon or a trout on the line, just by the way the fish fights," Doug says.

"Really?" I ask, untangling my hook from a set of particularly vicious branches. "Can they also tell different types of shrubbery?" Actually, I don't say this, but I do think about it.

The sky has gone from gray to blue-black, and the temperature, once refreshing and minty, is now bone-chilling. It can't be more than fifteen degrees. Warm, to most ice fishermen. Cold to me. While untangling my line, I prick an exposed finger on my hook and decide I've had enough. I set my pole on the ground, and after a few minutes Doug and Jeff join me. They, too, are over it. But on the bank on the opposite side of the canal, Carol Sue is still marching back and forth, back and forth, in her effort to catch a brown trout. We can barely see her face.

While watching her, I recall an article I'd read in a magazine about inner-tube fishing, in which fishermen use specially designed inner tubes with insulated legs to cast all day on a lake without ever having to touch dry land.

"Have you guys every tried that?" I ask Jeff and Doug.

They look at each and then back at me.

"No way!" Doug says. "Those guys are *nuts*."

A young man named Matt walks up to join us. Matt is holding a can of Busch beer, his third in the last forty-five minutes. He's also smoking a Winston Gold. He nods his head in Carol Sue's direction. "If she don't get her fish," he says to us, "you guys are fucked."

"No shit," Doug replies. He turns and looks at me. "You got room for two more people at your cabin? If Suzi don't get her fish, we don't want to be sleeping under the same roof with her."

Jeff shakes his head and says nothing to defend his wife.

We watch in silence for several long minutes as Carol Sue strides along the bank. Matt cracks open another beer. "Yep," he says. "You're gonna be fucked all right."

Unbelievably, another half-hour passes. It's now officially night, and all color has disappeared from the landscape. I look toward the water and notice a small red light has appeared. It's about the size of a frog's eye and is bouncing on top of the current.

"What's that?" I ask.

"A lighted bobber," Jeff says. "So you can see your line when it gets dark."

Matt's right. We are fucked. Carol Sue continues to march. The bobber continues to bob. Matt smokes.

Jeff tries, gently, to coax his wife out of her frenzy. When she doesn't respond, he addresses her again with a little more force. "Come on, Carol," he says. "We need to get moving." I feel a sudden swell of affection for this fine man.

"I wouldn't risk it if I was you," Matt says, exhaling.

Doug laughs. "Yeah, Jeff. You know how she gets."

But Jeff is kind and persistent and he eventually manages to convince his wife that it's okay to stop fishing for the day because she still has until noon tomorrow to catch her brown trout and qualify for the Grand Slam.

"Okay," she calls from across the canal. "But we have to get out here by 5:30 or 6:00."

• • •

I walk into the cabin where Angela has a hot yellow fire crackling in the wood stove. The cabin's windows have steamed over, and inside it smells like marinara sauce and spicy Italian sausage. I can't imagine stumbling upon a more appealing setting after the hard white ice of the day.

Angela smiles and begins to walk toward me extending a newly poured glass of red wine. But as she gets closer, the smile on her face starts to diminish, and I wonder if she's got some bad news to share. Some bad news that the wine will help with. She's been by herself in a snowbound cabin all day and normally that's something she'd like, given its environmental reminders of arctic dog sledding and all that. But the closer she gets, the more disturbed she looks.

When she reaches me, still standing by the door trying to peel off layers of clothing, she is practically grimacing. She hands me the glass of wine without offering any sort of welcome hug.

I look at her, perplexed.

"You stink," she says.

• • •

The next morning I wake at 9:25, thankful—deeply, deeply thankful—that I haven't been standing alongside an ice-cold canal for three hours already. Last night, Jeff had invited me along for the day, but I assured him that between the lake and the canal, I had indeed gotten a comprehensive view of winter fishing.

I walk into the living room of the small cabin, sit on one of the green-and-white gingham easy chairs, and try to understand the attraction to this sport. Yesterday, when I asked people why they fished, they told me about the rush that comes from hooking a ten- or twenty-inch trout and reeling it in for dinner. I, too, had experienced that rush, but it wasn't significant enough to lure me back out onto the frozen lake. Other people shared fond childhood memories of fishing with uncles and grandpas and dads. But people do a lot of things with uncles and grandpas and dads. Why does ice fishing stick for some and not others? Intriguingly, many more of the people I talked to hadn't the vaguest idea why they liked the sport.

"That a real good question," Doug said. "If you find out, let me know so I can tell my wife."

I settle back into the chair, take a sip of my coffee, and notice through the window a sheet of ice about three feet long hanging off the edge of the metal roof. It is approximately twelve feet across, a rigid ice skirt just waiting for a slight increase in temperature to loosen its grip and slide onto the forest floor. I decide to sit on one of the green-and-white gingham easy chairs and wait for the ice to fall.

The hours I spent fishing yesterday must have given me a new appreciation for the slower things in life. Things without any immediate satisfaction or reward. Things like watching ice melt. I wrap my hands around my warm coffee mug, stare at the sheet of ice, and wonder who I'm trying to kid.

• • •

The Three Lakes Ice Fishing Contest officially ends at noon, and at 12:30 I drive toward the weigh-in station to see if Doug and Jeff and Carol Sue—*especially* Carol Sue—have placed in any of the money categories. The sky is overcast and the air pressure is falling, as a long-awaited cold front from Canada descends on the Rocky Mountains. I drive past Lake Granby and look at the ice. Without the fishermen in their colorful parkas, it looks gray and lonely.

Since Jeff's cabin is just off the highway, I stop by. Carol Sue is the only one home. She's smiling and freshly blow-dried and... did I say *smiling?* As focused and intense and competitive as Carol Sue was last night, I'm surprised by how utterly joyful she appears today. The news must be good.

"Did you get your brownie?" I ask.

"Naaaah," she says, laughing. *Laughing?* "It wasn't meant to be this year."

"Is that okay?"

"Of course. I had a wonderful time. I love the derby."

This puzzles me. So, it's not about catching a fish, it's about *trying* to catch a fish? I have so much to learn.

"If you hurry," Carol Sue adds, "you can probably catch Jeff and Doug at the weigh-in station."

I find them standing amid a bevy of tired men in padded jackets, tractor hats, and several days' worth of stubble. The men are watching, intently, as the judges record the final weights in each category on a white board. The men remind me of Depression-era day laborers waiting to see who might get a job for a few hours.

Jeff and Doug walk up to me, and I find I'm inexplicably glad to see them. I didn't like their sport, but they were so gracious and accommodating that I realize I've grown fond of them.

"Well?" I ask.

"Nothin'," Doug says. "We didn't win a thing."

"Contests are tough," Jeff adds. "There's too many people on the ice. You should come out with me next weekend when nobody's around. Then you can see what real ice fishing is like."

"You're going back out *next* weekend?"

"Of course. I'll probably go out several times before then." Jeff smiles at me in a way that lets me know he knows his obsession is a little over the top—but that he wouldn't have it any other way.

I smile back at him. "No thanks."

"You sure you don't want to come?"

"I'm sure," I say.

"Well," he says, "if you ever change your mind, you know where to find me."

As he and Jeff walk me toward the car, I think about his offer, and how I'd like to take him up on it—really, I would—but I've gone ice fishing now and I can't conjure up a single good reason why I'd ever need to go again.

And this worries me because I'm now no closer to understanding passion—mine or anybody else's—than I ever was.

CHAPTER THREE
Birds of a Feather

"Boys will be boys and so will a lot of middle-aged men."
—Kin Hubbard

HERE'S THE PROBLEM AS I NOW SEE IT. ICE FISHING AND Barbie collecting are too white, too mainstream—in short, too much like me—for me to clearly see why they attract such rabid followers. To gain any hope of understanding fanatical passion in America, I will have to get out and experience more of America.

But truth be known, I'm hesitant. It's tense and uncomfortable being the gaping outsider, and if I fully commit to this quest, I'll be committing myself to outsiderness for a long time. I'll be signing up only to stand out and I don't know if I'm ready for that. It would be so much easier to call this off. To stay at home with my comfortable, well-worn set of friends who laugh at the same jokes I do. But then again, where would that get me? Giving up would only reinforce the fact that I tend to, well, give up. A lot. And isn't that what set me down this path to begin with? If I'm serious about uncovering my own brand of passion, I have to continue.

I decide that New York City, the subculture capital of the United States, will be my next stop primarily because I have a meeting scheduled there in a couple of weeks, and that, if nothing else, will provide an impetus to continue.

I scan the Internet looking for New York-based groups that catch my interest and am instantly overwhelmed with choices. I learn about hamster lovers, kazoo bands, checker players, and taphophiles, who are people with a passion for prowling through cemeteries. I read about soap opera fan clubs where loyalists get together and talk about *The Guiding Light*, *The Bold and the Beautiful*, and *Port Charles*, which has broken new ground in the world of daytime drama by introducing several vampire characters. Reading the daily episode synopses, I come across this entry: "Lucy convinces Ian that being a vampire isn't always a curse. Ian makes peace with the fact that he is a vampire and he and Lucy make love."

I continue to search and find people who study Jewish mysticism, revere Bob Marley, dabble in amateur astrology, and collect paper airsickness bags from airplanes. I contact one of the airsickness bag collectors by e-mail. He responds immediately with an offer to haul two Rubbermaid tubs full of airsickness bags from Boston to my New York hotel room. The bags are flat and stack easily, he writes, "except for the SickJon and Space Shuttle bags."

Now, being a journalist, I have grown quite accustomed to meeting with strange people in strange places. But here's some advice: When an airsickness bag collector offers to bring his airsickness bag collection to your hotel room, and when this offer involves driving between two major urban centers in the middle of the day, and when this offer comes within seconds—*seconds*—of you making nothing more than a casual inquiry about his airsickness bag collection, let's just say you should resist the temptation.

Continuing my search, I come across an article in the *New York Times* about a man named Frank Viola who's considered one of the best pigeon racers—or "birdmen" —in greater New York. I'm intrigued, for I've never heard of pigeon racing or met a birdman before. I arrange to pay Frank a visit.

Two weeks later, on an icy-cold February afternoon, I board a crowded subway car in Manhattan, squeeze into a seat between two teenagers in overstuffed jackets, and settle back for the ride into Brooklyn where Frank Viola lives. I gaze around at battered briefcases, frayed pant cuffs, an orange shopping bag, a dirty pair of white moon boots, and at the snag in the gray nylon stocking of the woman sitting across the aisle. I overhear music through the headphones worn by the boy next to me. Occasionally, though not very often, I catch the eye of a fellow rider. This is the delight of travel in New York City—to be wedged kneecap to shoulder among other human beings and still feel thoroughly alone.

During the ride, I wonder what attracts New Yorkers to pigeon racing. I grew up in San Francisco, have lived in Colorado most of my adult life, and have never come across birdmen in either of those regions. Granted, I wasn't exactly looking for them. But after reading the article on Frank Viola, I did some additional research and learned that New York is home to many pigeon clubs. I called several of them, and everyone I spoke with agreed: Frank Viola was the pigeon man's pigeon man.

The subway ride takes forty-five minutes, and the car stops several times along the way. People disembark at each stop, so that by the time I reach Frank's station, one stop short of Coney Island, the car is almost empty. I leave the subway platform and walk three blocks past small, nondescript apartment buildings and single-family homes to Frank's one-room basement apartment. I walk down a few grimy concrete stairs to the front door. Though the temperature outside is not above freezing, the door is wide open, and Frank calls me in. I walk inside, and my senses shift into overdrive.

Frank's apartment smells like decades of fried onions, and the ceiling is so low you can touch it with your fingertips. Every surface in the small room is heaped with a tumultuous array of clutter, including newspapers, canned goods, plastic sacks, remote controls, duct tape, envelopes, and plastic pill containers. A calico cat is sauntering through the chaos on the kitchen table. Beneath the cat, a dog of indeterminate lineage is engaged in a vigorous round of sniffing. The visual display is overwhelming, but so is the heat. It can't be more than thirty degrees outside, but it's approaching an equatorial ninety in here. Plus, Frank's television is broadcasting the five o'clock news at decibel levels high enough to reach yachts off the shore of Coney Island.

Frank is sitting behind a long oak table hooked to a silver cylinder of oxygen. Across from him sits his nephew, Peter Viola, a portly middle-aged man with thinning white hair.

"Hold on a minute," Frank says, as he searches for the off button on the television remote control.

Frank Viola is eighty-three years old and he's been racing pigeons ever since he could walk. Frank no longer has any discernable teeth, he requires round-the-clock supplemental oxygen, and you have to yell "FRANK! FRANK!" really loud to get his attention. Despite these infirmities, he still manages to maintain a loft of one hundred birds and plan one of the largest pigeon races in the country: The Frank Viola Invitational, a four-hundred-mile race between Ohio and Brooklyn that awards fifty thousand dollars to the fastest bird. In 2001, Frank's own bird, Mr. Viola, won the race against fourteen hundred feathered contenders. When he learned he'd won, he jumped to his feet, something that's no longer easy for him to do, and shouted, "Hoo! Hoo! Hoo!" It's this kind of rapture that keeps Frank going.

As his nephew Peter explains, "Most guys his age are meetin' their Maker, but not Frankie. Pigeons keep his mind sharp."

Frank finds the remote control, and the room falls strangely silent.

"That's right!" Frank agrees, shouting as if the television were still on. He adjusts the clear plastic oxygen tubes under his nose. "Pigeons also keep me away from women!"

Prior to coming here, I'd read that pigeon racing is not especially popular in America. Best-guess estimates put the number of flyers—as racers are known in pigeon parlance—at a scant 15,000. But what the sport lacks in numbers, it makes up for in devotion. Spend any time talking with flyers and you quickly learn that breeding, training, and racing pigeons is not a sport that participants choose so much as succumb to. A guy might, for the heck of it, get a pair of breeders from a friend and before he knows what's hit him, he's building a coop on the roof, spending hundreds of dollars a month on food and medication, and planning his entire social calendar around big-money races. Many flyers, by their own admission, would miss their own wedding for a good race. But *why?*

I clear off an oak chair in Frank's apartment and sit down to find out. "So tell me, Frank," I begin, "is pigeon racing becoming more popular these days?"

"What?" he responds, his smooth white hand cupping his left ear.

"PIGEONS, FRANKIE!" his nephew shouts. "SHE WANTS TO KNOW HOW POPULAR PIGEONS ARE."

"Ohhhh," Frank replies, with dawning awareness. "Pigeons fly *very* far."

"NO, FRANKIE! SHE DOESN'T WANT TO KNOW IF THEY FLY *FAR*, SHE WANTS TO KNOW IF THEY ARE *POPULAR*."

"Popular?" Frank asks, his face clouding in confusion. "No… I don't think I'm popular." Frank's mind may well be sharp, but his lack of hearing prevents me from witnessing it firsthand.

I try again. I ask Frank how much money he's won over the years and learn that, yes, he was indeed paid well during his fifty-year career as a construction worker. "I helped build the Twin Towers," he explains.

For half an hour, our conversation limps along in this fashion. I ask Frank a question in a normal tone of voice. Peter repeats it at a shout. Frank answers with some unrelated bit of trivia about the Knights of Columbus or spaghetti, and eventually we wind our way toward the correct answer. Our progress is hobbled and slow, but at least we're moving forward. I then make the mistake of asking Peter how the birds are timed during the races. Peter smiles at me and smoothes down the front of his blue-checked flannel shirt.

"That would be with this here Benzing Clock," he says. "It's made special for pigeon races."

Hoisting a brown metal box the size of a lunch pail onto the table, Peter begins to explain in precise detail the mechanical workings of the Benzing Clock. He lifts the clock's lid and fingers its brass components. He talks about calibration, timing, and how the clock's resilient tamper-proof design makes cheating virtually impossible. He removes nuts, spools, and rivets, and lines them up on the table. He speaks about lead seals and serial numbers and evidence tape. And as he speaks, I feel the electrical synapses in my brain begin to lose their charge until, after a time, I can no longer hear what Peter is saying. I become fascinated by his mouth, which simply keeps moving. And moving. It's as if he's been called to testify in front of a Congressional committee about why Benzing Clocks should be the official time-keeping machines of the American people. Never in the history of clocks and man has one man so loved one clock. By the time Peter finishes his dissertation, I cannot think of a single question worthy enough to follow such an impressive display. I stand, thank Peter and Frank for their time, and back my way out of the small hot apartment into the cold Brooklyn night.

• • •

As animals go, homing pigeons—which are the kind of birds racers use—*are* fairly remarkable. Take a pigeon two or two hundred miles from its home and it will almost always find its way back. Scientists who study such things believe the homing instinct is due to a combination of physical factors that allow birds to gain a sense of direction using the sun, stars, and the earth's magnetic field. Although they are not sure how these mechanisms work, scientists know from experiments that iron deposits in the birds' inner ears allow them to detect the earth's magnetic lines of force and this, in turn, directs them, much the way a compass guides backpackers.

In 2001, researchers in Japan released thirty-one pigeons from a field seventeen kilometers from Hiroshima. Nine of the birds had undergone surgery to interrupt the activity between the inner ear and the brain. All of the normal birds returned to their nests in Hiroshima within thirty minutes. Of the remaining nine, one returned to its nest three hours later; the others never did.

Human beings have long recognized and taken advantage of this unique talent. Egyptians used pigeons to carry mail three thousand years ago. Greeks used them during the first Olympic games to carry news of winning athletes to outlying villages. More recently, pigeons proved their mettle during World War II, when they were called upon to deliver vital intelligence after electronic communication failed. One of the most famous wartime pigeons was G.I. Joe. In 1943, this exemplary bird flew twenty miles in twenty minutes with a message that saved at least one hundred American soldiers from being accidentally bombed by the British. For his efforts, G.I. Joe was awarded the Dickin Medal of Valor, an award created by an Englishwoman to honor the gallantry and devotion of animals during the war. Of the fifty-three Dickin medals awarded, eighteen were presented to dogs, three to horses, and one to a cat—which is another story. But almost two-thirds of the medals, a whopping thirty-one, were awarded to brave battlefield pigeons.

Given the sport's distinguished history, I am determined to learn more about it.

• • •

The next day, I get off the subway at Park Chester in the Bronx and unfold the slip of paper on which I've scribbled the address of the Bronx Pigeon Club. Founded in 1955, with a current membership of thirty-five flyers, it is one of the oldest and largest pigeon clubs in Greater New York. If anyone can clue me in on the flyers' obsession, it will be these guys. I walk under the grimy metal subway bridge toward the address on White Plains Road.

White Plains Road is a busy, two-lane example of what not to do in urban planning. Brick, single-family homes squat next to blockish multi-story apartment buildings amid a dizzying array of retail establishments. In one three-block stretch I can bowl, play billiards, do my laundry, complete my taxes, buy love-birds or a couch, and choose from a multitude of salons in which to get professional African hair braids. Should I become hungry, I can indulge in Chinese take-out, goat curry, fish 'n' chips, fresh Ethiopian vegetables, a glazed donut, or a cold Coors—all of which suggests this is exactly the kind of place where you'd expect to find a pigeon club.

As clubs go, the Bronx Pigeon Club might be considered one of the nation's most prestigious, for it actually owns its club-house. It's a white, narrow, three-story apartment building that's easily identified by the pigeon coop on the garage in back. Members meet in a first-floor room that is accessed through a side door. I was told that on any given day of the week I'd find flyers here, mostly around lunchtime, which is when I arrive.

I stand outside the brown door and look at the address on my paper. I *am* at the right place, although there is no sign adver-tising this as the club's headquarters. It's as if I've stumbled upon a little boys' secret hideout. I turn the doorknob and enter a room that looks like the employee lunchroom at an auto repair shop.

Six men are sitting around a large white Formica table, and several jump to their feet when I enter. I'd planned to meet a man named Joe Musto—known in pigeon circles as the *Great*

Musto—but he hasn't arrived yet. Nor, apparently, has he alert-ed the others I was coming. They scramble to tidy up the place.

"Reno! Where are your manners? Get her some coffee."

"Vinny! You! Clean up the table."

"Sorry, ma'am. We wasn't expectin' ya. Like cream?"

"Here, have a seat."

"Oh. Sorry. We don't have cream."

"Here, talk to Kenneth."

"Will white powder do?"

Kenneth Tucker, a sixty-seven-year-old black man with kind eyes, takes pity on me and asks me to sit down.

"Tell me what this is going to enhance," he says.

I start to tell him that I'm here to enhance my knowledge of pigeon racing, but before I can get too far, I'm interrupted by someone behind me. I turn around.

"You don't listen to nothin' Tucker tells you," he says.

"You hush up," Kenneth replies. "You're just jealous."

"Jealous… yea. You wish."

The two continue their verbal ping pong, and I look around for a life vest. It comes in the form of a slim young man wearing a gray sweatshirt and green knit cap.

"Reno Truglio," he says, extending his hand toward me. "So, you want to know about the birds?"

Yes, I tell him. I'm here to learn about pigeon racing.

"Oh, it's the greatest sport on earth," Reno says. "The ab-so-lute greatest." Although Reno's relatively new to racing and is—at thirty-two—one of the youngest members of the club, he feels as if this is something he's been doing forever.

"You know how it is when you start doin' somethin' and it feels so good and so right that you know it's somethin' you could do everyday for the rest of your life?"

Well, no, I want to tell him. I don't know what that feels like, and that's exactly why I'm here. But before I get a chance to say this, the clubhouse door swings open, and a blast of cold air rushes in. Turning toward the door, I see a large man with dark hair, olive skin, and oversized gold-wire glasses walk into the room. He looks to be in his late fifties.

"Joe!" Reno shouts. He turns to me. "This here's the Great Musto. He's your man."

Joe ambles toward the table, nodding along the way at the other racers in the room.

"Hiya, Joe."

"Hey."

"Hey."

"How ya doin'?"

Joe walks around the end of the table to the seat directly across from me, where Reno is sitting. He waves his hand in front of Reno's face. Reno gets up and moves to another seat.

Joe takes the now-empty chair, sits down, and pulls a long brown cigarette out of a red package. He lights it, inhales, and then exhales slowly.

"Joe Musto," he says. "Pleased to meetcha."

Reno interjects. "Joe," he says, "I was just telling her about the birds and how..."

The Great Musto raises his hand, and Reno stops speaking.

"She's *come*... to *talk*... to *me*," Musto says.

"Yeah," Reno says, "I know. But I was just telling her that..."

Joe's hand goes up once again. Smoke trails from his cigarette. This time Reno sits back in his chair. At the end of the table, I see Kenneth Tucker roll his eyes. It seems that the older members of the club are not as inclined to give the Great Musto the deference he seeks. And when I start to ask Joe about the particulars of racing, all the present-and-accounted-for members of the Bronx Pigeon Club start talking at once.

My goal in coming here had been to get a calm, linear, Discovery Channel explanation about pigeon racing. But I immediately sense there's nothing calm or linear about this group. Members of the Bronx Pigeon Club argue repeatedly, prefacing each new quarrel with the phrase, "You don't know nothin'," as in, "You don't know nothin' and you're too stupid to even know that." They tell snickering side stories about Crazy Al and Cosmo and someone named Eddie Cowboy, who thinks he knows everything even though he ain't never won a major race. They express concern for my well-being.

"Joe!" they say, when the Great Musto lights his third long, brown cigarette in ten minutes." You're gonna give her *cancer*!"

Members of the Bronx Pigeon Club sit close and show me race charts. They stand and point to newspaper clippings. And they rearrange their seats with noisy, disorienting frequency. One minute I'm sitting next to Reno, the next, Cecil Coston, Jr., a young, newly retired police officer. If anyone starts to monopolize my time or attention, the Great Musto interjects and shoos them away.

"I said... she's here... to talk... to *me*."

Picture a group of pigeons flocking over a tossed breadcrumb and you have some idea how I feel. In a word: pecked.

• • •

As you might expect if you thought about this kind of thing at all, once telecommunications and long-distance mail service came into use, pigeons were no longer needed for their delivery services, and people began to race them for sport. Today, there are millions of flyers all over the world, with Taiwan and South Africa being among the most zealous bird-racing countries. In Taiwan alone, winning birds can earn up to two million dollars per race. But in the world of pigeon racing, no country comes close to Belgium in terms of sheer devotion to the sport.

"Nine out of ten houses there have pigeon lofts," Joe says, shaking his head as if he cannot *believe* how far American civilization has fallen behind the rest of the world.

To understand the particulars of pigeon racing, you must

first understand that every flyer maintains his own coop of birds, called a loft. All breeding, feeding, tending, and mending of the birds occurs in these lofts, which are generally built on rooftops to make it easier for the birds to find their way home. During the races, all birds are trucked to a common starting point, released—or "liberated"—and clocked on the journey back to their lofts.

Although the Benzing Clock that Frank Viola's nephew tried—and failed—to explain to me yesterday is still used by some clubs, the more advanced racing organizations use electronic scanners, much like those used by grocery stores, to time the birds. The scanners are placed at the coop's entrance, and when the birds fly in, the scanner's timer is activated by little electronic tags around the bird's legs.

Now, just so you know in case it ever comes up at a cocktail party, pigeons are timed based on yards-per-minute flown, and the average pigeon flies fifty miles an hour. Furthermore, because the birds fly back to their own coops, the location of the loft is very important in terms of speed advantage. Kenneth Tucker, for one, chose his house because it sat in the middle of the prevailing westerly wind flow, making it easier for his birds to sail home.

"You mean you bought your house so your birds could win more races?" I ask.

"Yep," Kenneth says, leaning back in his chair and clasping his hands behind his head.

"What did your wife say about that?"

"She didn't have nothing to say about it. I came home and told her I'd found us a new place to live."

Once a flyer has a loft, they begin to breed pairs of birds in order to create that year's racing team. Like owners of thoroughbred racehorses, flyers strive to breed speed into their birds by pairing homers with proven track records. A bird's pedigree is extremely important, and serious flyers have been known to pay thousands of dollars for a pair of birds with an award-winning lineage. The Great Musto once paid sixteen hundred dollars for a pigeon.

"Was it worth it?" I ask.

"Naah," he says.

Three weeks after breeding, the eggs hatch, and the baby pigeons grow rapidly. At three months of age, training begins. At first, the young birds are taken just outside their lofts and allowed to fly back in. Then they are driven a mile away. Then five miles. Then twenty miles. Day-by-day, flyers gradually increase the distance between the loft and the liberation point, so that birds can develop strength and endurance. Flyers typically lose a lot of birds during the early training period. They run into wires, get eaten by larger predators, or simply lose their way. Joe started the last racing season with one hundred and thirty-two birds and ended with thirty-six. Reno started with eighty-two and ended with eleven. They shrug as they cite these statistics.

"It's all part of the game," Reno says.

Just for kicks, let's say you decided to take up pigeon racing in your spare time. If you were a serious flyer, you'd pay serious attention to your birds' health during the training period. You'd clean the loft twice a day. You'd follow a steady regimen of vitamins and vaccinations. And if you didn't feel good about giving your birds synthetic supplements, you'd give them Echinacea, brewer's yeast, and something called pigeon tea, a loving home-brew of honey, garlic, and herbs.

You'd learn how to evaluate a pigeon's eye, including the size of the pupil, the pigment of the iris, and the eye's overall expression. Why? Because these things can tell you about the bird's nervous system, will power, and ability to win races. As experienced flyers know, an increased pupil means a decreased ability to finish long races.

If you were serious about winning races, you'd also learn

how to motivate your birds to win. You'd learn about something called widowhood flying, which is when you keep your cocks and hens separated until ten minutes before the birds are shipped off to a race. You'd put them together for several minutes, allowing them to get frisky and reacquainted. Then, just when they're ready to descend into connubial bliss, you'd remove the cock and ship him off to the starting point, where he'd be fueled to return by a frenzied desire for his mate.

Another motivational technique involves taking a young mother hen off a pair of eggs that are hatching, shipping her off to a race, and leaving the eggs behind.

Think it's cruel?

"Fuggedaboutit," Joe says. "Pigeons can be lazy. You gotta give 'em an incentive."

As the members of the Bronx Pigeon Club share these facts with me, I notice that one member has not said anything. He's sitting across the table, a slight man with a square face and square black glasses. Joe notices me eyeing him.

"He's someone you ought to talk to," Joe says. "He's one of the best flyers in the group."

I ask the quiet man what makes a good flyer, and he turns away from me and shields his face with his hands. I look at Joe.

"He's just shy," Joe says.

"That's not it," the man says, mumbling from behind his hand. "I don't want my name appearing in no book or magazine, 'cause I don't want my wife to find me." The other flyers nod. They too, apparently, have experienced their fair share of wife evasion.

So I ask members of the Bronx Pigeon Club what their wives think of their hobby, and for the first time in two hours, none of them has a thing to say. The room is silent except for the sound of a soap opera that's playing on a television mounted high in the corner. On it, someone named Bianca is talking to someone named Maggie about redefining their relationship.

"Well?" I prod. "What do your wives think of your hobby?"

They continue to look at one another.

Finally, Reno speaks up. "You ought to ask Joe about women and pigeons."

"Yeah," Cecil agrees. "The Great Musto'll tell you about women."

I look at Joe, who's surrounded by a white cloud of smoke.

"Let me put it this way," he says. "My first two wives all told me, 'It's me or the boids,' so I said good-bye." Joe waggles his two forefingers in a bye-bye motion. "So far, my current wife hasn't been so dumb. What you might say is that women and pigeons don't get along too good."

• • •

Okay. I'm starting to get the how of pigeon racing, but I'm still not getting the why. According to pigeon literature, people as diverse as Mike Tyson, Queen Elizabeth, Yul Brynner, Terry Bradshaw, Paul Newman, and Joanne Woodward have all raced pigeons at one time or another. Even Pablo Picasso was infatuated with the birds, naming his daughter Paloma—which is Spanish for pigeon—after them. But what is the attraction?

It can't be the money. Few guys ever win the big purses, and the birds are so expensive to maintain that the hobby is almost always a financially losing proposition.

It can't be the thrill of watching a race. Unlike other racing events, flyers can't even see their athletes perform.

I look around the table. "So why do you guys love this so much?" I ask.

"Let me put it this way," Reno says. "There ain't nothing that compares to that feeling you get when you see your bird drop outta nowhere. It's like no other feeling in the world."

The others nod, with silent reverence.

But even this is not without its stressors, because when race day dawns, the birds are hundreds of miles away, and flyers have nothing to do but wait for their return. And waiting, they say, can be excruciating. To pass the time, Kenneth paces. Cecil cleans. And Joe smokes. Several packs' worth. And he refuses to talk to anyone on the telephone. You want to get ahold of the Great Musto on race day? You get a walkie-talkie, 'cause there ain't no way he's coming off the roof to get no damn phone.

For Kenneth, one of the biggest draws of pigeon racing is the sense of community. "When I was in my twenties, I wanted nothin' more than to retire and hang out at the club every day." Which he now does, unless he has a doctor's appointment or must drive his wife to the mall. Looking around at the dark room with its cluttered counters and burnt-coffee smell, I have to wonder why no one suggested Florida as a possible retirement alternative.

Kenneth must sense my disbelief. "See, whatever you're doing, there's somebody here that knows something about it," he says. "If you need tires for your truck or a new TV, someone here always knows where the bargains are. A lot of us old guys are on medication now, so we spend a lot of time talking about that. We compare what we're on and the dosage and what the side effects are. And, yeah, we talk about pigeons. Of course. We always talk about pigeons."

So maybe it's the birds themselves. Maybe these guys love them like pets. I have trouble visualizing myself reading a book with a pigeon cooing in my lap, but who am I? Perhaps I'll understand all this a bit more if I can see the little winged athletes for myself. I tell the guys I'd like to go inside the loft.

"Great!" Cecil says, standing up to put on his coat. "I'll take you up."

I put on my coat and follow Cecil out the back door of the clubhouse and up a set of rickety wooden stairs to the roof of the garage. An icy wind whips through me, and I can hear the faint roar of traffic on the Bronx Expressway two blocks away. Spread above us are the bare winter branches of several large trees.

I pull my coat closer, step onto the flat tar paper roof, and walk behind Cecil toward a one-story plywood structure. Cecil opens the back door, and we step into a small walkway that separates two coops. The right coop, he tells me, holds the breeding pairs; the left coop holds birds that will start racing in April. Both coops are the size of walk-in closets and feature a series of wooden cubbyholes like those found in kindergarten classrooms. Inside the cubbyholes sit the birds.

I look at the birds who've been roused by Cecil's presence. There are brown and gray and white and blue pigeons, and though I'm impressed by the wide color variety, they are still, well, pigeons. To my untrained eye, these birds don't look any different from those I saw in Central Park yesterday.

The birds hear Cecil's voice and they begin to coo and flap their wings and fly from one cubbyhole to another. We step inside the breeding coop, and I feel breezy air currents generated by their wings. Cecil, who has a broad smile and a chipped front tooth, is happy to see his brood. Me, all I see is pigeon poop. Everywhere.

Cecil empties a can of grain into a long narrow wooden trough in the middle of the floor. He tosses the grain like he's emptying a bucket of water into the street. The birds flock to the floor and line up along both sides of the trough. They seem almost mannerly—and I have to admit the one with the little brown speckles is kind of cute. As pigeons go.

"What's his name?" I ask Cecil.

"He don't have a name," he says. "Birds don't get names until they win a race. Then they deserve it."

I continue to look at the birds on the cold roof of the garage and wonder about the attraction to them. Why is it that some people really, really like pigeons, and others really, really like dolls? I've long had this theory that God put people on earth with the exact combination of skills necessary for society to function. Some people are born carpenters. Others are drawn to farming or entertainment or law. The abilities needed for society to function effectively are somehow part of our gene pool and, even more remarkably, they are part of the gene pool in the appropriate percentages. We seem to have just enough accountants and translators. Just enough pastors and musicians. The upshot is that I understand how skills and interests can differ when we're talking about productive work, because I think it's part of some greater plan. But what kind of planning is involved when we're talking about hobbies. When we're talking about *pigeons*?

I look up and catch Cecil nuzzling the head of a grayish pigeon with the point of his chin.

"This here's Miss Grace," he says.

The pigeon, whose head is slowly becoming trapped between Cecil's neck and chin, looks sheepishly at the other pigeons in the coop. It's as if she's checking to make sure they haven't noticed her being embraced by this human, and if they have, she'd like them to know it wasn't her idea. I feel for Miss Grace. I used to get the same feeling while shopping at the mall with my mother.

Cecil continues to nuzzle Miss Grace, and I look away to allow him a moment of privacy.

No, even after seeing the pigeons up close, I don't understand the attraction to them. But I'm not sure it matters. In the middle of this busy, depressed New York borough, where people have little in common besides a shared zip code, pigeon racing is the thing that brings a select group of black, brown, white, young and old people together. It's not church. Or a bar. Or the neighborhood school. It's a pigeon club, and the members come here every day of the week even though racing season only takes place twice a year. If pigeons can foster that kind of acceptance and community, who am I to argue?

I leave the loft and make my way back down to the clubhouse, where the members of the Bronx Pigeon Club are leaning back in their chairs and looking at me, eyebrows raised. It's the same look I saw on the faces of the Barbie collectors and ice fishermen. It's a hopeful look, the look of people who want nothing more than to share their joy with others.

"Well?" they ask. "Whaddya think?"

I look at the guys around the table and, without thinking much about it, I tell them I want to come back during the fall racing season, sit on a roof, and wait for the birds to cross the finish line.

"Oh, you're gonna love it," Reno says. "There ain't no feeling like it."

• • •

On the rocking subway ride back to Manhattan, I think about the pigeon racers and the community they've formed. Most of the guys I spoke with work in blue-collar jobs. They're mechanics and pipe fitters and plumbers whose day-to-day lives don't seem to provide much in the way of control or career accomplishment. Pigeon racing, by comparison, provides an opportunity for them to routinely make key decisions about breeding, training, feeding, and health care. Best I can tell, having a loft of pigeons is like being the franchise owner of a team wherein you get to play all the parts: owner, coach, trainer, doctor, cook, cheerleader, statistician, and fan. Pigeon racing may be the poor man's route to team ownership. And why not? When their birds win, it is through their own diligent efforts.

Thinking about this, I wonder if people choose interests based on how much those interests can provide opportunities for self-expression they wouldn't otherwise have. Perhaps passions allow people to utilize drives and skills and talents that lie untapped. And yet… I don't think bird racing or ice fishing or doll collecting are solely about filling the gaps in one's life. They're also, in a weird way, about faith. The faith that it's okay to believe in something without hedging. The faith that simple pleasures by themselves are worth pursuing. The faith that leads people to connect with fellow believers in a supportive community.

I step off the subway at Grand Central Station and stop to wonder what kind of subtle brainwashing has occurred to cause me to make the leap from pigeon racing to faith.

Even more disturbing, I realize I've just publicly committed to attending a pigeon race.

CHAPTER FOUR

Meeting Up

"When they are alone they want to be with others and when they are with others they want to be alone... human beings are like that."
—Gertrude Stein

HERE'S A FACT APROPOS OF NOTHING IN PARTICULAR: ON any given day of the week you're likely to find more than 1,100 pigeons bobbing their way through Central Park.

Why should you care? Well, I'm not sure you should. But this is what happens after you spend time with pigeon racers. One day, you're going about your daily humdrum, happily oblivious to the world around you. The next, you start noticing pigeons *everywhere*. You spot cute little blue and brown and gray and white ones. And before you realize what's happening, you're talking to the Audubon Society about the technical name for park pigeons (Rock Doves), inquiring as to whether the population is growing or shrinking (hard to say), and questioning if park birds have the same homing instinct as the pigeons racers use (they do, but they haven't been bred to take advantage of it). Then you start bombarding friends with inconsequential pigeon facts. They stop accepting your invitations for coffee, and you begin to experience for yourself the lonely isolation that results from having an obsession that other people find insane.

No wonder the communities that grow up around bird racing or doll collecting are so strong. No one else can stand them.

Except, that is, for me.

Make of that what you will, but I'm starting to sense there's more to this than I originally anticipated. It's a phenomenon I sum up with this equation: passion + people = community.

Get people together around a common interest. Allow them to talk about that interest without fear of ridicule, and something transcendent occurs. The interest expands. Relationships deepen. And soon you've got a nurturing community wherein people are making quilts to help each other survive hard times.

Almost two hundred years ago, Alexis de Tocqueville wrote in *Democracy in America* that America was a nation of joiners. Whereas the English and Europeans allowed communities to form naturally around village and neighborhood lines, de Tocqueville observed that Americans seemed far more willing to create ad hoc communities around shared interests—or, what he called, "the smallest undertakings."

When you look at the breadth of America's subcultural landscape, it's clear this tendency to join together still holds true. In fact, some academics believe the desire for community is why America is the most religious country of all the industrialized nations. God is important, sure, but so are the bake sales, charity drives, and gift exchanges that come from church participation.

Dr. Steven Gelber, a leisure historian and professor at the University of California at Santa Clara, put it to me this way: "You can have a strong attachment to God or you can have a strong attachment to alpacas. From a community perspective, they are one and the same—except that you can see alpacas."

I'm not sure I'd go that far, but his point is well taken: Community is something Americans seem to yearn for, and they embrace it in myriad ways. Which of course makes me think of the pigeon racers, because that's what I'm thinking about these days. The flyers I met with get together every single weekday, even though they race the birds just a few times each year. This tells me it's not about the birds—or at least not entirely. It's about some personal, communal, relationship need that sitting together in a shabby clubhouse seems to fulfill.

I think back to *Bowling Alone* and Robert Putnam's conclusion that traditional communities are dying because of our commuter lifestyle, because of television and computers, and because young people aren't attracted to the same organizations their parents were. And yet these fanatical outcroppings seem to be thriving. I wonder: Is our all-American yen for community intact, but just being expressed differently? How prevalent are these obsessive subcultures anyway?

Seeking an answer, I contact the Roper Center, a public opinion research organization that has tracked the participation of Americans in social and community groups for decades, and was one of the prime sources of data Putnam relied on in *Bowling Alone*. I want to know if they track such things as doll groups or pigeon clubs. I send them a lengthy e-mail explaining my project. They respond with a brief note.

Sorry, it says. We don't track that.

Okay.

Fine.

The Roper people may not know much about passionate fanatics, but I'll bet Scott Heiferman does. Scott is the CEO and founder of Meetup.com, the website I'd stumbled upon in the University of Denver library. His site, created in 2002, helps people with similar interests—regardless of what those interests might be—find one another.

Back in Manhattan, I decide to pay Scott a visit.

• • •

Meetup's headquarters are located in a nondescript office building on Broadway north of Houston Street. On one side of the building, there's a hip Urban Outfitters clothing store; the other, a Duane Reade Pharmacy; across the street, a Stereo Exchange Electronics—all of which put Meetup squarely on the hypotenuse of a contemporary urban triangle of sex, drugs, and rock 'n' roll. This is indicative of something, although what, I'm not sure.

I walk past a uniformed doorman into a small elevator and push the button for the tenth floor. On the slow ride up, I envision Meetup's offices. I picture a colorful whirl of noise and activity. This is, after all, a company responsible for helping millions of people with similar interests find one another. Political junkies and stay-at-home moms form the highest concentration of Meetup users. But the site has also fostered connections between vampires in Jacksonville, skeptics in Tucson, belly dancers in St. Louis, and dog lovers the world over. They've introduced owners of boxers, bull dogs, spaniels, shepherds, pugs, pit bulls, Pekinese, and prairie dogs. Ground zero for all this slap-happy, tail-wagging community life would most certainly be jovial and interactive, a hang-out-and-gab-about-*The Sopranos* kind of workplace.

The elevator comes to an abrupt, bouncing stop. I cross the hall into a large, open room with hardwood floors, expansive windows, and uber-cool office cubicles made of iron piping, and see... exactly one person—the receptionist.

"May I help you?" she asks.

Prior to coming here, I'd tried to arrange meetings with several people at the young company because I wanted different perspectives on what all this fervent meeting up might mean, if anything. But apparently, the folks at Meetup are more inclined to help strangers meet with one another than to actually meet with strangers themselves. In addition to Scott, all I could arrange was a meeting with Allyson Leonard, the company's newly hired press representative.

The receptionist calls Allyson, and soon I hear feet clomping toward me on the hardwood floor. I turn and see a young woman with long straight blond hair, large hoop earring, and blue jeans.

"Hi, I'm Ali," she says. "Follow me."

Ali leads me into a small, dimly lit meeting room with a round white coffee table and two low-slung chairs that remind me of those chic-but-unfunctional chairs on display at the Museum of Modern Art. I sit down on one of them. The base of the chair is so low that my knees jut above my thighs, making me feel as if I'm sitting in a beach chair waiting for a hit off the bong.

"So," Ali asks. "What can I help you with?" She seems ignorant of how uncomfortable these chairs really are.

I ask Ali about Meetup and how much it's growing and who its members are, and it becomes clear immediately that Allyson's too new to the company to provide much insight.

"I don't know the answer to that," she says.

"Good question," she says.

"I'll look into that," she says.

Undaunted, I keep trying.

"Sorry," she says.

"Sorry."

"Sorry."

Allyson's foot begins to tap up and down.

I decide to switch tactics. Instead of asking Ali for insight into other people's interests, I ask about her own.

"My interests?" she says. "Well, I'm a member of the Philosopher's Roundtable."

Philosophy?

"I became interested in philosophy when I was very young and started questioning various theories of religion, although I've never studied it formally." Ali looks at the floor and thinks about her other interests. "Oh, yeah!" Her head comes up. "I also want to start a boxing meetup."

Boxing? Now we're getting somewhere. I try to sit up, but the chair's rigid design won't let me. Sighing, I lean back and ask Ali how long she's been a boxer.

She laughs. "No, I like to *watch* the fights. But I don't want to pay the fifty-dollar Pay-Per-View charge. That's why I think it would be cool to get a group together to watch fights, you know, like we used to do in college."

Staring at Ali, I never would have guessed this young woman with perfect white teeth would enjoy watching grown men beat the crap out of each other. And the fact that she does impresses me greatly. Philosophy *and* boxing? Ali's just confirmed my growing belief that you don't really know a person until you know what zany combination of interests they possess.

Intrigued, I ask Ali if she's planning to attend any other meetups.

"Well, there's one I know about but I'm not sure I want to go," she says.

I wait for her to continue.

"See, there's this whole category of meetups for people who have specific medical conditions. And, like, there's this one for people who have restless leg syndrome." Ali's own leg stops jack hammering the second she says this. She looks down at it.

"I mean, I didn't know I had a *syndrome*. But I'm not sure I want to go to the meeting, because I think, with all those legs banging up and down the room would get pretty noisy."

Boxing, philosophy, *and* restless–leg syndrome? I now *love* this young woman. I start to think of another question designed to unravel the crazy complexities of one Allyson Leonard, but before I get a chance, she picks up her notepad and glides up and out of her chair.

"Sorry I wasn't able to be more helpful," she says.

Oh.

This must be my cue.

I wriggle and hoist and heave and somehow manage to lift

myself out of the low chair. When at last I am standing, Ali gazes down at the empty chair and then back at me. Politely, she says nothing.

We walk into the large room filled with cubicles. It is almost eleven o'clock in the morning and there are now just two people at their desks.

Ali must notice my puzzled look.

"We start late," she says. "Stay here, and I'll get Scott."

• • •

Ali walks off to some hidden back room, and I'm left to wonder about the lack of people in this workplace. The number of cubicles suggests there are a lot more employees who work for the young company, but either they haven't arrived yet, as Ali said, or they're working from home.

I've always been a huge proponent of the work-where-and-when-you're-productive philosophy, probably because I was fired from the only full-time job I ever had. My boss at the time, a burnt-out forty-something with Scotch-induced facial redness, called me into his office one chilly October morning. While I don't remember his exact words, it seemed my termination had something to do with my inability to "mesh" with the eight-to-five office culture.

Mesh schmesh.

I've been self-employed ever since that cold October morning twenty years ago, and while I don't miss the regular hours or the boss, I do miss the collegial, gossipy sense of working with people in a small office.

I look at Meetup's empty offices and find it ironic that a company created to help re-establish community in this land of plenty is also affected by two of the very things responsible for dismantling it: technology; and the confounding preference people have, when given a chance, to spend time alone.

• • •

Several long minutes later, Scott walks into the reception area.

He's thirty-something, with sandy blond hair, wire-rim glasses, and a shy, intelligent manner.

I follow Scott into a large conference room just off the reception area and am relieved to see that the chairs in this room are normal conference-room chairs. The only light in the room is coming from windows that face Broadway. Because it's over-cast outside, the room has a chilly, gray pallor. I hear horns honking on the street below and am once again struck by the strange disconnect of talking about community in a place that, on its surface, has very little of its own. We sit down, and Scott pulls out his personal data assistant and checks it for messages.

Before coming here this morning, I logged onto Meetup.com and learned that the site currently lists more than five thousand different interests around which people can form a community—more than twice the number that existed when I originally logged on. Like Elvis and live in Baton Rouge? No problem. Eager to do some ghost tracking in Topeka? Meetup's got you covered. In the first two years of its existence, almost two million Americans used Meetup to find kindred spirits in their own communities, including fishermen, doll collectors, and birding enthusiasts.

Furthermore, the number of interests on the site appears to be growing by more than one hundred topics each month, and they are getting ever more specific. Where once there were Beatles meetups, now there are meetups focused solely on Sir Paul McCartney. Philosophy meetups have splintered into groups fashioned around Socrates, Ayn Rand, and Robert Pirsig, author of *Zen and the Art of Motorcycle Maintenance*. And cock-atiel-loving separatists can now opt out of the more general bird group into a meetup of their own.

Membership in civic organizations may be on the steady decline, but by golly, if you love ferrets and live in Houston you can get together with more than seventy other ferret lovers on the first Thursday of every month. It seems there's something inherently seductive and satisfying about sharing the thing you love the most with other people. As a pug lover explained to me recently, "If you love pugs and you meet someone who feels the same way you do, there's this instant connection that's like— wow! I can't explain it, but it's real."

The number of crazy communities on the Meetup.com site confirms my growing sense that passion is becoming the new community builder in our society. These subcultures are the new American tribes.

• • •

Scott decides there are no messages he needs to attend to. He shuts off the PDA and lays it on the table in front of him. I ask him why he thinks the number of micro-communities on the Meetup site is growing so rapidly.

He leans back in his chair.

"Here's what I think," he says softly. "I can go through my whole day interacting with literally nobody. I can wake up and instead of taking the subway, I can take a cab. I can go to work and instead of having meetings, I can send e-mail and instant messages. Instead of listening to music in the office and chit-chatting about that music, I can listen to my headphones. I can go to an ATM and order groceries on line—which I do—and not interact with a cashier or teller all day long.

"I mean, I think there is something comforting about being isolated and not having to interact, but it definitely goes against biology. Millions of years of evolution have created something in the species that gets something from face-to-face interaction. And if you don't interact with people, you tend not to trust them. But when you do, you start to think they are pretty okay."

I think about my encounter with Ali and how, in the space of twenty minutes, I went from thinking she's too young and inexperienced to share meaningful conversation, to thinking that she's pretty darn cool. As Scott talks, I find myself wondering if he thinks *I'm* pretty darn cool—which is, I admit, something I wonder on a fairly regular basis. Probably because I spend too much time alone.

For the next half hour, my conversation with Scott about American community life roams across widely diverse terrain. We talk about how old-style communities like the League of Women Voters may not be working anymore because Americans crave newness.

"We're in a new century and a new millennium," Scott says. "We want things freshened up a bit."

We talk about how people in America, unlike other countries, have the spare time and disposable wealth to be exuberant about things such as, say, blue parakeets.

"I don't know if people would come together around a parakeet as easily in Paris. It *is* sort of an indulgence. Certainly, a country has to be developed to a certain point before you have time to meet up about parakeets."

Which makes me wonder: Why organize around a parakeet at all? Why not love the little budgies on your own?

"Hmmm, good question," he says. "We recently did some research on the organizers of meetup groups, and when we asked them why they created these groups, they told us it was because they wanted to create a local resource."

Resource? I tell Scott I'm not sure what he means.

"It means they love the thing—whatever it is—so much they want to form some kind of established presence around it in their communities. The person who starts a local parakeet meetup does it because he thinks there should be a parakeet institution, so that other parakeet lovers have a place to go. I'm speculating a bit, but I suspect they've thought, 'Boy, when I first got into parakeets, it sure was lonely. I wish there was a parakeet resource where I could meet other parakeet lovers.'"

"So," I say, to make sure I'm following him, "as parakeet lovers, they've felt lonely or left out, and they want to remedy the situation for all future parakeet lovers."

"Ex-*actly*," he says. "I originally thought meetups would be all about getting together and having nice social experiences. But what happens is that these groups come together because they're not getting enough respect from the outside world. It's a pride thing. It's like classic labor or women's rights or gay rights organizing. When people feel like outsiders who aren't getting justice is when people have the motivation to organize. It's no surprise that the most popular dog meetup is the Chihuahua group. It's one of the most made-fun-of dogs in the world.

"See, I use the word *organize* deliberately. Many meetups come together because people in them feel disrespected and they want to mobilize their communities. The Chihuahua lovers have been petitioning Purina to make their pet food more Chihuahua friendly. Pug lovers organized a march on city hall to get the leash law changed."

And some people claim America has lost its relentless optimism.

Scott looks down at his PDA, and I sense he needs to go. But before he leaves, I have to ask him the question I've been asking everyone since I started this project. The question I asked Ali. The question I'm trying to answer for myself.

"So Scott, what are your passions?"

"I'm the organizer of the New York Technology Meetup, which is like a total gadget fest where people bring their latest cool things."

Darn. I was hoping for something a little more unexpected. "What about other meetups? Ever just pop in on one out of curiosity?"

"Well, once I decided to check out the sign language meetup, not really thinking that it would be a terribly poor experience, because the rule is you don't talk. And since I don't sign, I couldn't understand a thing. I was like, '*Okaaay*, great to meet you.'"

Scott stands to say good-bye. And as I gather my things to

join him, I find I'm pleased to discover that this tech-savvy entrepreneur has—at least once—made the kind of ill-conceived calculation I make on a regular basis. Case in point: I once signed up for an acting class and dropped out after twenty minutes when I discovered that I'd actually have to act. Why this didn't occur to me I'm not sure, but I can relate to Scott's dismay at having chosen to eavesdrop on a meetup where people didn't speak.

I think about what he said, about how you trust people more the more you are around them. But there's another part of this equation. Getting to know people—and learning what you have in common—also helps you *like* them.

• • •

On the cab ride back to my hotel, I think about our conversation and how the Internet is fostering connections between people that heretofore didn't exist. No wonder the number of meetup groups is growing so exponentially. It's as if ferret lovers have simply been looking for a way to break free of their solitary cages and romp together in ferret-loving splendor. Of course, Meetup.com is just one place where fanatics can find each other. Thousands of other groups maintain their own individual sites, or connect through other Internet portals, community newspapers, referrals from friends, or because of the odd flyer someone tacked on a kiosk at the local mall.

But regardless of how their ferret-loving paths are intersecting, it seems to me that they are—and in greater numbers than ever before.

I now have a new reason to continue my quest: I don't want to be left out.

PART TWO : *Immerse*

CHAPTER FIVE

Hitler Did Fine, But I Can Do Better

"This war will not be over by the next commercial break."
—News Announcer during the Gulf War

EVER HAD ONE OF THOSE DIZZYING MOMENTS, WHERE YOU find yourself standing among a crowd of people who are so thoroughly alien to you, so thoroughly Not Like You, that it takes every ounce of willpower you possess not to turn and run screaming home to mommy?

Me too.

In fact, I'm having one right now.

It's a sunny summer morning and I've just arrived at the World Boardgaming Championships being held at the Marriott Hunt Valley Inn in a suburb north of Baltimore. When I first heard about the Boardgaming Championships, I began to skip happily around my bedroom. Boardgames? Now *this* was something I could relate to. I envisioned rooms full of pleasant, well-scrubbed people playing Monopoly, Scrabble, Trivial Pursuit, and other games I've been known to play, enjoy, and gloat a little over winning. I was excited by the potential of finding an interest I could relate to; jazzed by the thought that maybe here I'd find my tribe—*my* pigeon racers.

I was also way off the mark.

I'm standing inside the doorway of a hotel ballroom named the Maryland Room. Inside, dozens of people are clustered around banquet tables holding board games, the likes of which

I've never seen before. Signs on the tables tell me they're playing "Robo Rally," "VINCI: The Rise & Fall of Civilizations," and something called "Merchant of Venus." I find a description of Merchant of Venus and read: "If you like your grease immortal, your sculpture psychotic, and your genes designer, then this is the game for you."

Huh?

Although I've never heard of games like this, it's not the games themselves that have activated my get-to-safety alarm. It's the participants. They are overwhelmingly male, predominantly white, and most look like they haven't shaven, combed their hair, crunched a fresh vegetable, or experienced a good night's sleep in days. Clad in rumpled and untucked T-shirts, the players look like men who, having escaped the civilizing influence of their wives, have found themselves descending into pits of slovenliness heretofore only dreamed of.

A few minutes ago, I watched a man with curly black hair thrust half a hamburger into his mouth—using the palm of his hand—while trying to discuss something with his tablemates. Unaided by chewing, the compressed burger sat idly inside the man's mouth, straining his left cheek to the bursting point, making conversation all but impossible. I felt sorry for that burger. All cramped up in the dark with nothing to do but wait for further instructions.

Perhaps recognizing the futility of trying to speak with a burger in his mouth, the man then swallowed it—wholly unchewed—in a feat of guttural capacity that could have merited a cover story in a scientific journal.

It's not the first time I've wondered whether hobbies like this are merely an excuse for men to get out of the house.

In fact, since I've been investigating passion, I've found it far easier to find communities of men devoted to singular interests, especially those that involve balls, pucks, bullets, drills, bait, breasts, engines, and bottles of oxygen. But perhaps I'm simply more intrigued by the male-dominated subcultures because they've always seemed so off-limits.

When I was a little girl, I'd spend summers at the family cabin in Northern California, playing on the Eel River with my five male cousins. They were always jokey and dirt-caked and full of stitches, and their fearless vitality thrilled me. I had no brothers and thus no direct daily experience with dirt bikes or dune buggies or playtime that involved imaginary fox holes and machine-gun fire. And I was fascinated by it all. My cousins spent summers backpacking in Yosemite, while my sisters and I worked on our tans.

As a kid, I yearned to sample a bit of that active male world but whenever I'd talk to my mother about, say, riding a motorcycle or scaling a mountain, I got her emergency room lecture. Mom worked in a hospital emergency room throughout my childhood and she knew from nightly experience what a motorcycle and mountain climbing could do to the human body. At one end of the spectrum: cuts. Stitches. Scrapes. Breaks. Burns. Sprains. At the other: death. Skiers landed in the ER. Daredevils landed in the ER. The *Kennedys* landed in the ER. Tame, sensible families like ours did not.

Appealing to my father was useless. He spent his young, active years teaching ballroom dancing at an Arthur Murray Studio in San Francisco.

With the world of male passions off limits, I, of course, craved them all the more. In college, I started camping. I learned to drive a motorcycle. I drank tequila shooters. But somewhere along the line I must have absorbed the message that polite restraint—not unchecked exuberance—was the consummate behavior to strive for. Whenever I forgot that, whenever I got a little stinky and sweaty and *involved*, my mother would reel me back in.

"Honey," she'd say, shaking her head at my silly attempts at tomboy behavior. "Only men and horses sweat."

Reflecting on this, it's no wonder I've been drawn to these secret male worlds with their no-holds-barred behavior. But now, as I look at the board gamers in their rumpled clothing and stale body smells, I believe I may have over-romanticized men and their passions.

And yet… I can't seem to pull myself away.

I leave Burger Boy and the Maryland Room behind and enter a hallway where many of the board games being played are on display. I browse their covers.

A game called Battle Cry boasts: "Recreate 15 Epic World War battles. There's just one difference. You are *there!*"

The cover of Cosmic Encounter tells me: "Armed with alien power, you are ready to colonize the galaxy."

Other games include Attila, Air Baron, Acquire, Liberty, Brute Force, Samurai, Attack Sub, Vanished Planet, Squad Leader, Greed, Pay Dirt, and PanzerBlitz.

Given the all-girls family I hail from, I wasn't aware they could build so much testosterone into a board game. The most violent it ever got at our house was when my sisters and I played Feeley Meeley, a game in which players shoved their hands inside holes cut into a cardboard cube and tried to find an object inside, such as a comb or whistle, using only the sense of touch. With four young female hands grasping inside for the same object, we endured our fair share of slapping, jabbing, poking, pulling, threats, tears, and piercing, high-pitched accusations of cheating. I shudder to think what viciousness a game like Air Baron would have unleashed.

Still, looking at the racks of games, I'm mystified by this slash 'n' burn, conquer-and-destroy mentality. Who plays these games anyway? The urge to flee has now given way to curiosity. Asking around for someone to help me, I am connected with Don Greenwood, the convention director.

• • •

Greenwood is a large man with a soft belly, oversized glasses, and bushy mustache. He's standing behind a dark wood registration counter, and when I tell him why I'm here, he looks at me and taps his pen on the counter without saying a word. I can't help but think it's because he sees me for what I am: Someone who is acting politely interested in boardgamers, but actually sees herself as a teensy bit superior to them—primarily because feeling superior is preferable to feeling left out. If I was Mr. Greenwood, I don't know if I'd talk to me.

His pen continues to tap.

"Okay," he says, finally, "but I have just ten minutes."

He steps from behind the counter and tells a woman standing nearby he'll only be a minute. Unlike other people I've visited with, Don doesn't seem particularly interested in recruiting me.

We begin chatting and he tells me that 1,100 people from around the world have come here to the fifth annual World Boardgaming Championships. This weekend, about 140 games are being played as part of the competition, but hundreds more are being played during open gaming.

"What do the winners receive?" I ask. "Money?"

"There's no prize money. That brings out the daggers."

I wait for Don to tell me what, exactly, they do receive. The silence lengthens.

"So… what *do* they play for?"

"Woods."

"Woods?"

"Yeah. Woods. Plaques." Don is no longer tapping his pen, but he might as well be.

"I see," I reply, although of course I don't see anything at all.

Don must sense my discomfort for he takes a deep breath, exhales slowly, and decides that since I'm not going away he might as well answer my questions.

"Okay," he says. "This is how it works."

Don explains that players get points for winning individual

events. These points are called laurels. The more competitive the game, the more people who play, the more laurels you get. At the end of a game, the person with the most laurels gets a plaque showing he is the winner of that game. At the end of the convention, the person with the most laurels overall is named the Caesar, the reigning king of the World Boardgaming Championships.

"We do it this way 'cause if there was prize money it would bring out the pros and we'd have to worry about cheating. This way, people play for honor and bragging rights only. This conference is for purists."

I tell Don that I'd expected to encounter more popular board games like Scrabble and Monopoly and maybe—ha-ha—Chutes and Ladders.

Don does not find this amusing.

"These are not party or social games like *you* might be familiar with," he says. "These are niche games. They are highly *involved* games that have *intricate* rules and are heavy on strategy. These games require a *significant* investment of time. They are *not* for the general populace."

Well then.

Don removes his ball cap and scratches his bald head. He has two puffs of curly hair over each ear and he smoothes these down before replacing his cap.

I soldier on.

I ask Don why he is attracted to boardgames, and he tells me it's because niche games are tense and exciting, and they allow players to stay involved. In Monopoly, if you get the right real estate, you push everyone else into poverty. In Scrabble, wordsmiths can out-vocabularize their opponents in no time. But niche games allow people to remain emotionally engaged and strategically involved throughout the length of the game. Plus, he adds, they offer a great intellectual challenge.

"Intellectual challenge?" I ask, thinking about the man with the hamburger.

"Absolutely. Many of these games simulate historic, real-world events. I especially like games where you set the parameters so historical events can occur the way you create them."

"So players need some knowledge of history?"

"That's good to have," he agrees, "but math is more important. In fact, most of the people here are extremely well-educated. There are lots of engineers."

I'll be honest. For the last several minutes I've been trying to convince myself that burger-eating boardgamers have nothing to teach me. It's just so foreign here, so *male*, even for my voyeuristic tastes. Plus, the whole gamey gaming environment just makes me want to shower.

But Don's comment about the educational level of participants reels me back in, especially since I had so recently concluded that pigeon racers did what they did because of the lack of intellectual challenge in their jobs. In fact, to date, most of the people I've been with have been predominantly working class. This has made it easy for me to conclude I don't have passions because I've got two master's degrees and thus am simply too educated (she says, head lifted with a misplaced bit of hubris) to bother with them.

But if what Don says is true, fanaticism is not the province of the underemployed, and the people here might have something to teach me after all.

Don looks toward his berth at the registration desk, and I suspect he's about to call time on our conversation. "Um, can I ask one more favor?" I ask.

He exhales again.

I tell him I'm researching passion and would like to talk with some of the most zealous gamers here. "Any suggestions?"

"Head over to the Worthington room," he says.

"The Worthington Room?"

"Yeah. It's what, Saturday now? The guys in there have been playing the same game since Tuesday."

"The *same* game?"

"You said you wanted passion."

• • •

I believe Don Greenwood was telling the truth when he proclaimed niche games were tense and exciting, but I've been standing in the Worthington Room for the last ten minutes and have yet to spot evidence of the action-packed, zip-a-dee-doo-da adventure he referred to.

Inside the room, clusters of men are gathered around large round tables covered by incongruously pink tablecloths. Like the players downstairs, these guys look rumpled and tired, and the room smells like adult male bodies that haven't seen the tiled interior of a shower stall for days. Most are quietly staring at game boards on the tables in front of them. The atmosphere feels heavy, like a room full of students straining to complete their college entrance exams.

A large man with four days' worth of white chin stubble notices me.

"How're you doing?" he asks.

His voice is craggy like that of a life-long smoker. I walk over to his table, on which sits a game board the size of a hood from a small sedan. He introduces himself.

Steve Voros, he says. Former material control specialist. Ford Motor Company. Now retired. He extends his hand.

I tell Steve that I'm investigating fanatical passion, and he tells me that boy-howdy, have I come to the right place.

"You have to be nuts to play this," he says. "I've been playing for twenty-five years and I'm *still* learning the game."

"*That's* for sure," says the man who's sitting across the table from him.

"Yeah, you wish," Steve replies.

"Are you two playing against each other?" I ask.

"Yeah," Steve says. "We've played four games since Tuesday. We're not like the guys over there." He cocks his head toward the table behind me.

I look over at the table. Steve tells me the men there are playing A World At War, which takes sixty or seventy hours of play time. He's playing its predecessor, Advanced Third Reich, which is not only easier, he says, but also requires a scant twelve hours to complete.

"*Only* twelve?"

"Yeah. We don't go as long, so it doesn't get as tense."

There's that word again. "Tense how?"

"I'll tell you how. You should've been here this morning at about three o'clock. There was a group of guys playing at that table in the corner." He points to a table that now sits vacant. "They'd been playing for about twenty hours straight without sleep when they got into a fight about the rules. One of the guys got so mad he picked up the game and overturned it. You do that, and the game's over."

"Did you see it?"

"Nah, I left about 1 a.m. I just heard the rumors this morning. But I know they're true. You take a bunch of guys who haven't slept, put 'em around a table where the Second World War is going on, and you can expect a few disagreements. Everyone here's pretty smart, so they all think they're right all the time. Just look around."

Steve turns and starts pointing toward the other players in the room. "That guy's a lawyer. That guy's got a Ph.D. in tree hugging. And see that sublime guy over there? He's a neurologist."

I gaze in the direction Steve's pointing but fail to find someone I would characterize as sublime. Still, I'm impressed. Don was right—brainiacs play these games.

Steve turns back to his own table and gestures toward his opponent, a small, slim man with wire-rim glasses. "And this guy here, he knows world leaders."

"Not quite," his opponent says. He has a thick German accent.

We chat, and I learn Steve's opponent is Herbert Gratz from Vienna, Austria. Herbert has attended the World Boardgaming Championships every year since 1991 and, when he's not playing games, he works at the International Monetary Fund at the Central Bank in Vienna. "It sounds impressive, but I'm just a policy advisor to management."

I ask Herbert why he comes to Maryland all the way from Austria every year. "Can't you play these games at home?"

"Oh, no. All the serious conflict-resolution games are published in English," he says. For a small man, he sounds eerily like Arnold Schwarzenegger. "In Germany, you can be legally prosecuted if you publish a game with a swastika on the package. That's why all the games Germans publish are about saving the environment. They all have funny little bunnies skipping through the forest."

Herbert says this with such disdain that I've no need to ask him why he prefers conflict games. Instead, I ask him specifically what it is about Advanced Third Reich that causes him to cross the Atlantic every year to play it for several days on end.

"Because I want to be like the Americans. I want to be like the maniacs that rule the world."

Herbert laughs in a manner that's intended to suggest he's kidding.

"But," he adds, "I also like eating the ribs they serve at the hotel. Of course, in Austria, we have ribs. But they're not as good as the Marriott."

Steve interjects. "You *do* like your ribs."

"I tell you, I do."

Herbert looks around the room at the other players and then turns his attention back to me.

"Okay, seriously," he says. "I started playing this game because I like complicated strategy games. When I was younger, I played chess and bridge. I liked the competition. But now it's not so much about competition. It's about companionship. Like with this guy," he says, pointing to Steve.

I look back and forth between the two men. The unexpected retreat of Herbert's Third Reich swagger takes me by surprise, and I find myself touched by his confession.

"It's true," Steve adds. "We've played together for years."

The two men start bickering over exactly how many years it's been. Five? Four? Six? Watching them, I'm once again struck by the unlikely friendships that form around common interests. How else would a retired autoworker from Detroit come to fraternize with an international money manager from Vienna? Although their interests may be the same, their lives aren't.

"So, tell me," I ask, in an attempt to stop their squabbling, "what is the aim of the game?"

"The victory conditions are not to clearly win or lose," Herbert says. "There are shades of winning. You play to lose by only a little. Of course, if the other guy whines…" he pauses and looks across the table at Steve, "that is also very positive and rewarding."

"Oh, brother," Steve says.

"You said you were on the fourth game?" I ask Steve.

"That's right," he says.

"Have you lost each one?"

"Oh, most certainly."

• • •

I leave to let Steve resume his happy losing streak and I walk over to a table where four men are sitting curved over a game board. I stand beside a man wearing a St. Johns ball cap. He's staring intently at the game board and chewing his thumbnail. The other players around the table are conversing. But their conversation is slow, as if their responses are time-delayed because of great distance.

"In my last Euro scenario, the Russians had rockets."

Pause.

"I hate it when they do that."

Pause.

"You going for pizza?"

Pause.

"I *said* are you going for pizza?"

"Nah, I'm gonna hang around here, because it looks like my brother is going to toast Japan."

Pause.

"Yeah. Japan is getting hot."

Pause.

"Will you be hitting me with the bomb?"

Pause.

"I dunno."

As the game proceeds, one of the players sitting close to me attempts to give me a brief, entry-level overview of A World at War. He tells me the game is a World War II strategy game in which two teams—one serving as the Axis powers, the other as the Allies—compete to gain world control. The game is designed to allow players to pursue their own wartime strategies. They build navies to suit their strategic requirements. They deploy armies and air force pools based on projected need. They worry about oil reserves, their nation's economies, and diplomatic alliances with other nation-states. All of these factors have an impact on the war strategies they can eventually put into place, and the options are endless. Japan could choose to invade Australia or India, for example. Germany could develop the atomic bomb. The British position in the Middle East could crumble.

"It sounds complicated," I say, capitalizing on my highly refined journalistic ability to state the obvious.

"Oh, it takes a good ten years to get to proficiency level," he says.

I continue to watch them play and realize that unlike the pigeon racers, these guys have not chosen a passion that utilizes untapped skills and talents. Instead, they are turning up the dial on intellectual strengths they use every day in their professional lives. As lawyers and doctors and academics, they've already developed the ability to synthesize information, think strategically, and create workable strategies. What A World at War appears to do is allow them to fully test these skills in a more intense environment. The fact that they don't have to sleep or shave or shower is merely an added bonus.

During one of the many long pauses, I ask the players how much they've slept over the past four nights and learn they've only broken for three-to-five hours a night—tops.

"And it's not restful sleep, either. You're tossing and turning and thinking about the game. Your adrenaline gets stuck in one mode."

"Yeah. I can't even imagine going back to work on Monday. It'll be like coming back from outer space."

The other players lean forward and appear to grow energized by the discussion of their extreme gaming accomplishments.

"We're like Navy Seals. They train like this too. A whole week without sleep."

"My philosophy is this. If we're gonna do this all week, we're *gonna do this all week.*"

"I totally agree. I had to play all the chits with the wife to come here. Hey… wait a minute! Did you bomb him?"

"Naaa."

"Come on. This game is called A World at War, but there's not much fighting going on. It should be called A World at Peace."

This last comment brings their attention back to the game. I watch them for a while seeking clues as to what they're doing. On a nearby chair, I spot the game's rulebook and lean over to pick it up. It's 196 full-sized pages, 8.5 point type, single spaced.

The man with the St. Johns ball cap sees me looking at it. "You ought to talk to the guy who wrote that."

"Who's that?"

"Over there, in the corner." He points to a man wearing a T-shirt from the National Air and Space Museum that features illustrations of World War II bombers. "That's Bruce Harper. He designed the game."

• • •

Bruce Harper is a forty-eight-year-old lawyer from Vancouver, British Columbia, who prosecutes tax offenses. He's got pale skin, short reddish hair, and deep purple circles under his eyes. He reminds me of Woody Allen, minus the glasses. He's sitting at the same corner table that was allegedly vacated at three o'clock this morning by the group of angry, overtired players.

In the last fifteen years, Bruce has designed four games: Wrasslin', Advanced Civilization, Advanced Third Reich, and Empire of the Rising Sun. He combined the last two games into A World at War, which—although it officially debuted only four days ago at the World Boardgaming Championships—has been under development for years.

Bruce got into game designing because he understands the importance of rules to a good game and how to write rules that people understand. In 1981, he was playing a game with friends when a question arose about the proper play procedure. He wrote a note to the company making a suggestion about how to improve the rules so as to eliminate such confusion.

"They put my suggestion in the next rule book and before I knew it, I'd become the Q-and-A guy for that particular game," he explains. "You see, for most people rules are sacrosanct. If the rules say that pigs fly, well then, pigs fly. For a game to be successful, the rules have to be clear. You don't want to spend your play time arguing about them."

Bruce speaks the way you'd expect a person who is concerned about the interpretation of rules to speak. He looks me directly in the eye. He prefaces each sentence with long, thoughtful pauses. And although he is eating a Marriott-issue hamburger much like the one compacted earlier by the man downstairs, Bruce takes time to carefully chew every bite before speaking.

"Why are strategy games like A World at War so popular here?"

Chew. Swallow.

"If you read a book about history, say, about World War II, you know how it will end," he explains. "But games like this are interactive. The players themselves decide the outcome based on their own strategic moves. People can say to themselves, 'Hitler did fine up until this point. I can do better.' The challenge of the game is not to recreate actual events, but to respond to different what-if scenarios. For example, what if Japan didn't bomb Pearl Harbor? If all the assumptions are reasonable, and all the rules make sense, then the game proceeds without a problem. But if you get a rule wrong, it can wreck the game."

"Do your skills as a lawyer help you design games?" I know the answer to this, but I have to ask anyway.

Chew. Swallow. Napkin dab.

"Probably. I've learned to write clearly because I understand the problems caused by a lack of clarity. There's an old law from England that's only one page long and has been massively litigated. There's been something like twenty thousand decisions on that one single law. But when a law is clearly written, the need for litigation is diminished. There's far less litigation with a long law than a shorter one because the answer is in the writing. Game designers who don't take time to clarify the rules so that people understand how to follow them, well, to me, that shows an astounding misinterpretation of human nature."

Bruce is clearly not a person I want to be caught jaywalking around.

"What other games do you play?" I ask.

"I haven't played many games besides my own over the last few years. It seems self-indulgent to play when so many people are waiting for my rules." Bruce says this as if the rules he's been working on hold the key to everlasting world peace. Which they might, for all I know.

"So playing games is your passion?"

"Definitely.

"When I'm playing a game like this, I'm totally focused. I'm not thinking about work or anything else. It's the way I relax. My wife relaxes by reading trashy novels. I relax by coming here. Really, there's no other way I'd rather spend a week than by playing games, acting like an idiot and not sleeping and eating."

Sensing Bruce will have an opinion on the subject, I ask him why it seems there are so many male-dominated subcultures.

"Because guys have to be doing something to get together. Women form social groups easily, but men need an excuse. One guy never calls up another guy and says, 'Hey, let's go have a few beers and talk.'"

"But isn't locking yourself in a hotel for a week pretty obsessive?"

"Obsessive, passionate. Whatever. They both describe the same kind of behavior. I'm proud that I've designed a game that might cause some loner to come out of his house and interact with others. I like to think that I've prevented some crazy guy from heading out onto the street with a rifle.

"I tell you who I feel sorry for," he adds. "I feel sorry for those people who don't have any passions at all. Passion is a great thing in life."

Sheepishly, I say nothing.

"I mean what harm does all this do anyway?" Bruce sweeps his hand from right to left in a room-encompassing gesture. "We're all old friends here, even the people who met just four days ago."

I thank Bruce for his time and walk through the tables to the exit. And as I do, I feel the familiar stab of envy return.

CHAPTER SIX

Mayberry Daze

"There are two rules around here. The first rule is to Obey All Rules."
—Barney Fife

EARLY ON A WARM THURSDAY EVENING, I DRIVE ON CURVY
wooded roads to the Cross Creek Country Club, find my way to
a large banquet room where a noisy golf-tournament dinner is
underway, and scan the room looking for a man I've arranged to
meet. The scene is exactly what you'd expect to find at a southern country club on a warm September night: sunburned golfers,
clinking glasses, and a buffet line that meanders the entire length
of the room. But this tournament dinner is different from others
I've attended in three distinct ways.

One, the master of ceremonies is dressed like Barney Fife.

Two, the person handing out awards is dressed like Floyd
the Barber.

And three, the person I've arranged to meet told me on the
phone that he wished to be known, this weekend at least, as Otis
the Drunk.

In real life, Otis the Drunk is a man named Kenneth
Junkin, a fifty-five-year-old communications worker from
Gordo, Alabama, who's never had a drink stronger than a wine
cooler, and even that was a long time ago. Most of the time,
Kenneth Junkin is quite content being known as Kenneth
Junkin, a man who doesn't drink. But not tonight. Not this
weekend. This weekend, Kenneth and thousands of people like

him will shed their everyday identities and concerns and indulge in their shared affection for *The Andy Griffith Show*, the situation comedy about small-town life that ran, first in black and white and then in color, from 1960 to 1968.

The occasion for all this indulgence is the Annual Mayberry Days Festival being held in Mount Airy, North Carolina, which is Andy Griffith's real home town as well as the inspiration behind the idyllic southern burg depicted on the show. The festival provides an excuse for more than 20,000 devoted Andy Griffith pilgrims to come together in the place that started it all.

Kenneth invited me to accompany him to this year's festival so that I, too, could experience the celestial aura that surrounds Mayberry.

"You're gonna love it," he told me on the phone. "It's like learning there really is a Santa Claus and getting to visit his house at the North Pole."

So that I could recognize him, Kenneth mailed me a 5 x 7 black-and-white photo of himself dressed as his Mayberry alter ego. The photo was signed, "Love, Otis."

• • •

I first learned of Mayberry Days years ago from a journalist I met on a press junket. One morning over breakfast, he told me about the annual festival and the people who dress like characters, and how Mayberry Days was hands down just about the funnest thing he'd done in more than fifty years of living.

He also told me about *The Andy Griffith Show* Rerun Watchers Club, a fan club with more than 1,200 chapters in places as diverse as Alabama, California, Thailand, and the United Arab Emirates. The Rerun Watchers Club was launched in 1978 by four college students in a dorm at Vanderbilt University. Today, there are more than 25,000 members worldwide.

"You think I'm crazy, don't you?" he asked.

"Oh, no," I assured him.

When I started this quest, I knew Mayberry Days had to be on my itinerary. There was just one problem: I'd never been a fan of *The Andy Griffith Show*. How could I begin to understand the activities at Mayberry Days without knowing who the characters were or what premise the show was based on?

So I started cramming.

A week before traveling to North Carolina, I popped two videotaped episodes into the VCR each night for a week. The first night, I sat down in front of the television reluctantly, as if being forced to watch a documentary about some obscure foreign war. The second night, I began whistling the Mayberry theme song. The third night, I started preparing for the show thirty minutes ahead of time. I got into flannel pajamas, made a cup of chamomile tea, grabbed a mini-Snickers bar, and screamed for Angela to hurry and finish writing her trial brief or else she would miss kind-hearted Andy Taylor, freckle-faced Opie, matronly Aunt Bea, and bumbling Barney Fife, and she wouldn't want to do that, would she? By the fourth night, I was hooked. How had I missed *this*?

If you're as shamelessly out of touch with *The Andy Griffith Show* as I was, here's what you need to know: Mayberry residents live the quintessential small-town life. They participate in talent shows. Plan local festivals. Date their neighbors. In Mayberry, life runs smoothly until some insignificant happening snowballs into a major fiasco, many of which are triggered by city slickers, escaped convicts and other interlopers who upset the small town's equilibrium. This being television, every misadventure is peacefully solved within thirty minutes, thanks to compassion, hard work, charity, or some other beneficial but underused human virtue. Watching the show and absorbing its moral lesson was like going to Sunday School and I couldn't believe how much I enjoyed it.

Still, as much as I liked the show, I couldn't envision myself trekking across the country in celebration of it. So, instead, I trekked across the country to learn more about the people who would.

• • •

Standing at the back of the banquet room at the country club, it takes me less than five minutes, thanks to the photo, to find Otis-né-Kenneth. I walk to his table and tap him on the shoulder.

"Howdy," he says, standing to greet me. Kenneth is a tall, large man with pink cheeks and a kindly smile. He bends over and hugs me as if we've known each other for years.

"I'm real glad you could make it," he says. "Real glad. You're gonna love this. Yes, you are."

He asks the people at his table to excuse us, and together we walk out of the banquet room to a hallway where it's quiet. We sit down in a couple of club chairs and I ask Kenneth how his love affair with *Andy Griffith* began.

"I'll never forget it" he explains. "The first show aired on Thursday, October 3, 1960. I was twelve years old."

Kenneth watched the show weekly during its prime-time run from 1960 to 1968. Years later, when it entered syndication, he began watching it almost daily. "The show was entertaining when I was growing up, but later on it became so much more," he says. "It became therapy for me. When I'd have a bad day— now, don't get me wrong, I don't have many—but when I did, I'd go home, start watchin' the show, and forget about it. I always wanted to go on patrol with Andy and Barney, have a pop with Goober, eat one of Aunt Bea's pies, and have a girlfriend like Thelma Lou."

Kenneth stares off at some unseen point in the distance.

"I know there's no such thing as a perfect world, but Mayberry is the closest thing to perfect there is."

From 1960 to the mid-1980s, Kenneth didn't share his feelings about the show with many people. But all that changed when he met Jim Clark, the founder and Presiding Goober of *The Andy Griffith Show* Rerun Watchers Club at a Mayberry reunion at Opryland in Nashville. It was then he realized there were legions of other fans who shared his obsession. Within six months, Kenneth had formed a local rerun watchers chapter called Hearty Eatin' Men and Beautiful Delicate Women. A few months after that, his chapter spilled onto Main Street during Mayberry Days, and Kenneth's life has not been the same since.

In the last twelve years, he's attended every Mayberry celebration and reunion ever held. He's refashioned two old Fords into Mayberry squad cars and now manages the Mayberry Squad Car Nationals, a rally where other owners of Mayberry squad cars come together to drag race and run obstacle courses. In one of the contests, drivers are required to get out of their cars and "arrest" a mannequin of Ernest T. Bass, the hillbilly villain of the show. Kenneth's own 1964 Ford Custom is the three-time world champion.

"She's not just pretty to look at," he says. "That baby can perform."

Kenneth's penchant for all things Mayberry has also allowed him to make a name for himself in Tuscaloosa, where he hosts a radio program devoted to the show.

"When people see me now—and this is not boasting—I'm considered Mr. Mayberry," he explains. "It's an honor the way people regard me."

Of course, he adds, all of these accomplishments pale in comparison to his died-and-gone-to-heaven experience of meeting and performing with many of the show's original cast members. Over the years, Kenneth has met George Lindsay who played Goober; Betty Lynn, who played Thelma Lou; and most importantly, Don Knotts, who played Barney Fife, Sheriff Taylor's hapless deputy.

"There's no person on earth I wanted to meet more than Don Knotts," Kenneth explains. "Ronald Reagan was close. But Don Knotts was my hero."

• • •

The next morning, I drive to downtown Mount Airy where Kenneth and I have agreed to meet for the first full day of Mayberry activities. Downtown Mount Airy is a five-block stretch of century-old brick buildings that house gift shops, diners, fabric stores, and consignment shops. I suspect that most days, the old downtown is fairly quiet, because there's a larger, newer shopping mall right off the highway. But today, the street is jammed with busloads of tourists.

The tourists have gray hair and white legs and dark socks and pastel sun hats. They carry video recorders and large purses and plastic bags with Mayberry souvenirs. The men walk the women across the street. The women gaze into shop windows. The couples argue about what to do or where to eat and what to buy.

I stand near a gift shop where the owners have set up a sidewalk table filled with all manner of Mayberry memorabilia, including monogrammed mousepads, T-shirts, ceramic bells, salt-and-pepper shakers, yo-yos, water bottles, and mock license plates that read, "This vehicle protected by Fife." An older woman near me is desperate to buy *Aunt Bea's Mayberry Cookbook* but her husband's putting the kabosh on it.

"We don't need another damn cookbook," he tells her.

"But this one's different. It's by Aunt Bea."

He walks away. She continues to flip through the book's pages.

I look up the street just as Kenneth rounds the corner in the bright morning sun. Whereas last night he was dressed like a golfer, today he is garbed in full Otis regalia: seersucker summer suit, fancy tie, black suspenders, and slightly crushed straw fedora. His left lapel sports a small U.S. flag pin. Upon seeing me, he lifts a brass key and key ring from his pocket and lets it dangle from his thumb.

"This is to the county jail," he says, smiling.

(Mayberry fact #1: Otis was a considerate drunk who

would incarcerate himself whenever he'd been on a bender.)

Looking at the key, Kenneth bellows, "I'm sober now, but I'll get over it!"

Kenneth starts to tell me about all the activities planned for the first day of Mayberry Days when we're interrupted by a woman with cottony white hair who's calling to him from across the street.

"Ooooooooo!" she says, like a child who's just spotted Mickey Mouse at Disneyland. "There's the drunk!"

The woman crosses the street, walks up to Kenneth, and points a bony finger at his large chest. "I'm going to have to ar-*rest* you," she says.

"But wait! I'm not drunk yet!" he says. Kenneth pulls back his sleeve and looks at his watch. "Course, there's still plenty of time."

He laughs.

She laughs.

Having satisfied the woman's need for a brush with Mayberry stardom, Kenneth pulls out a copy of the same black-and-white photo he sent to me, the photo of himself dressed as Otis. He uncaps a black felt pen and leans closer to the woman and two friends who've just joined her.

"Where are you ladies from?" he asks. "Lexington? Would that be Lexington, *Alabama*!?"

Kenneth arcs his back as if this is the most startling piece of geography he's ever heard of. "Well, that's a mighty nice place." Holding the pen's cap in his teeth, he autographs the photo. "To Helen: Otis Campbell."

Kenneth begins speaking to Helen's friend, and together they discover they have some kinfolk in common. They actually use the word kinfolk.

"I used to live within hollerin' distance of him," Kenneth says. He actually uses the word hollerin'.

Kenneth signs another autograph, stands for a photo with

the group, and tells the women they really ought to get one of them pork chop sandwiches at the Snappy Lunch.

(Mayberry fact #2: Andy and Barney used to get pork chop sandwiches at the mythical Mayberry Snappy Lunch, which was named after the authentic Mount Airy Snappy Lunch.)

Kenneth as Otis is kind and cordial and charismatic. He looks his fans directly in the eyes. He lets them know they *matter*. Like a popular politician, Kenneth-as-Otis is both larger than life and one of the little people. The fact that the "real" Otis—that is, the fictional TV character Otis—was inebriated and irascible matters not a whit to Kenneth Junkin or his fans. Once in the land of Mayberry, people see what they want to see, and that vision is invariably down-home and friendly, like a pitcher of icy lemonade on a hot summer's day.

"Sorry about that," he says to me, after the women leave. "That tends to happen when I'm dressed like…" Another clutch of older women interrupts us.

"Hiiiii Oooootis!" croons one of them. "Are you sober?"

"I'm sober now, but I'll get over it!"

• • •

Last night, Kenneth explained to me that his role as Mr. Mayberry entailed many responsibilities, not the least of which was writing and managing the annual Mayberry Days Trivia Contest. The contest, he said, is not designed for casual fans who might tune in now and again. It's geared toward true Mayberry scholars, the kind of people who understand the critical importance of memorizing Mayberry license plates, street addresses, and the cost of a deluxe lunch special at Morelli's Restaurant as announced in episode #132. (Answer: $1.85.)

For the last three years, the hands-down winner of the contest was a woman known to Kenneth only as The Lady in Red.

"No one can beat her," he explained. "Last year, she was the first person in Mayberry history to correctly answer every single question."

As Kenneth attends to his growing fan base, I notice a woman down the street wearing a red dress, red earrings, and red straw hat. Wondering if it might be the infamous trivia queen, I walk over and introduce myself. It seems pointless to ask if she's the Lady in Red because she is, in fact, a lady in red. Instead, I ask if she's the reigning trivia champion.

"Oh, yes, honey," she says in a syrupy southern accent. "That would be me."

Her round white face breaks into a broad smile and I sense how proud she is to be recognized. Up close, her features are plain. She's got a slightly overweight, middle-aged middle. And her clothes, while neat, are clearly not designer-label expensive. But the careful coordination that went into her outfit—the red bracelet, the red lipstick, the red bow tie in her hair—tells me this is a proud woman who cares about details.

We begin chatting, and I learn her name is Pat Bullins. Pat is a fifty-five-year-old homemaker from Walnut Cove, North Carolina, who first entered the Mayberry Days trivia contest six years ago. That first year, she correctly answered thirteen questions out of twenty-four. Defeated, she went home, studied the reruns more closely, and the next year managed to snag the title of second runner-up. The third, fourth, and fifth time around, Pat took top honors—and this afternoon, she'll be vying for her fourth straight win.

"Are you nervous?" I ask.

"Oh, yes, honey. They's still a lot I don't know." She fans her face with a cardboard Mayberry Days fan that features a black-and-white caricature of Aunt Bea. "By myself I can't do it. See, it all depends on the Lord."

Pat stops fanning her face and opens the fist of her right hand.

"See this here," she says, looking down at a small black Bible the size of a matchbook. "I found it in the parking lot at Wal-Mart. Now, don't get the wrong idea. It's not for good luck.

I'm a Christian, honey, and we don't believe in luck. I don't believe in rabbits' foots or any of that silly stuff. I carry this Bible 'cause it helps me to think. Helps with the butterflies, you know. God is the one who wins the contest, not me."

Pat is so earnest, her belief in the Lord's contribution so resolute, that she actually has me believing God cares about *The Andy Griffith Show.*

Pat squeezes the Bible in her hand and holds her hand to her heart. "God willing, I'll do fine today."

I ask if her friends at home know of her accomplishments.

"Oh, no, honey. Nobody at home knows 'bout all this. Well, they know in our church. That would be the Freedom Baptist Church in Rural Hall, North Carolina. But I don't do this to brag. That wouldn't be right."

An older man with gray hair and a round belly walks up to us. "This is my husband, Melvin," Pat says.

"Did she tell you she's got glaucoma in one eye?" Melvin asks.

"Oh, Melvin, she don't need to be hearing 'bout that."

"Sure she does. It's hard for you to see details. You work hard at this contest." Melvin turns his attention back to me. "Course, she also has a photographic memory."

I can't tell whether Melvin is making the point that winning trivia contests is easy or difficult for his wife. Or if maybe he's angling for a little of her glory. Behind us, I hear someone whispering, "*I think that's the Lady in Red.*"

Because I'm curious how a person memorizes all the minutiae necessary to win the contest, I ask Pat how she studies.

"Well, for a long time, I literally wrote down all the words spoken in every episode. But the contest has gotten harder and harder, and now I also have to notice all the little bitty details. Sometimes, they is things in there for just a fraction of a second, and if I want to win I have to pay attention to 'em. Like the license tag on the laundry truck that appears in one episode. I watched the show but I couldn't quite see the license number. I studied and studied and I *still* couldn't get it. Then, one night, I was asleep and a number was goin' through my head over and over and over again. I woke up and I knew—I just *knew*—it was the license number. I put in the tape, and sure enough that's what it was. Like I said, honey, the Lord helps me with all of this."

"It sounds like you've been working hard," I tell her.

"That's for sure," says Pat's adult daughter, who's been standing nearby. "She's got binders and note cards and yellow sticky notes all over the living room. She works at this almost every day."

Every day? "What's the most episodes you've ever watched in a week?"

"The most? Hmmm, probably about forty."

"What do you watch during an average week?"

" 'Bout thirty-nine."

"Thirty-*nine*?"

"That's right," Pat says. Her face breaks into a broad smile.

This means that Pat Bullins spends close to twenty hours in front of her television every week watching reruns of a forty-year-old show. Do the math and you realize that each calendar year she manages to watch every episode ever broadcast at least eight times.

It's now clear this afternoon's trivia contest is not between Pat and the other participants. The sole contestants in this Mayberry tête-à-tête are the God-fearing Lady in Red and Mr. Otis-the-Drunk Mayberry. Can he stump her this year, or will hard work and heavenly intervention allow her to triumph? I don't know the answer, but I'm now fairly gleeful in anticipation of the real-life drama about to play out in fictional Mayberry.

Before leaving to rejoin Kenneth, I wish Pat luck.

"Thanks, honey. God willing, I can do it again!"

• • •

Craig Flockerzie and Jennifer Cole started dating several years ago. At some point during all their cuddly, getting-to-know-you talk, the young couple from Ohio realized they shared a deep cellular love for *The Andy Griffith Show*. Both had watched reruns of the show with their parents, and the memories of those times were so fondly strong they decided when the time came they'd get married in Mayberry—or rather, Mount Airy, the closest real-life equivalent.

According to the official Mayberry Days program, the time has now come. The Flockerzie-Cole wedding will take place on the steps of the Old City Jail in twenty minutes. It is the first official wedding to occur at Mayberry Days, and everyone who wants to is invited to participate. I find Kenneth, and together we walk up Main Street and over a block to the steps of the Old City Jail. I know it's the old city jail because there's a sign that says "Old City Jail." The turn-of-the-century brick building is painted baby blue. It sits next to a gift emporium and in front of a large public parking lot.

About two hundred Mayberry tourists have gathered in the parking lot under the hot midday sun. They are listening to the mayor read a proclamation affirming the pride of Mount Airy residents in its native son and the clean-living show he created. Lined up along the brick wall behind him are people dressed like characters on the show. I see Opie, Goober, Ernest T. Bass, Howard Sprague, Briscoe Darlin', and Floyd the Barber. I find these look-alikes amazing, not because they exist, but because I've now spent enough time in Mayberry to know who they are.

Kenneth, too, sees the look-alikes, and he starts plotting how to make his way through the crowd to join them.

"Hmmm. I could go inside the Old City Jail and stumble down the stairs," he says.

I nod in encouragement.

"Nah," he says. "That could be rude. But then again, it could be funny." Kenneth scratches his chin and considers his options. I turn my attention to the presentation.

The mayor finishes his proclamation and hands the microphone over to a man named David Browning, who is the emcee for this event. Browning is dressed like Deputy Barney Fife and does an impressive job capturing the deputy's twitchy personality and eye-popping facial expressions.

Someone yells out, "Why'd you let Thelma Lou get away?"

(Mayberry fact #3: Thelma Lou was an office worker on the show, and she and Barney frequently dated.)

Barney-né-Browning looks wounded. "Whaddya mean?" he asks, frowning. "Didn't you see *Return to Mayberry*?"

(Mayberry fact #4: A reunion show held in 1986 showed the deputy and Thelma Lou rekindling their long-lost love.)

The crowd eats it up.

I turn to Kenneth, who's still trying to devise a way to join his look-alike colleagues. "He's good," I say.

"Yes, he is," Kenneth says. So good, in fact, that Browning is able to make a full-time living posing as the Mayberry deputy at sales conventions, on television commercials, and at grand openings of car dealerships throughout the South. He's been so successful that his wife quit her job to manage his career.

"He now makes about eighteen-hundred dollars a day," Kenneth says.

Which serves a lesson to anyone who thinks you can't make a living doing what you love.

After a few minutes of friendly bantering with the crowd, Browning introduces Earle Hagen, who wrote *The Andy Griffith Show*'s famous whistling theme song. Hagen, who looks to be pushing about eighty, is one of the festival's honorary guests. As he walks slowly to the microphone, the crowd of fans assembled in the parking lot starts whistling the theme song together. At first, the whistles are disconnected and choppy, without an audible tune to unite them. But within just a few beats, they find their rhythm and the clearly whistled tune rises and floats in the air above us. Suddenly, the hot, sun-baked lot starts to feel lighter and cooler than it did just seconds ago. I find it all a little erotic, although I'd never admit that to anyone here. It's my first mass whistle.

A minute later, the song ends and the whistle fades away. Hagen makes a few cordial remarks to the crowd, and finally the event we've been waiting for is about to commence. The look-alikes leave the stage, the lectern is removed, and the Flockerzie-Cole bridal party—complete with black tuxes, a white gown, and plum-colored bridesmaid couture—assembles on the steps of the Old City Jail. The bride's got long sandy blond hair and a fresh, eager, Midwestern face. She looks like a young Priscilla Presley. The groom appears a little dazed, but seems to be making the best of it. A young blond flower girl looks up at the two of them like they are fairy tale-royalty.

An Elvis impersonator in a red jumpsuit walks up to the young couple and starts the ceremony.

"Wise men say only fools rush in..."

About halfway through the song, someone grips my left arm. Startled, I look down to see a short, gray-haired woman with thick glasses. She waves the festival program in front of my face.

"I thought this didn't start until noon!" she yells. "That's what the paper said!"

I shrug. I mean, it's not like *I* have anything to do with the planning.

She walks off, disgusted to have missed the very first moments of the very first Mayberry wedding.

Elvis finishes the song, and the minister begins to address the crowd. "We are all gathered here, before friends, relatives, in the site of God..." The spectators quiet down and give the man of the cloth and the young couple in front of him the respect they deserve, and less than ten minutes later, Craig and Jennifer are pronounced husband and wife. They kiss, the crowd cheers, and the happy couple get into a black-and-white Mayberry squad car—complete with a red siren light on top—and they are driven, one assumes, toward years of nuptial splendor.

As the squad car passes, it dawns on me I may be spending too much time with these subcultures because things like a Mayberry wedding and a squad car limousine are starting to seem somewhat normal.

• • •

The wedding crowd begins to disperse and Kenneth is once again happily encircled by fans. While waiting for him, I chat with some of the other look-alikes about their attraction to the show. They all start talking at once.

"I like all this because it helps me get back to how life used to be. You know, safe and all."

"*Andy Griffith* was about real life, not vulgar one-liners."

"If you like the show, you've got to have love in you."

"Sheriff Taylor was a moral man. He reminds us about the right way to act."

Their comments remind me of the conversation I had with Dr. Steven Gelber, the leisure historian who made the link between God and alpacas. Gelber has extensively researched American hobbies and come to the conclusion that people choose pastimes based, in part, on how well those activities reflect cultural values that are important to them. A person who values teamwork and competition, for example, might spend evenings playing in a softball league. A person who values aesthetics and creativity might collect dolls and sew her own costumes.

As I listen to the predominantly white southern fans assembled here it strikes me that Mayberry folks are, like the Lady in Red, a reverent bunch. They are people who do unto others, turn the other cheek, and value a world in which you'd never, ever, not in a coon's age or longer, think of beddin' down with someone other than your honey. They are people who thank the Lord for breakfast. They are people who plan, God willing, for a long healthy future. They are people who believe in kindness and chastity and manners—above all, manners. They are people who believe in the better world that once existed, and the better world they hope to create.

In fact, the moral point of the show and the values it espouses have even inspired a Bible-study program called "Finding the Way Back to Mayberry," in which church-goers watch videotaped episodes, identify the show's moral points, and read corresponding scripture.

But while fans recall the show as a realistic depiction of the idyllic days of yore, in reality, *The Andy Griffith Show* aired during a time of significant social unrest, a time when the Vietnam War and the Cold War competed for headline space with the race riots in the South. And yet, none of the troubling social issues of the sixties ever made it onto the show.

This unrealistic portrayal of the South is why critics take issue with *The Andy Griffith Show*. Mayberry, they claim, was seemingly the only town in America immune from war, crime, class issues, racial unrest, drugs, snotty adolescents, venereal disease, traffic jams, the N word, peace signs, and tie-dyed T-shirts. Detractors will tell you that Mayberry was not a real place, but a mythological space that glorified the kind of clean-living family life that never really existed.

All of which is merely academic blabbing to the devout fans gathered around me. Life may never have existed the way it was portrayed on the show, but they believe it's certainly an ideal worth striving for.

• • •

In America, small towns with economic struggles go to great lengths to attract tourist dollars. Abita Springs, Louisiana, invites visitors to see the Bassigator, Louisiana's version of the Jackalope. Clinton, Montana, hosts the annual testicle festival in honor of the ranching industry and the bulls who sacrifice their manhood. And Mount Airy has the idealistic Mayberry and its native son, Andy Griffith.

An hour ago, Kenneth left to review his questions for the trivia contest, and I came here, to the Mount Airy Visitor Center, located in a charming, sky-blue Victorian house. The center houses a museum devoted to the largest collection of Andy Griffith memorabilia ever assembled in one place.

Here, every surface is covered with treasures from Griffith's life. There are old record albums, television scripts, the suit he wore on *Matlock*, and even a white-and-orange plastic wrapper that was once the casing for an Andy Griffith Whole Hog Sausage. Altogether, there are three rooms of memorabilia. I walk through them slowly, not by choice, but because my progress is impeded by the Mayberry bride in her white wedding dress.

Evidently, the honeymoon can wait.

On his own, Andy Griffith has certainly been enough to put Mount Airy on the map. But upon walking into the main room of the Visitor Center, I learn that the town actually boasts, in addition to Griffith, a curious trio of famous citizens: Donna Fargo, the singer best known as The Happiest Girl in the Whole U.S.A; and Eng and Chang Bunker, the "original Siamese twins," who settled in the area in the 1830s. Whereas Griffith has three rooms devoted to his life, Donna, Eng, and Chang share but a single wall. Still, it beats neutered bulls and bassigators.

On my way out of the building, I pick up a business directory and notice how fully this small town has embraced its Mayberry legacy. The listing of local firms includes Aunt Bea's Barbecue, Goober's Service Garage, and no less than twenty-nine businesses with the word Mayberry in the title, including Mayberry Alarm, Mayberry Auto Sales, Mayberry Consignments, Mayberry Heating and Air, and Mayberry Septic. Mount Airy may have inspired the fictitious Mayberry, but Mayberry has had an unmistakable and perhaps life-saving impact on the small town.

• • •

Just before four o'clock, I walk back through the small, brick-lined downtown to The Andy Griffith Playhouse, an old brick building where Griffith himself used to go to grammar school. Here, in a small grassy park, is where the trivia contest will be held.

On the lawn in front of the playhouse, vendors are selling funnel cakes, onion blossoms, Nehi soda, homemade ice cream, blue cotton candy, Krazy Fries, and German link sausage—but no beer. Like Mayberry itself, Mount Airy does not promote the consumption of evil spirits. The town is not technically dry—beer and wine are available— but you have to know where to look. I order fresh-squeezed lemonade and search for a place to sit on the grass and watch the contest, which isn't as easy as it sounds.

The trivia contest is one of the festival highlights and already there must be close to three hundred people jammed into the small park. I step over Styrofoam coolers and between small children and ultimately find a small square patch of grass. I wedge myself into it and wait for the contest to begin.

To my right is the stage and to my left, toward the back of the park, I can see Pat Bullins waiting beneath her red hat. She's waving the Aunt Bea fan in front of her face. She's not smiling.

Minutes later, Kenneth walks onto the small wooden stage and explains into a microphone how the contest works. Each contestant, he says, should grab one of the Aunt Bea fans that have been distributed throughout the festival. Once a question is asked, anyone who knows the answer must run up to the stage and whisper that answer into the ear of one of three judges. If the answer is correct, the judge will place a sticker on the back of the fan. At the end of the contest, the person with the most stickers wins. The process sounds straightforward, if a bit inefficient.

Kenneth calls out the first question: "On a quiet Sunday morning, Tucker experiences car trouble outside of Mayberry. What is the highway number that he broke down on?"

I hear someone yelling from the back of park, "I think I know!"

I turn and see Pat Bullins running toward the stage, weaving her way through the people sitting on the lawn. She's waving the Aunt Bea paddle as if trying to gain someone's attention. Amazingly, several other people think they too know the answer, and Pat has to wait in line behind them. When at last she's in front of a judge, she leans close, cups her hand around her mouth, and whispers the answer into his ear.

He shakes his head.

"Sorry," he says.

Pat walks, face down, to the back of the park. *What?* How could this be? By my calculation, Pat Bullins has watched more than two thousand *Andy Griffith* reruns over the last twelve months.

Kenneth asks the second question: "Who called Andy Griffith and told him there was a car inside the courthouse?"

This time, Pat seems more confident.

"Oooo, I got it!" she shouts, running on tiptoe toward the judge. She whispers her answer, and this time he smiles.

"Yes!" she cries, balling her hands into fists. He places a sticker on her paddle, and she returns, through the crowd, to her position at the back of the park.

Three questions come and go, and the Lady in Red scores on each one of them. She knows how much Doc Andrews charged per visit (five dollars). She knows who invited Andy and Barney into membership at the Esquire Club in Raleigh (Roger Courtney). She knows what street John Masters, the Mayberry Choir Director, lived on (Elm). Each time, she winds her way through the people sitting on the grass to the stage, receives an affirmative nod, and then winds her way back. Her laborious trek through the park makes me wonder why she didn't stand closer to the stage.

By now, the other spectators have started to notice her.

"Who is she?" asks the woman sitting behind me.

"She's here every year," her companion replies. "No one can beat her."

Kenneth announces question number six: "Who in Mayberry will not admit to having two sets of false teeth?"

Pat runs to the judge and whispers into his ear and this time, I'm not the only one watching her. She seems to have gained the attention of everyone in the small park. We wait, eagerly, for the judge's response.

He looks at her and shakes his head.

"Oooooooohhhhh," the crowd replies.

Question number seven, Pat Bullins is one of only two people to answer correctly. Question number eight, she's the only one. Question number nine, she runs to the judge, takes a deep breath, and whispers her answer. The judge smiles. Pat looks skyward.

"Thank you, Lord!" she screams.

The contest continues, and so does Pat's run of success. At the beginning of the contest, about a dozen participants tried to answer each question. But now that we've reached question number eighteen, only one or two people attempt to take her on. Kenneth asks the next question.

A woman near me nudges her husband in the ribs. "*You* know the answer to that," she says.

"Why bother?" he says.

Finally, Kenneth asks the last question of the contest: "What was the identification number of the airplane Aunt Bea took flying lessons in?"

Kenneth told me earlier this was a throw-away question, the kind anyone at Mayberry Days would be able to answer because a caricature of Aunt Bea sitting in her plane is on this year's official Mayberry Days T-shirt. The identification number is clearly visible on the shirt, which is worn by many people in the crowd.

Several people run up to the judges, and each one gets an affirmative nod and sticker. Pat, however, is still waiting at the back of the park, her head down in concentration. Kenneth is watching her, and so are the other judges. Like me, they seem to be wondering why she isn't running to the stage. Seconds pass. I smell onion fries and cotton candy from the vendors behind me. I hear someone ask, "What's the *matter* with her?" I look at the registration number on the T-shirts and try to will her to the stage.

C'mon, Pat. Come *on*.

Finally, her head flies up. "Wait! I *know* what it is!"

Once again, she high-steps her way through the obstacle course of people sitting on the green lawn and whispers her answer into the judge's ear.

He looks at her, his expression serious. She looks back at him. She moves the fan quickly back and forth in front of her face. Then, slowly, the judge's face breaks into a broad grin.

"Right!" he says, and although I don't know for sure, I suspect Pat Bullins is the only one here who knew the answer without cheating.

Pat hands him her paddle, and he counts the stickers on the back. Out of twenty-three questions, she answered twenty-one correctly, making her the World Champion of Mayberry Trivia for the fourth year in a row. No one else was even close.

The crowd begins to disperse and I walk over to Pat to congratulate her. Her round white face is shiny from the heat and excitement of the afternoon.

"Oh, honey," she says. "It wasn't me. It was the Lord."

• • •

After the contest, I decide I need some down time, some time away from the Aunt Beas and Ernest Ts. Dinner and a glass of wine, emphasis on wine, would be nice.

I recall seeing a restaurant downtown named Merkiff's that is one of the few in Mount Airy to serve anything stronger than

Mountain Dew. It's located above a gift shop, not far from the Old City Jail. I walk there and ask the hostess for a table for one.

"One?" she replies. Her freckled face looks puzzled.

"Yes," I say. "One please."

She shows me to a table in the corner and hands me a menu. Two minutes later, a young woman with cropped blond hair comes to the table.

"Hi, I'm Amanda," she says. Her name tag, however, says her name is Chris. Why is it that everyone in Mayberry seems to have two identities?

I ask Amanda/Chris for a glass of Chardonnay.

"Chardonnay?" she repeats, with the same puzzled expression as the hostess.

"Yes, please. Chardonnay."

Amanda/Chris clearly doesn't approve of my selection, but she does have a job to do. She leaves to get the wine. A few minutes later, she returns and places it on the dark wooden table in front of me. She then writes down my order for the nightly dinner special: butterfly shrimp and mashed potatoes. She finishes writing and looks up.

"You ain't from around here, are ya?" Her southern accent is so strong you could tune a fiddle to it.

"No," I say. "I'm from somewhere's else."

She nods as if this was just what she expected. "Well, welcome." Amanda/Chris turns and flounces back toward the kitchen.

And as she does, I take a sip of my wine, sit back in my chair, and realize with a minor bit of alarm that I've just used the expression, "somewhere's else."

• • •

The next morning at 7 a.m., I meet Kenneth and two of his friends at the Snappy Lunch for an early breakfast. The old diner has a long Formica counter with swivel stools and a separate room lined with booths. The place smells like grease and coffee and cigarettes and is already busy despite the early hour.

The four of us squeeze into a booth and order breakfast: biscuits, eggs, and gravy all around. As we wait for breakfast to arrive, I chat with Allan Newsome, a Floyd-the-Barber look-alike who's been friends with Kenneth for years. Allan, who's dressed this morning in full-on Floyd regalia—white smock, bristle brush, silver scissors—is a family man from Huntsville, Alabama. He tells me that this weekend he's handed out more than one thousand autographed photos of himself as Floyd.

"How long have you been dressing like Floyd?" I ask.

"Since 1994."

"Yeah," Kenneth adds. "He's been doing this so long that sometimes he won't answer to the name Allan."

Allan shrugs. "Sometimes being Floyd does cause a few problems."

"How so?"

"I work at the Redstone Arsenal and because of my security clearance, I have to declare any aliases. Last year, I dressed in a pink barber smock and glasses and adopted the name Pink Floyd. I had to get that cleared through company security and, well…" he looks down at the table, "it was a little awkward."

Kenneth's other friend, Kevin Snead, laughs at this.

"So what's your alias?" I ask Kevin.

"I don't have one," he says.

We begin talking, and I learn that just because Kevin hasn't adopted a Mayberry alter-ego doesn't means he isn't obsessed with the show. In fact, Kevin recently purchased a 32,000-square-foot warehouse on which he's constructing a new façade. When complete, the façade will be like a street right out of Mayberry, complete with Floyd's Barbershop, Foley's Supermarket, and Wally's Service Station.

"I watched the show all my life," he says, by way of explanation. "I seen every episode at least a hundred times."

When breakfast arrives, the three men start reminiscing about the many Mayberry pilgrimages they've taken over the years. They tell me about the time they traveled to Southern California to see Don Knotts get his star on the Hollywood Walk of Fame. The ceremony wasn't until eleven thirty, but the three were so excited they arrived at 7:30 and helped city workers set up chairs, sweep the sidewalk, and polish the brass star.

They tell me about the time they used old black-and-white aerial photos to identify the Desilu studio back lot in Culver City, California, where *The Andy Griffith Show* was filmed. Overlaying those photos with current maps, they were able to pinpoint the exact location of the Mayberry jail and Sheriff Andy Taylor's desk. It is now a security checkpoint next to a film soundstage.

"We went and got our pictures took on that *exact* spot," Kenneth says.

They tell me about the trip they took to Franklin Canyon Lake in Beverly Hills, which was the lake Andy and Opie walked by at the beginning of every show. "We all picked up several rocks and threw them into the water," Kevin explains. "Just like Opie."

They tell me these stories lost in Mayberry rapture. Here, surrounded by their flock, these men don't have to hedge or make excuses or pretend that Mayberry doesn't matter like it does.

When breakfast is over, the men push away their plates, and talk turns to the parade that will start in a couple of hours. The three of them trailered Kenneth's squad car here all the way from Gordo and were hoping to ride it in the parade. But regretfully, something has happened to the transmission, and they haven't been able to fix it.

"Yeah," Kevin says from across the table. "The transmission went out completely yesterday. I had to drive her in reverse on the Andy Griffith Parkway for well over a mile."

The Andy Griffith Parkway is the main interstate highway that serves Mount Airy. I envision the black-and-white squad car with its cherry red top light driving backward against three lanes of highway traffic and can't help myself. I start laughing.

Kevin smiles. "It *was* pretty funny," he admits. "But I got a nasty kink in my neck from looking over my shoulder while trying to steer."

We get up to pay the tab, and on the way I ask Allan, the only one of the three who's married, what his wife thinks of his fascination with Mayberry.

Kenneth answers for him. "She's *won*-derful," he says. "If I could find me a wife like that, I might be persuaded to give up my single ways."

Kevin agrees. "She is great, even though Allan sometimes forgets and starts talking like Floyd at home."

I look at Allan.

"It's true," he admits. "The other day my son came up to me and said, 'Daddy, you're talking like Floyd again.' 'No, I'm not,' I said. Then my wife called out from the other room, 'Yes, you were, dear.'"

• • •

At ten o'clock, I make my way to the corner of Cherry and South in downtown Mount Airy to watch the annual Mayberry Days parade. The crowd of spectators is lined three-deep along both sides of the street. I find a spot on the corner near the post office and wait for the parade to begin.

I've spent the last two days immersed in the real-life manifestation of the fictional Mayberry. I've wondered why a single nondrinker dresses like a lascivious drunk; why a devout homemaker devotes so much time to Mayberry trivia; why a relatively straight-laced electrical engineer dresses like a goofy barber. It's almost too easy to say that these people do what they do because something is missing in their lives. That Kenneth Junkin finds love and admiration that is missing from his home life; that Pat Bullins finds achievement that being a homemaker doesn't provide; that Allan Newsome gets to shed the day-to-day seriousness of working at a weapons arsenal by walking around in a smock and asking would-be customers if they need a trim. That may all be true. Mayberry mania may be nothing more than a compensatory exercise that backfills the holes in one's life. But I'm not so sure this is all that different from watching baseball or gardening—and yet we don't claim those people are missing something.

The parade begins, and two Mount Airy police cars slowly make their way down the crowded street in the bright sunshine. The police cars are followed by a predictable succession of small-town parade entries, with a decidedly Mayberry twist. The marching band is playing the show's theme song. The majorettes are dressed in denim overalls and carrying fishing poles with yellow cardboard fish. The Pork Princess is followed by the Barbecue Queen who's followed by Miss Mayberry Days who's followed by a dark green convertible with a white piece of cardboard dangling from the driver's-side door. On the cardboard, written in black felt pen, are the words: "I ain't drunk yet, but I'm working on it. Love, Otis." I look inside the convertible and am pleased to see that Kenneth, in his crumpled straw hat and black suspenders, has not let the lack of a squad car stop him from participating in the parade.

I wave at Kenneth energetically. And as I do, I find that I'm happy to be part of this celebration. Perhaps I do have a passion after all. Perhaps what I love is spending time with people who just don't give a damn what other people think. I may not be completely comfortable here—after all, I am from somewhere's else—but these Mayberry fans are teaching me what it feels like to be fully yourself without apologies.

The parade continues peacefully for another half hour until all at once the people around me start to point up the street and jostle for better viewing positions. I look at them, trying to figure out what's up.

"Barney's coming," they say.

"There he is."

"I can see him."

"Get out your camera."

I step off the curb and squint up the street where a Barney Fife look-alike is signing autographs and teasing the crowd. As he moves closer, I notice it's not the Barney Fife look-alike who wowed the crowd at yesterday's wedding ceremony, not the Barney Fife look-alike who makes $1,800 for appearances. This is a new Barney Fife look-alike, one I haven't seen before. The people around me also start to notice he's not the one they're used to.

"Eww, who's *he?*"

"I don't want a picture of *him.*"

"He's not the *real* Barney Fife."

They put their cameras away and stand back on the curb. I don't care what anybody says. You've got to love a world wherein reality is suspended to such a degree that people will only accept the most well-known fakes of fictional characters.

• • •

The afternoon arrives, and I discover I'm sad my time in Mayberry will soon be coming to an end. I watch some reruns of the show at a local coffee shop. I stand in line at the Mount Airy Post Office to get postcards imprinted with the official Mayberry Days postmark.

Finally, at four o'clock, I go with Kenneth to the last event: the annual meeting of *The Andy Griffith Show* Rerun Watchers Club, where we eat boxed dinners containing barbecued pork sandwiches. The meeting is attended by representatives from chapters all around the country whose names come from lines in the show: "A Cherry for Thelma Lou" is here from Decatur, Illinois. "What's Wrestlin' to Some is Dancin' to Others" has traveled all the way from Kansas. My personal favorite is a chapter from Newcastle, Indiana, called "This Is the Body of a Judo Fighter: I'm a Deadly Weapon!"

The meeting proceeds, awards are handed out, news is shared, and within ninety minutes the meeting is over. I walk outside with Kenneth. It's early evening now, Main Street is deserted, and it's begun to rain. A wet autumn chill has settled over Mount Airy. I tell Kenneth I'm a little sad to be leaving.

"That's how I always feel," he says. "But I know there's always next year."

He bends over and gives me a big ol' Otis bear hug.

"Thanks, Kenneth, for sharing a bit of Mayberry with me."

"Oh, it was my pleasure, really it was," he says. "The way I look at it, this is like getting together with family for a reunion, only we get to pick the family. Now you're a part of that family, y'know."

I smile, not quite sure if this is true or not.

Kenneth leaves, and I walk into Weaver's Department Store, which is located next to the old theater. Normally, the store is called Specialty Collectables and Keepsakes and sells Christmas ornaments, mantel displays, and other arts and crafts. But this one weekend every year, the store becomes Weaver's in honor of the fictional Mayberry establishment. I walk in and see that the entire front half of the store has been given over to Mayberry products. There are twirling wire racks with Mayberry greeting cards, turnstiles with Mayberry sweatshirts, and countless shelves stacked with Mayberry books, advent calendars, trivia games, mugs, and shot glasses. I find myself wanting a little something to commemorate the weekend.

I take my time walking through the displays and eventually choose a coffee mug, several greeting cards, a key chain, and a black-and-white mousepad that says, "This Computer Protected by Fife."

Several months ago when I started down this road, I was pleased to be given a Malibu Barbie doll at the Annual Barbie Doll Collector Convention. Today, I'm forking over my own hard-earned money in an effort to share a bit of this passion.

It's not much. But it's a start.

CHAPTER SEVEN

Spreadin' the Josh

"You raise me up to more than I can be."
—Josh Groban

"DOWN HERE! DOWN HERE! I CAN SEE THE BUSES BEHIND
the fence and I think we can get in this way!"

"Is there an opening in the fence?"

"I don't know, but I'm willing to climb over."

I give up.

Just when I'm starting to grasp the slippery mysteries of
fanatical passion I find myself late on a Tuesday night rushing
around a wind-swept, near-empty parking lot outside the SBC
Center in San Antonio, Texas, with a passel of pop-star groupies.
We are scrambling to get close to the bus that will shuttle Josh
Groban, the international singing sensation, from the stadium to
his hotel. With me are a fifty-six-year-old grandmother, her
nine-year-old grandson, a divorced trombonist named James, a
woman who keeps a life-sized cardboard cutout of Josh in her
walk-in closet, and a devout Christian from New Jersey who's
willing to do anything to get close to Josh's bus.

"You know what I'm saying," she says. "*Anything.*" She
slows down and looks at me. "Well, anything that's not illegal or
immoral."

These people are on a mission. What do they want? An
autograph would be ideal. A handshake exquisite. But even a

glimpse of Josh's curly brown hair through the tinted window of the bus would be deeply satisfying.

One of the groupies jogs past me. "Heck," she calls, "I'd be happy just to see his *musicians*."

Sighing, I rush to keep up with her.

• • •

Several months ago, I'd never heard of Josh Groban, even though his recordings have sold more than ten million copies worldwide. Then I got a call from my friend Allan, who was aware of my quest.

"Shari," he said, "you've got to check out the Grobanites."

"The *Who*banites?"

"The Grobanites."

Allan told me the Grobanites were predominantly women, predominantly middle-aged women, who were utterly devoted to the twenty-four-year-old boy singer. He told me many followed Josh from concert to concert like a post-modern menopausal version of the Deadheads. He told me some of them had taken out second mortgages to do this. He told me some had marital problems.

I asked Allan how he'd come to be so well informed and he explained he'd been to a concert and sat next to a Grobanite. "She talked through the entire concert about Josh and his fan base and how she and many of the other Grobanites had never felt this way about anything before."

And that's when he had me. Women going agog for the first time in mid-life? Maybe these people *could* teach me something.

A few weeks later, I posted a note on an Internet forum explaining my interest in talking with some Grobanites. I happened to mention that I'd already spent time with Barbie collectors, ice fishermen, and pigeon racers. Within a few hours, 247 people had viewed the post, and several responded.

"Are you saying we're weird or something?"

"Yah… I don't really understand how Josh fits into any category with Barbie."

"*Before, the press has turned us into psychotic no-lifers… they make it seem like we have no other purpose in life than to follow Josh around, mesmerized, with drool coming from our mouths, waiting to wipe his butt for him. And that's not true. Only some of us do that.*"

This last writer made it a point to say she was kidding. But she also warned me: Grobanites were very protective with their reputation—and Josh's. The message: I could attend a concert and talk to whomever I pleased, but I'd better be careful.

Realizing the land of Grobanites might be more difficult to enter than anticipated, I contacted Linda Story Omalia, the fifty-six-year-old Grobanite who'd inducted my friend Allan into the club. My question: Would she be willing to introduce me to a few Grobanites and let me attend a concert with her?

"Absolutely!" she said, over the phone. "Shari, I read all those posts on the forum and have to say some of those Grobanites are just a *little* too sensitive. I mean, this *is* kinda weird."

We devised a plan I would fly to Houston where Linda lives, meet up with her and several other Grobanites, and travel with them by car to San Antonio where we'd attend a Grobanite Meet 'n' Greet before heading off to Josh's concert that evening. "That way," she said, "you'll get to meet a lot of us crazy Grobies."

After all the admonishment suffered on the Josh Groban forum, I was grateful Linda was so willing to help me understand all this.

"Don't mention it, honey. We call it spreadin' the Josh."

• • •

My tour of Grobania began early this morning at the Houston airport, where I was picked up by James Matej, who works with Linda at Stewart Title Company. As I was buckling my seat belt, he turned to me. He was about my age, with a kindly face and a dark beard.

"Just so you know," he said, "I'm *not* a Grobanite."

"That's okay. I'm not a Grobanite either."

With that out of the way, we exited the airport and drove toward the office park where we'd planned to meet Linda. Along the way, James explained that he was a musician, a trombonist actually, and while he'd been successful early on, he'd taken that success for granted, got married too young, given up his music, raised two kids, got divorced, and was now desperate to reclaim his space in the musical world. Unfortunately, the underwhelming demand for solo trombone acts was making his re-entry difficult.

"Oh, listen to me," he said. "I'm just yacking away, and you're not here to learn about *me*."

"But I am here to learn about passion, and you seem pretty passionate about music."

"You could say that. Actually, that's why I'm going tonight. Josh's opening act is a solo trumpet player. I thought I might be able to pick up some ideas."

James then turned the subject back to the Grobanites. "I'll be anxious to see what you think of them," he said. "Do you know Josh's music?"

I confessed I'd only heard a couple of songs.

He smiled at me, crow's-feet crinkling the sides of his brown eyes. I couldn't tell what his smile was saying, but I sensed that James, with his musical background and avowed non-Grobanite status, was going to be a useful counterbalance to the day's activities.

A half hour later, Linda came screeching into the company parking lot behind us.

"Hi, Shari!" she said, jumping out of her dark gray Chevy Suburban. "Glad you could join us!" Linda Story Omalia is a tall, thin, I-beam of a woman. She was wearing a black sweatshirt from the University of Grobania and lipstick the color of valentines. I liked her instantly.

James and I climbed into the middle row of seats and were introduced to our traveling companions—Kathy Blum, who's forty-seven and works as a part-time manager for a chain of movie theaters; Denise Hampton, also forty-seven, who works at a Build-a-Bear franchise; and Sean Smith, Linda's nine-year-old grandson.

"I Grobanized him a long time ago," Linda explained.

We got underway and all four of the Grobanites began talking at once. They talked about the upcoming concert. They talked about the souvenirs they were planning to buy. They talked about the price they paid for tickets.

"I got a front-row ticket online this morning for less than a hundred dollars."

"Oh, my heart be still. I had to spend four hundred for my ticket."

"Four *hundred?*"

"Yes, but the husband thinks I only spent two."

The energy inside the car reminded me of the nervous, I-hope-my-hair-looks-good feeling I used to have before high school dances.

Accelerating onto Highway 10 westbound for San Antonio, the office parks gradually gave way to open fields, the anxious excitement of the Grobanites gradually settled into silent anticipation, and the next two hours unfolded, for me, like a Berlitz course for foreign visitors to Grobania—complete with detailed information about the language, culture, and customs of its residents.

• • •

The first thing visitors to Grobania need to understand is that it's virtually impossible to speak about Josh Groban without using Joshisms. All subcultures possess their own vernacular, of course, but the Grobanictionary, as it's called, is unparalleled in its linguistic scope and creativity. For instance, Grobanites are often severely afflicted with Grobanitis, a contagious infection that causes them to continuously play Josh's CDs or check his website or look twice whenever they see a man with curly brown hair. They are also prone to Grobanian slips, suffer from Joshmares, become scatterjoshed, and are seized by Joshfright when they finally get a chance to meet their idol. Older fans take Joshtrogen. Younger fans believe he is drop-dead gor-josh. And fans with children have been known to throw Grobantrums when their kids want attention—and they'd rather gaze at the latest Josh video. The Grobanictionary is so exhaustingly extensive it's not uncommon to hear several terms strung together in one sentence, as in, "I'm a hopeless Grobantic Grobanite who's willing to enter the state of Holy Joshimony with someone Joshilicious."

Having a working vocabujosh is important in Grobania, but at best it will merely get you a green card. Fans seeking permanent resident status must demonstrate a much longer list of characteristics. Such as? Well, for starters, a true Grobanite remembers the very first time she heard Josh's operatic baritone. Linda was eating in the kitchen with her husband and when she heard his voice on *The Ali McBeal Show* she dropped her fork, got up, and stared, dumbstruck, at the television. "The next morning, I went to work and looked him up on the Internet," she explained. "After that, I just went crazy."

Second, by their own admission, Grobanites are Grobanites from the get-go. This is not the kind of passion you have to plant and let germinate. Either you love Josh or you don't, end of story. And if you do, you won't keep his music to yourself. Instead, you'll understand that Josh, who sings pop ballads in the classical style, many in Italian or Spanish, is not easy to classify. He's not *really* a pop star. Not *really* a classical musician. And the top forty radio stations won't touch him. Because of all this, you'll take it upon yourself to spread the Josh far and wide. You'll give CDs to friends. You'll slam music critics who've written unfavorable reviews. You'll join forces with other Grobanites to get him more visibility.

"We spammed Oprah to get him on her show," Linda

explained. "And when he finally did appear, Oprah came out and said, 'Okaaaaay, Grobanites, I got your message. It's okay to stop now.'"

Third, card-carrying Grobanites possess a deep, encyclopedic knowledge of all things Groban. They know Josh likes sushi with blueberry sauce, herring and cheese, coffee crisps from Canada, and Rice Krispie squares. They know that blue and purple and black are his favorite colors; *The Simpsons*, his favorite TV show; and that he is equally enamored with Sting, Pavarotti and Linkin Park.

"And don't forget Fiji Water," Kathy said, holding up her own bottle of Fiji from the passenger seat. "Because Josh likes it, this is all I drink now."

Fourth, Grobanites can also detail Josh's musical training, family life, and list of bad habits—which aren't many, Linda stressed. "He's a sloucher and drives too fast."

But don't be misled into thinking all Grobanites are alike. Yes, Grobanites are predominantly female. Yes, many are middle-aged. But if you were to take a snapshot of the audience at a Josh Groban concert you'd see everyone from four-year-old girls to eighty-five-year-old grandfathers. Among them, you'd find doctors and lawyers and school teachers and hairdressers. Some are only mildly fascinated. Others plan their lives around Josh.

One of the most rapturous is a Grobanite known as the Pillow Lady, so named because of the handcrafted pillows she makes that feature color photos of Josh. The Pillow Lady is forty-seven years old and completing a Ph.D. in accounting. She's also highly critical of the woman Josh is dating and has been kicked off the forum several times for dissing his girlfriend.

But she's just one example among many, Linda said. One Grobanite followed Josh into a hair salon to retrieve his curly clippings from the floor. One tried and failed to trademark the name Grobanite. One took out a forty-five-thousand-dollar second mortgage in order to buy Josh merchandise and fly to concerts. One has a life-size stuffed doll that looks like Josh, which she puts in the playpen with her grandson.

Linda is obviously a proud Grobanite. But because she also seems to possess a healthy basecoat of skepticism, I had to ask: Did she think any of this was a trifle excessive?

"It is, for many people," she admitted. "We haven't heard of a bankruptcy yet, but I wouldn't be surprised. I know a lot of people who've maxed out their credit cards. I try to put a limit on it. I'll say, 'That's it. I'm Joshed out. I'm not going to the concert in New Orleans.' But then, the time came, and I went. I mean, you can only hear him sing the same thing over and over so many times."

Kathy interjected, "I'm not there yet." She waved her bottle of Fiji for emphasis. "I'm going to every concert I can until I can actually meet him."

"But why? What does Josh do to people?"

Linda thought about this for a moment, her thumbs tapping the sides of the steering wheel at the ten and two o'clock positions.

"Here's my theory," she said. "My theory is that the women who end up going to his concerts more than one time, well, they won't admit this, but I think he touches a small part of us inside. Whether we're beautiful or not beautiful. Whether we're rich or not rich. He touches someplace inside that nobody else has been able to."

• • •

Just outside of San Antonio, we stopped at Wendy's for a bathroom break. Denise, who'd been quietly playing with Linda's grandson, climbed over the backseat and accompanied me inside. She's a fast talker with a Jersey accent packed into a short, tennis-shoed body.

"You want to know what people like about Josh?" she asked. "I'll tell you. I believe Josh is a gift from God. Now, I'm no Holy Roller. I don't go around knocking on people's doors.

But I do believe the end is near. The world is setting itself up for Armegeddon. Children have no respect for themselves. There are so many weird things in the world. But Josh, his voice alone is going to bring together generations of people that would not have been together otherwise. There's this girl on the Josh Groban forum. We call her Annabanana. She's twelve or thirteen years old. I was e-mailing back and forth with this thirteen-year-old, and we were both understanding each other. What were we talking about? *Josh* of course! He's does that to people. Where else would I be talking to a thirteen-year-old?"

I followed Denise into the restroom, and we each took a stall. I sat down thinking we'd take a break from conversation while we, you know, did our business. But Denise continued, raising her voice to be heard over the top of the stall door.

"I remember the first concert I went to," she said. "The night before, I was praying for traveling mercies. Then God woke me up in the middle of the night and told me to get some stuff to give to Josh from my trip to Israel. I'd spent two weeks in Israel—without the husband, he didn't want to go—and it was the best two weeks of my life. God told me to get some things from that trip. So I did. I put together a little gift box. Inside was a shekel from Jerusalem, a dried flower from the Mount of the Beatitudes, seashells from the Mediterranean, an olive branch from the Mount of Olive. Oh! And rocks from Caesarea, where Jesus went to start his ministry when driven out of Bethlehem."

Sitting in my stall, listening to Denise, I vacillated between two wildly different thoughts. One, that this was shaping up to be one of the more memorable bathroom chats I'd ever had. And two, that I hoped Josh appreciated her gift.

"So," I said, overcoming my own polite bathroom restraint, "how did you get the box to Josh?"

"Linda had a backstage pass! I gave her the box, and she passed it on. I inserted a note telling Josh that God asked me to do this. I signed my first name, but not my last. God did *not* ask me to do that."

Her story complete, we flushed, washed our hands, and walked back outside. I recalled her comment about spending four hundred dollars for tonight's ticket and asked if God had also encouraged her to do that.

"No, God did *not* encourage me to do that. I work at Build-a-Bear in the mall for minimum wage, so you can imagine how much money that is to me. When the ticket thing came up, I said, 'Lord, that's a lot of money.' I told Him what I was about to do, and then a calm came over me. I felt it was the right thing to do 'cause, you know, at my age, it never occurred to me that I would feel this way about anything again. Besides, I haven't been healthy. I have rheumatoid arthritis, fibromyalgia, and hepatitis C. Everything was fine for years, but then the medication started to affect my eyesight, and my jaw bone deteriorated. Now I've got dentures. You know what I'm saying? I was thinking my life was basically over. Then I heard Josh, and he touched me in a way I hadn't been touched in a long time. So I decided to do this. Just this once. Even if I did deceive the husband. But I won't do it again because, you know, there are too many hungry people in the world. I couldn't live with myself."

Denise climbed into the back seat. "You know what else?" she said. "I think we Grobanites have more in our lives than most people do. If you have nothing in your life, you think of nothing but yourself. It's important for people to find something to appreciate—Jesus or music or ballet or whatever. That way, instead of centering on themselves, they can center on something else and maybe find that life isn't as bad as they thought."

"I agree," I said.

• • •

Forty-five minutes later, we pulled into the Best Western Hotel in downtown San Antonio, which had been chosen as the official resting place for out-of-town Grobanites. After checking in, I walked to the elevator with Kathy and Linda and her grandson. Three other Grobanites held the door for us. One was wearing a large round pin on her lapel with a color photo of Josh.

"Are y'all Grobanites?" she asked, her face all pink and smiley.

Not sure how to answer, I faked deafness.

"You bet we're Grobanites!" Linda replied. "Well, except for her." She pointed at me. "She's a Baby Grobe. This is her first concert."

The pin lady looked at me. "Awww, that's soooo cute. You're just gonna love him."

I'd like to report that I graciously accepted the pin lady's well wishes, but in fact, all I could manage was a thin smile.

Several long seconds later, the elevator opened onto my floor, and Kathy and I stepped off into a narrow hallway. At the end of the hall, a gaggle of Grobanites were collected around a brass luggage cart. They looked up at us.

"Hey!" they called. "Y'all Grobanites?"

Shit.

Not again.

No, I wanted to say. *No, I am* not *a Grobanite.* But that seemed insulting somehow. These were perfectly lovely people having a perfectly lovely time. But claiming to actually be a Grobanite would be equally wrong. Perhaps worse. Panicking, I began to fake an intense interest in the flat white plastic of my hotel key. Finally, Kathy spoke up behind me.

"*I'm* a Grobanite!" she said, and a squeal rose in the hallway.

I reached the door to my room as the group of women scuttled, en masse, past me and toward their new tribe member. Once inside, I shut the door, leaned against it, and realized Grobanites aren't the only people who resist being lumped into a category at odds with their own self-perceptions.

• • •

The hotel room was decorated with Mission-style oak furniture, sage green walls, and dim Tiffany-style lamps with geometric patterns. I checked my watch. Three thirty. We didn't have to leave for the Meet 'n' Greet for over an hour. I climbed onto the patterned bedspread and lay down for a quick nap.

But I couldn't sleep. My mind was a bubbling bouillabaisse of impressions. I couldn't figure out how to characterize the Grobanites. They could be pious, eager, enthusiastic, and charitable. But they were also defensive, petty, protective, and rebellious—which meant I probably had more in common with them than I cared to admit.

And yet the idea of celebrity worship is one I don't inherently understand. In the interest of full disclosure, I should probably reveal that when I was eleven years old I did kiss the glossy magazine photo of David Cassidy that hung on my bedroom wall. And I did this more than once. But I haven't gone ape over anyone since then, and if anything, this lack of understanding makes me the oddball.

Prior to coming here, I'd clicked around the Internet and learned that a team of British and U.S. researchers had discovered at least a third of Americans suffer from celebrity worship syndrome, and many of the rest of us are at risk of developing the condition. After all, we live in a paparazzied, *People* magazine culture, wherein Madonna and Elvis receive far more Google hits than Darwin and Einstein.

Read the journal reports and you get the distinct impression that researchers find fanatical fans a bit off. Celebrity worship, they say, is at the top of a slippery slope that can lead quickly to depression, anxiety, psychosis, social dysfunction, loneliness, and a distinct need for spiritual sustenance. As conventional wisdom has it, fanatics are either impressionable fools or dangerous stalkers.

But in among all the articles about the psychosis of celebrity worship, I also uncovered some contradictory reports that claimed celebrity worship is actually a beneficial, biologically driven behavior that can help with social bonding. How? By giving us something to gossip about. You might have nothing else in common with your coworkers, but at least you have Michael Jackson to talk about. Some psychologists also believe whom we worship helps define who we are. By dissecting the personality and lifestyle choices of Josh Groban, Grobanites are, in effect, learning about and reinforcing their own underlying values.

Lying in the quiet, dark room, I reviewed the things I'd been learning about the Grobanites in search of clues to what those underlying values might be. Certainly, they shared an appreciation for music. But the one thing continually emphasized by the Grobanites—both in their responses to me on the forum and during my conversations with Linda—was the importance of giving.

"People get charitable because of Josh," Linda said. "We're moved by what a sweet person he is."

Linda told me about the time she and eight other fans worked to help the brother of a Grobanite who'd become a vented quadriplegic in a car accident. The man's name was David. He could no longer speak, his wife had been killed in the same accident, and he had a little girl at home.

"We wanted to get David some specialized equipment to enable him to enjoy life more," she explained.

Calling their efforts the Campaign of Compassion, they solicited donations from other Grobanites. They made crafts and sold them at auctions. They formed a card chain and mailed cards to David every single day. It took many long months, but eventually they were able to buy a customized laptop to allow David to type—and thus communicate—by tapping his tongue inside his cheek. But that wasn't all. Her team also worked tirelessly for more than a year to get David a motorized wheelchair. Talk to any Grobanite, Linda had suggested, and you'll hear a story like this.

All of which leads me to believe that perhaps I shouldn't get so defensive when Grobanites try to Grobanize me in elevators.

But then again…

Oh my Josh.

This is all so confusing.

• • •

An hour later, this charitable drive was on full display at the Grobanite Meet 'n' Greet held at a Mexican restaurant on the Riverwalk in downtown San Antonio. The restaurant's walls were covered with sepia-toned photos of the Alamo, mounted Texas longhorns, and signs featuring the five-pointed Texas star proclaiming Liberty or Death. But the history of the region as it relates to Texas independence couldn't have been further from the minds of the sixty women and five men who came to socialize and raise money for charity by buying lots and lots—and lots—of Josh Groban souvenirs.

The silent auction tables were heaped with Josh Groban calendars, mugs, picture frames, pillows, stationery, T-shirts, magnets, snow globes, tea trays, and other lovingly crafted homemade merchandise. I sat down at a table across from Linda and noticed a white-handled lunch bag resting on my placemat.

"That's your gift bag," Linda said.

I burrowed into it and discovered three photo magnets, two CDs, a package of Rice Krispies treats, a couple of pens, and a tattoo of Josh's head that I could temporarily apply to my arm or another bare piece of flesh.

"It's not a *bad* gift bag," Linda explained. "But there've been better. This one doesn't have any thud pills."

"*Thud* pills?"

"Yes, you use them after Josh takes the stage and you faint and go 'thud!'"

Linda, who'd applied a fresh coat of lipstick and changed

clothes in preparation for the concert, was obviously getting excited about the show.

After a buffet dinner of tacos and enchiladas, the live auction got underway. The premiere item was a handmade quilt with eighteen panels of different Josh Groban photographs. A stout older woman with short, white, gym-teacher hair took the microphone.

"Come on, ladies," she shouted, her voice rough like an emery board. "Wouldn't you like to curl up with this?"

The bidding started and quickly leapfrogged from thirty to sixty to eighty dollars. "One hundred!" the auctioneer shouted. "Do we hear one hundred dollars?"

Linda's friend Kathy, who'd been counting the bills in her wallet, raised her hand. "I've got $104!"

The room fell quiet. The smell of refried beans hung in the air. Kathy's fists shook like rattles. It looked, for one long suspended moment, like she might get the quilt. But then the bidding jumped to $110. Then $115. Then $120. The curl-up-with-Josh quilt ultimately went for $130 to a woman who looked to be well into her sixties. She grabbed the quilt and wove her way back through the tables and stopped in front of one of the other, lower bidders.

"Here," she said, handing the quilt to the other woman. "This is for you."

Astonished, I turn to Linda. "She just *gave* it away?"

"Yeah," she said. "Grobanites are like that."

• • •

Fueled by the frenzy of the Meet 'n' Greet, the Grobanites and I rushed back into Linda's Suburban, rocketed through downtown San Antonio toward the SBC Center, and became instantly, dizzyingly lost. Kathy, who'd been reading the map, had somehow missed a turn.

"I thought you had this all worked out!" Linda screamed. "You've always been so organized!"

"Well, I *did* know how to get to the Center from the hotel, but not from the restaurant!"

"Oh, this is hilarious."

"There's Houston! That's the street we want to be on."

"You sure?"

"Positive."

"Well, if not, I'm going back to the hotel and I'm starting over."

"At this point, I don't know if I can get us back to the hotel."

"Ohhh, I'm going to kill you!"

"But it's only six thirty! There's still plenty of time to find our seats and buy merchandise."

"Obviously, what we need now is some Groban Dust to give us luck." Linda leaned over the steering wheel and blew. "Fffft, fffft, blow, baby, blow."

"Slow down!" Kathy said. "There's a police officer."

"I don't care about him! I'm going to pull that policeman over and say we are Grobanites and we are not from this city and we're lost, and I'm gonna start cryin' like a baby if I can't find the SBC Center."

"We'll find it," Kathy said. "We'll find it."

And amazingly, we did. Less than five minutes later, we pulled into the parking lot and the furor in the front seat, instead of settling down, started all over again. Kathy directed Linda to the number *four* parking lot, which was the cheapest. But Linda wanted to go to the number *two* parking lot, which was closer to the stadium, which meant we'd be closer to Josh's tour buses, and since it was *her* car and *she* was driving it was *her* decision to make.

Kathy sighed. "I'll bet the buses are way back there where we started, and now there's not a chance in hell we're going to see him after the show."

Linda was not happy with Kathy's sudden display of pessimism. She pointed to a lot, across from the entrance. "*That's* where I'm going." The sign above the lot said, "Media Only."

A parking attendant tried to stop the Suburban from entering the media-only lot, but Linda wouldn't hear of it. She rolled down her window and mumbled something that somehow managed to sound both desperate and official at the same time. Perplexed, the attendant let her pass. She pulled into a space directly across from the entrance and threw the Suburban into park, causing us to slam forward like crash-test dummies.

Linda marched toward the door, followed in a line by Kathy, Denise, Sean, James, and me. On the way in, I could hear Denise muttering, "This is like one hundred Christmases."

• • •

Once inside, Denise and Linda and Kathy got into the back of a long line at the souvenir stand, and I stood to the side with James. He'd been quiet all day, respectful of the others. But as we watched the fans clamor for sweatshirts and posters and CDs, he confided in me.

"This is all sort of amazing considering that Josh is not very good," he said. "I mean, he's getting better, but it's interesting how popular mediocre talent can be in this country."

• • •

James and I found our seats on the arena floor fourteen rows back from the stage. I sat down next to a plump woman named Danielle, who wore a red feather boa and displayed a breathtaking line of cleavage.

Danielle told me it was her twenty-ninth birthday, and she'd left her husband and two kids home in Albuquerque so she could celebrate by doing what she loves best: adoring Josh Groban.

"My mom was a Parrot Head who followed Jimmy Buffet," she said. "I thought she was the biggest dork ever. I mean, you know, she went to concerts with a *parrot* on her head. Now look at me. Everything I do, my mom used to do. Like, tomorrow I'm going to get a Josh tattoo on my wrist." Danielle stroked her boa as she thought about her present to herself. "It's going to be his curly-haired signature."

Just then, Danielle saw some of her fellow Grobanites sitting in a nearby section and wriggled her way past me toward the aisle. A piece of her red boa caught on the chair in front of me, and a single feather floated down onto my lap. I picked it up and showed it to James.

"Uh-oh," he said. "I think you've just been Grobanized."

Ten minutes later, the lights dimmed, Danielle returned, and Chris Botti, Josh's opening act and the trumpet player James had come to see, took the stage and the crowd responded enthusiastically. They listened and clapped and whistled as if Botti were the man they'd come to see. In my history, *no* one has ever whistled for the opener. But Linda had warned me about this.

"Josh fans don't just love Josh," she said. "They love everyone associated with him—his keyboard player, his drummer, his opening act—we support all of them, too."

Which was great. For the Grobanites.

But after the steady day-long ramp up to the concert, after wondering for hours if I might possibly swirl into Josh's orbit along with the rest of the Grobanites, after being tickled for forty-five minutes in the left cheek by Danielle's boa, I was ready for Josh to appear.

And when he finally did, the crowd went completely, utterly, bodaciously berserk. The sound of their stomping feet rumbled throughout the concrete arena. I expected the Grobanites to rush the stage immediately, but instead they seemed to follow some kind of silent pre-established protocol. They waited politely for him to finish his first song, and *then* several fans made their way to the stage to hand him gifts. They gave him a white angel bear. A basket of Coffee Crisps. A black cowboy hat. I turned to James.

"I feel bad I didn't bring anything."

"That's okay," he said. "I didn't either."

Josh thanked each gift bearer personally. He shook their hands. He placed his right hand over his heart. And then he returned to his act, backed up by members of a local high school choir and several members of the local symphony—something Danielle explained was de rigucur for a Groban concert.

Whether he was singing in Italian or Spanish or English, Josh's baritone was rich and clear. His voice easy to listen to. But something about his demeanor made me think that all the fan adoration made him uneasy. His voice cracked at one point, and he said, "Uh-oh. It's going to be a puberty night."

I cringed.

But I was the only one.

It seemed that this aw-shucks-I'm-human-too persona was exactly what the Grobanites liked about Josh.

The songs continued, the gifts continued, and when the concert ended two hours later, a third of the fans sitting on the stadium floor stampeded toward the stage for a chance to touch Josh's hand. It was all very sweet and pleasant. But frankly, after the two-hundred-mile build-up, the concert itself was a little anti-climactic. I don't know what I was expecting. Elvis, maybe. Or Jesus. But Josh struck me simply as a nice young man caught up in the middle of something larger and far more mysterious than he is.

• • •

I didn't share these impressions with my personal Grobanites when we met up again after the concert. The show had made them lively and impatient, like hummingbirds, as if they didn't know what to do with themselves now that the concert they'd waited all day-month-year for was over. They flittered between and amongst each other, looking for a way to release the energy.

Kathy zoomed up to me. "Oh, my God," she said, holding her right hand tight against her chest. "I touched his hand. I squeezed it soooo hard. I can't wait to tell my friends and family that I touched him." She wasn't talking to me. Not really. She just had to talk, and once she did, she buzzed up the stairs toward the concourse. I met up with her again outside the restroom.

"Oh my God," she said. "It's hitting me now. I can't believe it. I actually *touched* him."

We floated amid a tide of fans toward the stadium exit. I assumed we'd head straight for the Suburban, but once outside, Kathy and Denise started plotting how to get to the tour buses. The collar of my black leather jacket flipped back and forth in the icy wind. But instead of being deterred by the cold, Kathy and Denise seemed energized by it. Even Sean, Linda's grandson, became more animated than I'd seen him all day.

"Down here," Denise yelled, jogging in front of us. "I think if we go to the end of the chain link fence, and then work our way through the parking lot, we can reach the buses."

• • •

So here we are. We've spent the last half hour walking through the parking lot, around the perimeter of the arena, and back again. There is no break in the fence, no way to get to the chariots that will whisk Josh and his crew back to their kingdom. We can see the tall beige buses in the distance, but there's a security guard blocking the way.

We wait for ten, twenty more minutes, hoping that if we can't get to the buses, maybe they'll drive toward us. But there's no sign of movement, and the thermometer's draining mercury by the second. Finally, Linda says, it's time to go back to the hotel. Quietly, the Grobanites agree. They turn and follow Linda, heads down, through the dark, now-empty parking lot toward the Suburban.

I get inside and rest my head against the back of the seat thinking about the sage green walls of my hotel room. But just as I'm starting to relax, Linda suddenly speeds up, makes a sharp left, and turns back into the lot.

"Oh, heck," she says. "Let's see if we can *drive* closer to the buses."

Denise and Kathy and Sean become so incredibly, joyously happy with this decision that they start directing Linda all at once.

"Straight ahead."

"No, I think you should go left."

"Whatever you do, just hurry."

We veer this way and that, zigzagging over the original path we took into the lot six hours earlier. This time it's easier because there are no cars, but Linda still manages to run over one orange cone and fling another off to the left. Five minutes later, it's the same story: The buses, the Holy Grail, the pot at the end of the rainbow, Josh Groban—all out of reach. Instead of discouraging the Grobanites, though, the impossibility of this mission has re-energized them. Collectively, they decide to drive back to the front of the stadium and just wait for those damn buses to leave.

Which we do, for about ten minutes.

"I hate to tell y'all this," Linda says, her optimism waning, "but I think Josh is probably already back at his hotel. He usually takes a car, not the buses."

She's telling us this *now?*

Linda expresses sympathy with the Grobanites who've not yet had the pleasure, as she has, of meeting Josh and his entourage. But it's close to midnight now, and she really thinks we ought to head back to the hotel.

She exits the parking lot, speeds onto the highway, and discovers several minutes later that she's going the wrong way. She takes the next off-ramp, circles under the highway, and stops to let two buses go by.

It takes a second to register.

"Oh, my God!" she says. "Those are the buses!" Linda pulls up right behind them and we follow Josh Groban's tour buses onto the highway. Everyone assumes the buses will take the exit to the Riverwalk, where the band has been staying. But that exit—which also happens to be our exit—comes and goes. So does another one. And another one. And still, the buses roll down the highway, the Suburban in hot pursuit.

"They don't seem like they are going back to a hotel," Linda says. "I think they might be heading to Phoenix, where the next concert is."

"I don't care!" Kathy says. "Let's just follow them through the night. What else do we have to do?"

We travel in silence, watching the black windows and red tail lights of the large buses ahead of us. I wonder how long it takes to get to Phoenix from here. I wonder what the Grobanites will do once they get there. I wonder about the flight I have to catch tomorrow.

Finally, Linda gives up. "No," she says. "I don't think we ought to do that."

Quietly, reluctantly, she turns the Suburban around and slowly makes her way through the dark empty streets of San Antonio, back to the Best Western, back to the mundane life of jobs and alarm clocks, back to husbands that don't understand, back to the secret special place that resides in each one of them, where dreams of the next Josh Groban concert can begin.

• • •

As I follow the Grobanites into the hotel, I realize I've just spent fifteen hours with them and have managed to avoid even partial Grobanization. Surely, this is an achievement of some sort, but I'm not sure if it's an achievement that represents success or failure on my part. I've been on this quest several months now and have come to understand and even appreciate the passions of others. But my own remains as elusive as Josh's tour buses.

Ahead of me, I hear Linda's grandson talking in his high-pitched nine-year-old's voice about the concert. Though one chromosome and four decades separate him from most of the Grobanites in the lobby, he's got the lingo down.

"Josh on!" he screams as he runs through the lobby, his little-boy fist raised in the air. "Josh on!"

And that's exactly what I intend to do.

CHAPTER EIGHT
Smart Camp

"It's life captain, but not life as we know it."

—Captain Spock

TELL SOMEONE YOU'VE SPENT AN EVENING BOMBING around San Antonio with a car full of Grobanites, and after you explain what a Grobanite is and why they exist, these are the words you'll hear: freaks, weirdos, wackos, geeks, goofballs, nut buckets, headcases, and crazies. No wonder they get so defensive.

But it's not just Grobanites who are subject to such slander. It's anybody with an interest people don't understand. It's people like Ron and Tara Oakes, a pleasantly plump couple from Wheaton, Illinois. Ron and Tara are defiant science-fiction fans, devout Christians, and see no contradiction in these beliefs whatsoever. And, frankly, they're tired of people who do.

"I'm afraid to tell my science fiction friends about being a Christian, because they will look down on me," Ron says. "And I'm afraid to tell my Christian friends about being a science fiction fan because *they* will look down on me."

"Well, not anymore," says Tara. "At church, they know we're geeks."

The couple is leading a discussion on Christian fandom at To Be CONtinued, a science-fiction and fantasy convention being held this weekend in Schaumburg, Illinois. Ron and Tara, who opened the meeting with a prayer, are on a mission to help other Christian science-fiction fans accept themselves more fully—to not, as Ron explains, let life pound the life out of them. To bring their talk down to earth, so to speak, they've been relaying some of the more peculiar experiences they've encountered as out-of-the-closet Christians.

"People are always wanting to put us into narrow categories," Ron says. "But we believe in the Bible. We really *are* Christians. And we *also* like science fiction and think science is pretty cool."

"Yeah, but we get challenged," Tara says. "A guy came into a Christian party at one con and said, 'If I'm from Alpha Centauri and die, then according to you, I must be going to hell, because Christ died for you, not for me.' We had a forty-five-minute debate with this guy. We told him that the Bible is not science-fiction, it is not a textbook, it is not science. It's about God's relationship to man. If you *are* from Alpha Centauri, that's fine. The Bible doesn't say anything about God not relating to you."

The audience members sitting near me nod appreciatively, as if they, too, have often had to reassure misguided Centaurians.

"At another con, a guy barged into our meeting and started arguing with us about Christianity. It got really tense until a Klingon wandered in and started talking about his battle glories. He really camped it up. Soon, everyone was laughing. Afterward, we couldn't believe that a Christian party was rescued by a Klingon."

Talk about Christ and Klingons and why it's okay to love both continues for an hour. When the session ends, Ron stands to thank us for coming. "I love it when I go to a convention and find other Christians," he says. "That way I know I'm not the only one here."

I find Ron's comments oddly reassuring. Not because I'm a Christian or a science-fiction fan, but because it helps me to know I'm not the only one here who feels like a belt without a buckle.

. . .

You'd think I'd be used to this by now. But yesterday, when I arrived at the Schaumburg Marriott and registered for the convention, I was smacked with that familiar, scratchy, outsider feeling. I wasn't sure who I'd expected to find at a sci-fi/fantasy convention, but it wasn't aging hippies with wiry Einstein hair and tie-dyed T-shirts, or earth mothers in commodious peasant skirts, or young girls with spiky pink hair, or pale twenty-somethings wearing leather pants and studded dog collars. Yet, they're all here. On its own, this group would be enough to induce curiosity in even the most world-weary hotel clerk. But there are also, I might add, pirates. One kept walking back and forth in front of me. He seemed angry for some reason, as if the deck had not been properly swabbed.

"Ayyyye," he said, as he stormed by, the chains on his tall boots rattling.

At first, everyone in the lobby looked strange to me. But the more I watched, the more aware I became that *I* was the one who stood out in my black capri pants, neatly sprayed hair, and toenails painted with a color called God Save the Queen's Nails. It was as if everyone else had been invited to a masquerade, and I'd shown up eager to buy Tupperware.

Part of the problem is that I don't know much about science-fiction or fantasy or the whole "con" world, which is linguistic shorthand for fan-related conventions. And the program I printed off the Internet doesn't shed any light. On the roster for the next two days are programs on belly dancing, stand-up comedy, filking (*filking?*), Farscape, Buffy the Vampire Slayer, gaming, karaoke, Japanese anime, and, oddly enough, Legos. From the outside, it's hard to tell what binds these people together—and that's exactly what I aim to discover.

I initially chose to attend this con because I assumed it

would attract some Trekkies and, as I've discovered, you can't talk about fanatics in America for any length of time without Trekkies beaming their way into the conversation.

"Have you talked to them Trekkies yet?"

"Fanatics, huh, you mean like them Trekkies?"

"You'll want to check out them Trekkies, that's for sure."

I wasn't particularly interested in them Trekkies. But after a while, after about four-thousand Trekkie suggestions, I threw my hands in the air and promised to at least take a look at science-fiction fans. At the suggestion of a friend, I logged onto the To Be CONtinued website and quickly realized that this con— in addition to luring Trekkies—served as an intergalactic crossroads for all kinds of fans. And this cinched the deal. The con was a seeker's one-stop passion paradise. But upon arriving, I became baffled. What *do* Trekkies and Lego users have in common anyway?

Seeking an answer, I headed to the Lego room, a large Marriott meeting space that had been transformed into a colorful mélange of plastic sculpture. On long conference tables around the perimeter of the room were bright Lego castles, bridges, spaceships, clocks, and towns. I didn't play with Legos as a child. I was more of a Tinker Toy girl. But even if I had, I suspect I still would have been impressed by the intricate sophistication of the plastic brick structures. In one corner—a gorgeous white replica of a cable-stayed bridge in Toledo; in the other, an elaborate gray space station. After the pirates and peasants and punks in the lobby, the Legos seemed quaintly mainstream.

Felix Greco, an attractively fit, dark-haired thirty-one-year-old who's a year away from completing a doctorate in neurochemistry, was the man responsible for bringing Lego to Schaumburg this weekend. He admitted it was not typical for Lego fans to cavort with science-fiction fans, but his goal had been to recruit "sleepers"—people who are Lego fans but don't know it yet.

"But why here?" I asked.

"Because," he said, "geek attracts geek."

Unfortunately, his fellow Lego fans, who tend to be conservative, well-educated white guys in tennis shoes, had to be convinced. Nevermind that they spend long hours constructing intricate Lego sculptures in their basements. (Because building on the coffee table in the living room is verboten.) Or that some of them spend tens of thousands of dollars on Lego bricks. (One told me he'd spent $150,000 in the last seven years alone.) Or that problems with the missus are not uncommon. Felix himself admitted that he chose to attend this weekend's convention instead of celebrating his tenth anniversary with his wife. (Was that okay? I asked. No, he said. It was not cool at all.) Nevermind, in other words, that by some measures adult Lego fans might seem a bit eccentric. By their own reckoning, they are *normal*. But science-fiction fans? Ha! They're nothing more than a bunch of amoral people who are into S&M. Or so they believed.

Thinking their worries ridiculous, Felix overruled them. But once he arrived and had a chance to witness the wide assortment of humanity collected at the con—like me, he began to have second thoughts.

"Can I ask you a question?" he asked. "Do you ever think you stand out here? I mean look at you. I'm sorry, but you don't look like you belong."

I wasn't entirely sure what Felix was getting at, so I said nothing.

"Well, I mean, I was the one who wanted the Lego people to come here and now, looking at everyone, I'm not sure *we* fit in."

• • •

I woke this morning determined to fit the puzzling pieces of this convention together, which is why I chose the workshop on Christian fandom, and why I'm now sitting in the back row of one entitled "What is Filk?" Earlier, I spoke with a man at the registration desk who explained that filking was a type of folk music sung on science-fiction, fantasy, and computer themes. Often, he said, filk songs are parodies of hit songs with the lyrics changed to convey a more science-fiction theme. But, he stressed, the boundaries of filk are murky.

Murky indeed.

As the filk session gets underway, it becomes immediately evident that even filk fans aren't sure what filk is all about. The moderator, a bearded, pony-tailed musician named Steve Macdonald, asks for questions.

A young woman raises her hand. "So how do *you* define filk?"

"We're a community that welcomes outcasts," he replies. "If you walk into a room of filkers, you will be immediately welcome."

"But who *are* filkers?" someone asks.

"If you self-identify as a filker, then you are one."

"Is 'Rocket Man' by Elton John considered filk?"

"If it's sung by a filker, it is."

"Is a recorded song filk?"

"Not a professional one."

A woman wearing several long necklaces comments that these were the same debates she heard about folk music in the sixties.

Steve laughs. "I think it's important to know that filk is a very supportive community that does not expect or require perfection—in music or anything else," he says. "Think about it. You take kids in kindergarten and ask them what they want to be when they grow up. They'll immediately tell you singer, dancer, whatever. By the time they're in sixth grade, they don't do that anymore. Society has already gotten through to them about what they *should* and should *not* do. But with filking, there are no shoulds. This is a community about self-expression and inclusion. Here, everyone is welcome."

I look at the people scattered around the small bright meet-ing room. Is it just me or is there a theme developing? One con-vention. Three different groups of people. All struggling to belong.

. . .

The third session circled on my schedule is called Finding Fandom. I walk into a large moss green conference room just as the moderator, a young man named Robert Spencer, asks people in the audience to share stories of when they first became fans. Hands raise, and row by row, seat by seat, participants reveal what sparked their love-at-first sight relationship with science-fiction and fantasy stories.

"It was *Star Trek* for me."

"B-horror movies."

"*Conan the Barbarian*."

"*Ursula LeGuin*."

"*Godzilla*."

Robert nods his head appreciatively after each declaration. When the confessions end, he offers his own.

"Well, for me," he says, "I'm glad to say that I don't remem-ber living in the world that existed before *Planet of the Apes*."

I sit there for a moment, trying to discern how the world was different before Roddy McDowell and Kim Hunter suited up as simian scientists. Then I notice that Robert's looking right at me, eyebrows aloft. Oh! It must be my turn to share.

"Um," I say. "I'm, uh, not a science-fiction fan, but…"

The faces in the room swivel and glare at me with suspi-cion, as if I'm a gatecrasher here to steal their secrets—which in a way, I suppose I am. But because this is a small group whose members seem eager to communicate, I decide to be honest. I tell them I'm curious to learn what unites the people at this con-vention. I tell them I don't understand why Legos and filking and karaoke and anime and origami and belly dancing have been brought together at a science-fiction conference.

"I mean, I understand the sessions on space exploration, and whether or not humans will be able to colonize Mars. But I don't know what unites the rest of the group."

A small, quiet man with dark eyes is the first to speak.

"I'm a Mensa member," he says, "and going to cons is like going to Smart Camp. You get a certain group of intelligent, introverted people together, and certain things they will all find cool, like origami."

The moderator, Robert, nods his head in agreement. "That's right," he says. "What you're looking at are overlapping interests. Everyone here has a primary fandom, such as science-fiction or anime. But we all have an appreciation for other things. That's important, because when you get outside this group, no one appreciates any of it."

"But why?" I ask, temporarily forgetting that I don't have an appreciation for this stuff either.

Robert takes a deep breath, subtly indicating this is a topic far bigger than we have time for at the moment.

"You see," he says, "this a general con that provides people with the opportunity to go to a place where, for the most part, eccentrics are accepted as the norm—as not eccentric, in other words. So the walls they've built up in the mundane world come down and are softened. At work, many of the people here may not say anything about their interests in anime or science-fiction, but once they come here, they can talk with others openly. That openness extends to their appreciation for other genres. I may not personally be into gaming, for example, but if I come here and meet other people who are then I can accept them because, on some level, they are like me."

Robert has obviously thought about this stuff before.

"An anthropologist would say by nature we are communal creatures, that we display a pack mentality. But it's tough for some people to find the pack they belong to. Now, thanks to the Internet, you have a tool that offers a way for that communal need to be expressed. A way for people with niche interests to find each other. Many of the people here first met each other online."

A young woman in the front row turns to face me. She's got long hair, short bangs and glasses, and seems eager to add to the conversation.

"I grew up in a small town with no fandom community," she says. "I was into *Star Wars* and because of my love for that movie, I majored in aerospace and now work in aeronautics. I read all this sci-fi stuff as a kid, but I didn't know other people did. It was only five years ago that I discovered online there was a whole group of people who liked *exactly* the same things I did." The young woman speaks rapidly, as if hurrying to confess her story before losing her nerve. "Now, I'm part of a group that dresses like the TIE Fighter Pilots from *Star Wars* and when we get together, I couldn't be happier. I express my normal side at work. But I express my geek side—my *real* side—at conventions."

A young man sitting next to her interjects. "Here's the best way to explain what all this about," he says. "In school, there is segregation that starts in the first grade. There are sections for The Smarts, sections for The Cools, and sections for The Jocks. I was left in the 'I Don't Fit' Section."

The expressions of the other people in the room tell me his story is not unusual.

"At my first sci-fi convention," he says, "I walked around wondering, 'Who *are* you people?' Then I began to realize they were people just like me, people who didn't fit anywhere else. It was like finding my long-lost family."

My chest sinks at his unexpectedly honest confession. The room has grown silent. And warm. He continues. "The bond here between people is one that can't be taught and can't be learned. It's just something that's there." He looks at me, his face open and expectant. "Do you understand?"

"Yes," I tell him. "Yes, I do."

• • •

I think about his comments while eating lunch in the hotel café. In an effort to look busy and important, like I always do while dining alone, I make a list of the basic facts of my life:

1. I'm gay;
2. I don't have children;
3. I've never had a real job, preferring instead the exhilarating uncertainty of freelancing;
4. I live 1,200 miles away from my family of origin;
5. I've never been able to participate in a single group for very long without getting antsy to discover what *other* groups might have in store for me; and
6. My job as a writer means I'm forever peering through the windows at others.

Looking at the list, the lesson become clear: I'm an outsider too, which makes me exactly like everyone else at this convention.

And I'm not quite sure what to make of this.

• • •

An hour later, I head to the lobby to meet with Robert Spencer, the *Planet of the Apes* fan who moderated the last panel. I liked what he had to say about the nature of science-fiction fans and sensed he had more to say on the topic.

Robert is a thirty-six-year-old substitute teacher and disc jockey from Indianapolis. He's tall, wears large gold-rim glasses, and is overweight in a huggy-bear sort of way. Today, he's wearing a *Star Wars* T-shirt that asks, "*Got Wings?*"

We settle onto blue plaid wing-back chairs, and Robert tells me his love of science-fiction was ignited with *Star Wars* when he was just nine years old. As a boy he was instantly captivated by the film's romanticized military aesthetic, particularly that of the TIE fighter pilots, the cocky-but-dedicated fighters who were forever loyal to the Empire.

"They were the bad-guy aliens in black," he says. "They had that menacing edge. I fell in love with them."

That romance led Robert to enlist in the Army after high school, where he spent eight years working on attack helicopters. He'd planned to become a pilot, but that dream was shot down by injury. Eventually, Robert left the Army, but the world of space and all its vast possibilities didn't leave him. Today, he's a convention addict who regularly attends large cons, small cons, general cons, and cons devoted specifically to *Star Trek, Star Wars,* anime and science-fiction. "I guess you could say I'm interested in all genres," he explains. Along the way, Robert also managed to marry twice and procreate three times. "Yes," he says, "I'm one of those geeky fans who's actually been involved with females and reproduced."

Robert sits back in his chair and crosses one enormous white tennis shoe over his knee. He tells me that his involvement with the science-fiction community generally, and the TIE fighter pilots specifically, have imbued him with a sense of cultural identity lacking elsewhere in his life.

"In the United States, we don't have one overriding identity," he says. "There are Japanese and German and Croatian and Hispanic neighborhoods where people exhibit culture that is important to them. Me? My family is from England. I have some Macedonian blood, but I grew up in Indiana. I *guess* that makes me an American, but what does *that* mean? I grew up celebrating Christmas, Thanksgiving, and the Indy 500. But I didn't have an overriding feeling of any other sort of cultural identity—like I would, say, if I was a Catholic from Ireland. By not having an overriding tradition imposed on me, I take elements from literature and film and make them my own. Like the Three Musketeers and the image of the Samurai warrior. I like the honorable warrior stereotype. You know, one for all and all for one. In fact, my love for the TIE pilots even caused me to join an international group called the 501st Legion, which is a costuming organization that celebrates the bad guys from *Star Wars.* I'm a member of the Bloodfin Garrison in Indiana and I hang out with lots of other TIE pilots. Groups like this give us a cultural identity and affiliation. It gives us a community and culture to be a part of.

"The other important thing cons provide is ritual—like the ritual traditions in pagan and Christian traditions. Overall, ritual is lacking in our society. We don't have a hunting and gathering culture. When boys become men, it happens without fanfare. There's no circumcision. No being taken on the hunt. No ceremony to mark the move to manhood. But here, at cons, we have ritual. We have an opening ceremony to welcome guests. We have a closing ceremony to mark the successful end of the celebration. We have a masquerade, in which we don costumes just like tribes of primitive people who would dress up as warriors, or god-like figures, or antelopes and bears. At our masquerade, when a Klingon performs with a sword, he is re-enacting a grand moment in our shared cultural history, which for us is the movies. That is a big cultural bond in America. Finally, we always have a dance to celebrate festival and revelry, like the mating rituals of ancient tribes."

As Robert speaks, I become both enchanted and chagrined by his insight into the nature of these communities. I've logged several months and more than twenty thousand air miles in an effort to uncover the attraction behind trivial passions, and in the space of ten minutes, Robert manages to identify and uncloak several relevant mysteries.

"But you know," he continues, "although we cling to higher ideals, we still bicker. In the early days, the *book* sci-fi people didn't accept the *movie* sci-fi people. The Asimovs didn't like the Trekkies. There was the split between science fiction and fantasy fans. And there's *still* a split between the older Trekkies and the younger *Star Wars* fans. The younger folks are considered more aggressive. They are predominantly male and ex-military. They think 'Chicks dig us'—and to a certain extent, they are right. I mean which would you prefer: A heavyset older guy dressed like Captain Kirk, or a young, built guy dressed in armor?"

I smile at Robert's obvious reference to his own, foreboding, dressed-in-black TIE pilot demeanor. "You like dressing up as a fighter, don't you?" I ask.

"Absolutely," he says. "I've walked into a bar in costume with Darth Vader, Storm Troopers, and TIE Pilots, and we get treated like we're the Rolling Stones. We get drinks bought for us, whereas *nobody* buys drinks for a substitute teacher and broadcaster. I mean, look at me. I'm slightly heavyset. I wear glasses. I have brown hair. But in costume, I'm silent and menacing. Women stroke the hoses on my helmet while telling me that I frighten them... but that I excite them too."

Robert blushes, and for some reason so do I. So I change the subject. I ask him what one thing everyone at the con—Lego fans, Filkers, Christians alike—share in common.

He tilts back his head and looks toward the overhanging plants on the level above us. "I would say it is a unique personality quirk that makes us somewhat disconnected from society as a whole."

His comment surprises me.

"But *you* don't seem disconnected from society."

"Well, it runs the gamut," he says. "A lot of people here are socially inept people who don't know how to fit into their surroundings. For them, chitchat is hard. But here," Robert spreads his arms, "here they can meet someone and *talk*. I mean really talk, in that strange, smart language they have. For that brief moment, they will not be a single, alone, bipedal, carbon-based mammalian life form. They will be part of the collective human body."

• • •

Outside the hotel, an enormous white party tent has been set up for special performances. After leaving Robert, I walk into the tent and sit down in preparation for the night's activities, which include filking, a gong show, and a costume contest. There must be a hundred and fifty white folding chairs set up in the tent, but only about twenty of them are currently filled. I sit down in an empty row and wait for the performance to begin.

The small, dark-eyed Mensa member I spoke with in the seminar earlier walks up to me.

"Hi," he says.

"Hi," I say.

"Anyone sitting there?" He point to the empty seat next to me. I look at it, and at the fifty other open seats around us. I shake my head.

He scooches in front of me and sits down in the narrow chair. I lean to the right to give him room.

The show begins, and it occurs to me that I'd get better photographs if I was closer to the stage.

"I think I'll move closer," I say.

"Okay," he says.

I move forward several rows, sit on the end seat, and look up startled to realize that Mensa Man has followed me and is now waiting to take the seat next to me.

"Oh!" I say. "Sorry." I move aside and he sits down.

"This is closer," I say.

"Yes," he says. "Closer."

For the next two hours, Mensa Man and I tap our feet to the filker, witness a fantastically disorganized gong show, and watch a parade of people in costumes, including characters named Lord Aurelius, Pansy the Politically Correct Pirate Queen, Purple Haze, and Farscape Baby. We watch these events without speaking. When the performance ends, he stands up.

"Thank you," he says.

"You're welcome," I say.

He turns to leave and I watch his small, single, bipedal, carbon-based mammalian life form move slowly toward the exit.

• • •

When I first saw on the schedule that the convention would include a luau, I found it an odd choice for a gathering of science-fiction fans. Odder still was the start time: 10 p.m. But given how the day has evolved, a Hawaiian dinner party that doesn't start until ten o'clock now seems perfectly logical.

I arrive at the luau at 10:45 when the revelry is well underway. The hotel meeting room has been transformed with cardboard tropical fish, plastic flamingos, and tiki totems. The pirates are blending strawberry daiquiris with Captain Morgans at the back of the room. The full assemblage of hippies, punks, and earth mothers is dancing to a 1980s cover band.

I lean against the wall and watch them. One by one, the Lego fans I didn't meet yesterday come up to chat. Felix had explained to me that adult Lego users tend to be introverted and rather wary of strangers. But they must be used to me by now, for each one wants to tell me something special about his experiences with Lego, be it traveling to Holland to the Lego factory, or using Lego in museums as a way to get kids interested in science.

Smitten by their enthusiasm, I allow myself to be lured by one fan into the hotel's common area where on top of a grand piano he opens his laptop and shows me his brand new online Lego magazine. It's gloriously designed, and he clicks through every single page like a little boy who's just drawn the coolest spaceship in the universe. Just as we're finishing up, I hear a commotion in the lobby.

I look up to see a storm trooper, bounty hunter and two TIE fighter pilots from *Star Wars* come marching assertively toward us. The tallest of the TIE pilots walks up to me and leans over.

"Hi, Shari," he says, his voice deep.

It's Robert with his sexy hoses!

Twelve hours ago, I couldn't tell a TIE pilot from a pilot light, and now here I am effervescing in Robert's evil presence.

Within minutes, the foursome has attracted the attention of people in the luau, who crowd into the hallway to join them. Cameras are pulled out, and people begin to line up to have photos taken with the warriors. They only do this—I must point out—after seeing *me* orchestrate several photographs of myself with the group. Robert was right: they are like rock stars.

When the crowd eventually thins, Robert walks back over to me. "I told you," he says, breathing heavily through his dark helmet. "Now, follow me."

I follow Robert and the other costumed characters into the dance, where the situation in the hallway repeats itself. And before I know what is happening, I'm jumping into the fray to get even more photos of myself with the four intergalactic heroes. And I don't even like *Star Wars*, Obi-Wan. But here I am, kneeling on the floor with my hands behind my head, as the four warriors point their weapons at me.

Looking around, it appears that I'm not the only one who's been won over by the infectious con spirit. When I get up, I see that Felix, the Lego organizer, is also kneeling on the floor for a photo. He's got his hands clasped together in front of him, a dog collar around his neck, and a pirate woman—a piratess?—is holding him by a thin black-leather leash. I wait until the photo is taken and ask Felix about it.

"It's for all the guys who thought this was an amoral S&M conference," he says. "I figure if I can't beat 'em, I might as well join 'em."

Taking a cue from Felix, I give in and order a strawberry daiquiri. I raise my glass in gratitude after the pirate hands it to me.

"Aaaaye," he says.

"Aaaaye," I say.

Looking around, I still don't know why pirates are at this convention. I haven't attended an origami demonstration. I've yet to meet the belly dancers. And I've only caught brief glimpses of the anime films. But the kaleidoscope of differing interests no longer seems to matter.

In the early morning hours, after following the TIE pilots and storm troopers around the hotel, after having met every last Lego user at the convention, after popping in on the karaoke contest, I collapse on the bed in my hotel room.

Lying in the dark, listening to the hum of the air conditioner, something occurs to me. Originally, I said that I chose this quest.

I'm now beginning to believe this quest chose me.

CHAPTER NINE

Nature. Nurture. Novelty?

"Heredity is a splendid phenomenon that relieves us responsibility for our shortcomings."

—Steven Wright

SO I'VE BEEN THINKING.

The presence of all those smart, introverted people at the science-fiction convention got me wondering how much genetics and biology influence a person's choice of passion.

Seeking insight, I head to the library and dive into a collection of scientific databases. My initial findings seem quite obvious: that personal traits such as physique, aptitude, and personality all influence a person's recreational choices. A strong, well-coordinated, and competitive person is more apt to sweat it out on a roller derby league than to sit quietly at home quilting. Furthermore, external factors such as age, geography, and income have a lot to do with the leisure interests a person chooses. Whereas a wealthy widow from Florida is unlikely to be found baiting her hook in an ice-fishing tournament, a smart person with some disposable income *is* likely to travel to a science-fiction convention. Simply put, how we choose to play is influenced by that mysterious marriage between nature and nurture.

Felix Greco confirmed as much when he theorized in an e-mail that he was drawn to Lego because of a presumed genetic ability to conceptualize in three-dimensional shapes.

But, he added, "I will freely admit that my pursuit of Lego as a hobby had to with a very melancholy childhood. I was alone and neglected as a child. Lego reinvented itself as a toy with each thing I made. My parents were too poor to buy me new toys, so I was able to make new ones."

In Felix's case, the love for Lego was generated early on and happened to correspond with an innate ability he possessed. But what about people who choose hobbies later in life? What about the Barbie collector who didn't play with dolls as a child? Or the Grobanite who didn't hear Josh until she was in her fifties? Why doesn't the Barbie collector become a Grobanite or vice versa?

I continue searching and come across an intriguing study on identical twins by researchers at the University of Minnesota—which tells me that the answer may lie in the Rubik's cube of DNA that lies deep in our genes.

In the study, identical twins who were reared apart and met for the first time as adults, were amazed to discover they shared the same quite specific interests. One set of twins enjoyed working in dusty basement-carpentry shops. Another set were captains of volunteer fire departments. Two other twins were both amateur gunsmiths. The shared interests of these twins were too eerily explicit—and in the case of amateur gunsmithing, too uncommon—to be attributed solely to preferences based on physical attributes or environmental influence. Genetics, it would seem, influences our choice of passion in ways we can't even begin to understand.

Excited, I start digging into books with titles like *Genome* and *On the Psychobiology of Personality*. The authors advise caution to anyone trying to make a definitive link between genes and personality and interests. There would be no way to find a specific gene for boardgaming or pigeon racing. There are simply too many variables at work, they say. But in recent years, geneticists have found a link between a gene on the eleventh chromosome and people who are considered to be novelty or sensation seekers. And *this* catches my interest.

I sit up in my chair and go through the list of attributes ascribed to sensation seekers. In general, those ranked high in sensation seeking are people who are drawn either to risky vocations such as the military, or highly stimulating but non-risky occupations such as journalism. Check. They are people who prefer an ever-changing menu of spicy and ethnic and gourmet foods to bland, customary dishes. Check. They choose abstract art over representative works, foreign travel to lying on the beach, and when they watch television, which isn't often, they are more apt to continually click through channels than settle on any one program. Triple check. Sensation seekers get their jollies, in other words, through exposure to new, unexpected, and cognitively stimulating events. But. *But.* They only get those jollies for a certain length of time. Novelty seekers are so jazzed by novelty that once that novelty wears off, the interest fades and it's back to square one.

And I thought it was just me.

In turns out that this need for constant stimulation is associated with the D4 gene, which is a dopamine receptor, and dopamine is the brain's pleasure and reward chemical. Too little dopamine, and a person lacks initiative. Too much, and a person is easily bored and frequently in search of new stimulation. What researchers have discovered is that people with "short" D4 receptors can get their dopamine fix in relatively short order because they need less of it. Consequently, they are more easily satisfied by simple, routine activities, activities that might include watching *The Andy Griffith* show over and over again, for example, or staring into an icy hole on a frozen lake.

But when you're endowed with a "long" D4 receptor, you need bigger hits of dopamine to get the same happy buzz. In search of these dopamine hits, you'll discard the tried and true for the new and different. And you'll do so over and over again.

And you won't be able to help it. Your long dopamine tentacles will forever be leading you out into the world in a hungry ongoing grab for pleasure and stimulation.

The presence of a long D4 gene has also been associated, perhaps not surprisingly, with Attention Deficit Disorder, drug abuse, and sexual promiscuity—none of which I'll comment on, other to say that in the arena of sex, drugs and rock 'n' roll, I once held club-level seats. But that was back in college. Now that I'm older and in a happy relationship and can't sleep if I've sucked up too much wine, I've needed to satisfy my dopamine needs in more age-appropriate ways. Like going to places I'd never before considered. Like ice fishing in the Rockies. Or boardgaming in Baltimore. Or pigeon racing in the Bronx.

Suddenly, this is all making much more sense.

Of course, I can't be certain I actually have a long D4 receptor without submitting to genetic testing. And there is some controversy among researchers as to whether the link between novelty and dopamine and motivation is a clear one. But in my case, the evidence adds up. And it helps me to understand why I chose this quest to begin with, and why, during the science-fiction convention, I started to sense this quest was teaching me about something more than my own perceived lack of passion. But what is that something more? And why do I feel so compelled to continue this journey?

I'm not sure. I only know it is far from over.

CHAPTER TEN
Misfit Furries

"I only hope that we don't lose sight of one thing—
that it was all started by a mouse"

—Walt Disney

I'VE NEVER BEEN MUCH OF A DÉJÀ VU PERSON. YOU KNOW, those people who have woo-woo been-here-before experiences that cause them to stagger backward in cosmic wonderment. To me, déjà vu people seem sort of reactive and not terribly deep, like members of the Senate Armed Services Committee.

But I'm now having a déjà vu moment, which just goes to show you can find something in common with just about anyone. I'm not having a big, capital-letter moment. I'm not sensing I've been in *exactly* this place before. What I've got is déjà vu lite—I'm experiencing feelings I've had before, the feeling I don't belong, the feeling I had in Schaumburg, Illinois, when I was surrounded by pirates and hippies and, well, we don't really need to rehash all that now, do we?

It's a warm, sunny Friday afternoon, and I've just walked into the Holiday Inn in Costa Mesa, California, for the Califur Conference, an annual gathering of furries and followers of furry fandom.

I know.

Fur *what?* you're asking. That's exactly what I want to know.

I first heard of furries several months ago, and best I can tell from my googling, furries are people who share a love for the anthropomorphic representation of animals. They don't fancy real animals like the lumbering polar bear in the zoo or that excitable golden retriever next door. Rather, they like animated animal characters like Scooby Doo or Bambi or the Teenage Mutant Ninja Turtles. Furries like animals who speak English and wear vests and clean house; animals who rise above their limited intelligence in order to gossip and plot and plan and teach lessons to their young-uns, like Donald Duck was always doing with Huey, Dewey, and Louie. Furries like what these human-animal hybrids say about human values. They appreciate the creativity, the art form, the *cuteness* of it all.

But it doesn't stop there.

According to my research, many furries also identify strongly with their inner, animalistic selves, some to the point of adopting animal alter egos. One story I read talked about a computer programmer who woke up one day feeling he was missing something. Several long months of soul-searching later, he realized that the missing something was a tail. He tried to ignore it; he tried to convince himself that the desire for a tail was merely a brain fluke. When that didn't work, he eventually succumbed. Today, whenever his social situation allows, he happily suits up in a bushy black-and-white skunk's tail, with ears thrown on for added effect. Say what you will, but to me this is not terribly different from those people in Green Bay who don cheese heads four months out of the year.

Okay. Maybe it's a little different.

But wait, there's more. If you believe popular television— and who doesn't?—furries also have a darker side. Furries have been depicted on shows like *CSI* and *MTV* as sex-crazed fetishists who lose all control and inhibition when they see someone dressed in a full fursuit. Don't know what a fursuit is? Think Pluto and Pooh in the Disney parade. Apparently, a sizable portion of furries like to dress in full-body costumes, and for some, the sight of clumsy overstuffed cartoon animals is enough to put even the most mild-mannered among them into heat.

But even that's pretty mild compared to the "plushies," a subset of furry fandom that consists of people who collect stuffed animals to use as objects of sexual stimulation.

I'm sorry.

I know that I've conditioned you to believe this was a G-rated quest. And now here I am luring you down a much more lurid path. That certainly wasn't my intent. But let me ask you this: if you were a genetically predisposed sensation seeker like me, would *you* be able to resist a furry convention?

That's what I thought.

• • •

I walk over to the Califur registration table and stand in line behind several people wearing various sets of tails and ears. There are little bobtails and long cat tails, and other tails whose species is hard to decipher because they are dangling from the backs of blue jeans as opposed to the fuzzy haunches of real animals. Honors for the most arresting ensemble would have to go to the gent with the long brown donkey ears.

I give the thin young man behind the registration desk my name so that he can create a badge. He asks what I'd like my furry name to be.

I look at his laminated name tag. It reads, "Loial Otter."

Oh, dear. Do I give Mr. Otter a furry name and pretend to be part of the pack? Or do I keep some semblance of objective, journalistic distance? Do I try to fit in, or consciously remain an outsider?

"Marlowe Kitty," I tell him. Marlowe is my cat's name, and I think she'd be honored to be recognized in such a manner.

"How do you spell that?" Otter asks.

Before I can reply, a short young man wearing pointy white ears interrupts us. "I lost part of my tail!" he says, holding up the limp remains of white fur dangling from his butt. Otter and I look at him. "It was white fox," he says. "It was *real*." The three of us back up and begin scanning the ground for the missing tail part.

"I don't see anything," I say.

"I don't either," Otter says.

"Maybe it came off in the chair over there," the fox says. He prances toward the lounge area, and Otter looks back at me.

"What was your furry name again?" he asks.

"Ummmm, never mind. Just use my real name."

• • •

With each group of enthusiasts I spend time with, I've come closer to understanding the roots of shared passion, but the furries confound me. And truth be known, that is exactly why I'm here. I mean, when you see a man trotting around the lobby like a donkey, Grobanites and boardgamers start to seem so normal. So Starbucks. If I can grasp the realities of this subculture, if I can understand what it is about animals and art and tails that brings them together, then I fully believe I would, ummm, well, I'm not exactly sure what I would understand. But the mere existence of a furry convention seems to indicate there's something out there for everyone.

Seeking to ground myself in the ins and outs of furry fandom, I ask around for the conference organizer and meet a man named Robert Johnson. Furry name: AlohaWolf. Wolf is a tall, large man with dark eyes that struggle to make contact with my own. I tell him I'd like to get some background on the conference. Looking at something above my head, he says, "Follow me."

I follow AlohaWolf outside of the cool air-conditioned lobby onto a warm patio surrounded by a profusion of plants with glossy green leaves. We sit down at a glass-topped table. Wolf lights a cigarette and gazes at the hedge across the walkway.

"So, Robert," I say, looking to gain a foothold in this shape-shifting world. "How do you define furry?"

He exhales smoke. He looks over his right shoulder. He fiddles with his walkie-talkie. He must not have heard me.

"So... Robert!" I say, this time a little more loudly. "How do you define furry?"

He looks at the glass doors behind me and sighs. "A furry is someone who says they are a furry. We all have our own definition."

I wait for him to elaborate.

He taps his cigarettes on the table.

He's not going to elaborate.

"So," I prod gently, "what is *your* definition?"

"I don't define it. I leave it blank."

Blank. That's helpful.

AlohaWolf picks up his walkie-talkie.

"Mark?" he says. "Mark, are you there?"

Great. I've been here five minutes and already I'm going to be thrown out of the convention. I feared this. Expected it, actually, for I've discovered furries can be a little paranoid. I originally tried to attend a furry conference in Ohio, and the organizer told me in no uncertain terms that curious nonfurries with notebooks would not be welcome. As Robert talks into his walkie-talkie, I devise a backup plan. If I'm tossed out, I'll just march down to the local costume shop, find myself a Bullwinkle fursuit and return incognito. I'll become my own Deep Throat.

AlohaWolf finishes talking, and we sit in silence waiting for the mysterious Mark to appear. I picture a large foreboding furry, a growling grizzly with enormous claws and a billy club who will grab my thin white arm and drag me outside.

A couple of minutes later, a short quiet man with long gray hair and glasses walks up to us. Wolf introduces him as Mark Merlino, also known as Sylys Sable. "I'll let you talk to Mark," Wolf says. "He's better at this than I am."

Mark sits down, and I learn that he's fifty-three years old, lives in Garden Grove, and has his own company that has something to do with telecommunications engineering. But like every other fanatic I've met, Mark does not want to talk about his work life. He wants to talk about this life. The *real* life. The furry life.

As it turns out, Mark is one of the people who put furry fandom on the map. This was back in 1985, when he and some friends who were interested in animal art sponsored a party for other animal art fans at a science-fiction convention in Sacramento. Word of the party got out, and several people showed up with their own artwork. What so amazed them was that without knowing why or how, they'd all been drawing in the same style, a combination of Marvel Comics and Disney. Their art was not funny animal cartoons, but underground comics in which they used Fritz the Cat to poke fun at the adult world. It was art drawn by adults for adults. At the party, one of Mark's friends suggested the group call themselves "furries," and the name stuck.

That first furry party was held at Mark's house. The second year, the fledging group rented a hotel room. And within a few years, the party had become so popular that Mark and his friends created ConFurence, the first full-scale furry convention anywhere and a predecessor to this weekend's Califur convention. Today, thanks to the community-building power of the Internet, there are furry conventions all over the world, including Malaysia, Argentina, and Russia, and best-guess estimates put the number of furries in America at anywhere from 200,000 to well over 800,000 people—and growing rapidly.

Mark looks wistful as he thinks back to those early days of furry fandom. "This was a time when the furry center in all of us was being activated," he says. "It was like a cultural virus."

Which implores me to ask: how does the furry center get activated in anyone?

"For me, it was seeing *Bambi* when I was a kid," Mark says.

"There's a very strong Disney connection to all this. The first-generation furries were cartoonists and fans of the art form who were inspired, like me, by *Bambi* and *Lady and the Tramp*. People who came afterward were inspired by *The Fox and the Hound* and *The Aristocats*."

As he speaks, I can't help but think how tame and Middle America all this sounds. Disney? Tramp? *Bambi*? Even though I may be rushing things a bit, I ask him about the alleged sexual elements of furry fandom. Are the rumors real?

"Oh, they're real all right," he says. "You can't separate sexuality from fandom. And I blame Disney for this. Think about it," Mark pauses. "Name a Disney film you've seen."

"*The Lion King*," I say.

"Okay. Do you remember the scene where Nala and Simba are rolling on a hillside, and she is looking up at him? Did you notice how they were rubbing against each other all the time?"

"Yeeeees."

"Well, there are scenes like that in all Disney films. Think about *The Lady and the Tramp*. Tramp is a lady's man-dog. He goes after anything female. When he finally finds the sweet cocker spaniel, he sets his mind on seducing her. And that's just one example. There are lots of erotically powerful animal images in our culture. Think about werewolves, or the Catwoman from *Batman*."

I stare at Mark, wondering how it is I've so misinterpreted American culture.

He continues. "When puberty hits, many people start having vivid dreams involving animals. For males, it is often the black male leopard. For girls, it is often domestic dogs or horses. See, the fascination and attraction to animals starts early. You show me a kid crawling like a cat, and I'll show you a potential furry."

I nervously flash back on all the times I whinnied and galloped around my backyard as a kid. "Is it *always* sexual?"

"Let me put it this way," he says. "There are chemical changes that occur in the body when we see something beautiful or attractive. Many people get an endorphin rush from looking at sunsets. That's what happens to furries when we look at furry art. We get a tightening in the chest. It may be related to sexuality, but not always."

Mark finishes speaking just as a man walks by who looks remarkably like a tiger. He's got alternating orange and black stripes on his cheeks, chin and forehead, a long tiger tail, and it looks like his face has been modified to give it more cat-like dimensions. My gaze follows him down the leafy walkway.

"That's Stalking Cat," Mark says. "You'll want to speak to him. He's been surgically modifying his body for years in order to more fully embrace his tiger fursona."

"*Fursona?*" I ask, feeling as if I'm being lured down a rabbit hole.

"Almost everybody in the furry community has a fursona, which is their personal furry. The fursona is you, it's who you really are, it's the animal you most relate to."

"So what's your fursona?"

He points to the plastic name badge hanging around his neck. "Sylys Sable is my fursona. Sylys is a pine marten, a type of weasel. Weasels are small carnivores that can be eaten by bigger carnivores. But they don't know that; they think they are indestructible. They survive by being clever, by fluffing others. Having a weasel as my fursona has helped me a lot in real life. It helps me realize I don't have to be large or musclebound, which I'm not. I can just be a weasel."

I think back to my near-miss putting Marlowe Kitty on my name badge. Is my fursona a domestic cat—aloof and independent and easily bored?

I ask Mark about this and he shrugs. That's for me to determine. But there's not only the whole fursona thing to work out, he says; most furries also have totems, which are psychologically deeper. Totems are spirit guides, the animal that gives you guidance. You might choose a horse if you want more strength. Or a wolf, if you seek family. Or an eagle, if you crave freedom and nobility. The totem represents your ideal, the animal you wish to be more like. Mark tells me his totem is a sleek black leopard, an animal with strength, mystery, power, and beauty.

I look at Mark, who has pale skin, thinning gray hair and a reedy voice and am flooded with a wave of unexpected empathy.

Then the rabbit hole widens.

"I have three partners," Marks says, "and knowing our fursonas and totems really helps us all get along."

I sense immediately he is not talking about the kind of partners sanctioned by the secretary of state. I blurt, "There are *four* of you sharing the same relationship?"

"Yes, that's the great thing about being an adult and being a furry. When you're born into a family, you don't get to pick your family members. This way, we get to pick our own."

And Mark's chosen family is amazingly complex. There's Rodney, who's a mink and an otter; Bill, who's a house cat and a wolf; and Bob, who's both a calm, domestic lion and a powerful lion of total wisdom. I do the math. Four humans plus four fursonas plus four totems, and you've got twelve different beings sharing one romantic relationship. Knowing how complex it can be navigating the world with just one human, I'm impressed by Mark's matter-of-fact confidence in the arrangement.

"It sounds like furries are very self-aware," I say.

"Oh, yes. Being a furry is all about claiming your identity. In this country, what are you really? Are you your name? No. That was given to you by someone else. Your social security number? No. That's just a number. Your job? That's something you do to make money. But when you choose a fursona or totem, you are choosing a more acceptable representation of who you really are. In so much of society, there are so many layers of bullshit. It's hard to be yourself. But the whole fursona thing is really cool. It strips away human reluctance in many forms. For example, in our culture there is a personal ethic about personal space. Not here. Here, it's common that when a furry runs into another furry, the personal space boundaries go down, and the two will start hissing, rubbing up against each other, and rubbing noses.

"One of the interesting things is that you can be anything else and be a furry. You can be an animal rights extremist and be a furry. You can be a hunter and be a furry. You can follow Christ and be a furry. See, we aren't pretending to be furry; a furry is what we really are. The human being is what we are stuck with."

• • •

After Mark and I finish talking, I head over to the session on furry gun collectors, which is being led by Stalking Cat, the tiger-human crossbreed who walked by earlier. I'm not particularly interested in guns, but I am particularly interested in Stalking Cat. I stand in the hallway and watch from a distance as he dismantles a rifle and talks about its various components. I can't catch all of what he's saying, but the gist of it seems to be that using a rifle to kill animals is a God-given right of all Americans. And although Mark warned me about this, I have trouble coiling my consciousness around the idea that someone can be a furry, dress like an animal, adopt a fursona, and still want to blow the bejesus out of the little buggers.

• • •

I spend the remainder of the afternoon trying to make all this make more sense. I attend a workshop on how to build a fursuit and learn how to make tails and eyes and ears, and how to paint stripes onto fur, and the various pros and cons of buying animal noses from a taxidermist. "They are extremely lifelike and adaptable," the presenter tells us. "A bear nose can serve as a wolf nose in a pinch. But although it's a good look, these noses are hard and can hurt people."

I attend a drawing class taught by a furry artist, who tenderly encourages beginners to experiment without self-recrimination. "Dude," he says, "your work doesn't have to be right the first time. I mean, we're doing frikkin animation, not frikkin anatomy!"

I cruise over to the furry art show and dealer room and browse among tables of authentic wolf and raccoon tails, framed illustrations of Disneyesque characters, furry comic books, and art-on-demand furry characters produced by sketch artists. While in the show, I notice, sectioned off from the main display area, an exhibit labeled "Adults Only." Intrigued, I slip behind the felt panels.

The first illustration I see depicts two sexy rabbits with large human breasts, whips, and black leather boots, playing hide-and-seek in a forest. Fearing I may already stand out, being tail-less and all, I try to act as if rabbits with erect nipples are something I see every day. Stupidly, I nod at the painting as if the artist is standing next to it. Against my wishes, my feet propel me deeper into the display where I don my best non-reactive art-critic face. A nude adult male with antlers, cloven hooves, and a penis? Hmmmm, great use of color, depth, and perspective. Two cats in bustiers unlacing each other on a couch? Hmmm, so postmodern. So evocative of the more hidden aspects of the psyche.

When I reach the end of the display I walk back into the main showroom and accidentally bump into a young man in a tight white T-shirt and dark glasses. He looks like Keanu Reeves.

He stares at me, puzzled, and asks, "Are you somebody's *mother?*"

• • •

I'd like to tell you I'm not mystified by all this—that men with three partners and tigers who hunt and rabbits with breasts all strike me as perfectly reasonable forms of expression. But this group pushes me. This group forces to the surface some things I'd rather not see about myself.

Throughout this journey, I've prided myself on the ability to boldly march into the hot molten center of any subculture, to go beneath crusty surface impressions and understand what and why and how people love what they do. I've fancied myself to be a loving, open-minded combination of Mother Theresa, Henry Kissinger and Mister Rogers. Part care. Part tact. Part cardigan. But here, I'm floundering. I will myself to the edge of the rabbit hole and just as quickly back away. I want to find Wonderland, but I keep encountering Oz. Don't be silly, Toto. Scarecrows can't talk.

Seeking the input of another outsider, I head to the long wooden bar just off of the lobby and begin speaking with the bartender. He's a middle-aged man with a crisp white shirt, brocade vest, and the kind of nonjudgmental bartender smile that invites weepy, Scotch-induced confessions. I ask about his dealings with the furries.

"Well," he says, "earlier I heard someone barking in the parking lot. If you didn't know it was a person, you'd swear it was a dog. He was really good." The bartender drums his fingers on the bar top. "Oh! And another kid came up with two small bowls of what looked like cat food and asked me to microwave it."

My eyes widen. "Was he going to eat it?"

"I didn't ask. Some things you don't want to know." He puts a white paper napkin in front of me. "What'll you have?"

I ask for a gin and tonic. Extra lime.

A woman sitting nearby has been listening to us. She's the quintessential southern California gal: curly blond hair, ample chest, and accompanied by a tanned, muscle-bound man in a tank top.

"Know what I think?" she asks. She looks around and lowers her voice. "I think these are people who have no freakin' lives and spend too much time on their freakin' computers. They come here to have sex. I know. I saw that *CSI* episode." She shakes her head.

The bartender sets down my drink and looks at her. "You're sounding kind of old and judgmental," he says, a comment that strikes me as pretty direct for a bartender, until he explains that he's known her for a long time.

The blond woman shakes her head. "No, I'm *not* being judgmental. It's true. These people need to get a life." She says this as if the furries do what they do solely to irritate her, which for some reason irritates me. I turn my attention back to the bartender.

"So what do you think of them?" I ask.

He wipes the bar top with a rag, folds it neatly, and places it over the edge of the sink. "Nothing fazes me," he says. "I'm from New York. I lived there twenty years. We had everything there. Punks. Mohawks. You name it. I once saw a woman in Greenwich Village walking a sheep on a diamond-studded leash. They all came to the Village so they could be themselves. This is the same thing. What's the big deal if someone wants to wear a tail? What's it hurting? Anymore, I don't think anything is weird."

The blond woman rolls her eyes and pays the tab. She leaves, the tanned man following behind.

The bartender asks what I think of the furries, and I tell him I'm not sure. Their love of cartoon animals is apparent, many of the art pieces and fursuits are delightful, and the furries seem quite relaxed and friendly with one another. But I confess that the strangeness of it all bothers me, and it *bothers* me that it bothers me.

He looks toward the lobby at a pride of young furries. They're all thin, with close-cropped hair and an assemblage of silver piercings. Most look to be about twenty years old. The bartender shrugs.

"You know, who cares really? These people are young. They're obviously searching for something and they seem to have found it here. This is America. This is what we're all about.

My dad fought in World War II to make sure that Americans have the right to express themselves any way they want."

He glances down at my glass. "Want another?"

"No thanks. Just the tab."

He leaves to get the bill, and I think about what he's just said. He's right. I know that. But something about the furries tugs at me, and I sense the discomfort is trying to tell me something.

• • •

After speaking with the bartender, I now believe I'm ready to visit with Stalking Cat. I skew up my courage and find him standing in the lobby with a unicorn. I introduce myself, and we head back to the bar in search of a quiet table. As we are getting settled, the bartender sees me and smiles approvingly.

Up close, Cat is even more mesmerizing than from a distance. His eyes are the eyes of a Halloween cat—feline green with vertical black pupils. His teeth are pointed, with long white incisors. He's got round cheeks, and his upper lip has been cleft, split down the middle and curling up on each end in a Cheshire grin. I find myself wanting to touch his face the same way I'd touch an unfamiliar melon in the supermarket.

We begin speaking, and several young furries gather around our table, to listen attentively to Stalking Cat's every word. They're like seekers in the presence of the Maharaji, schoolkids in the thrall of Harry Potter.

In the mundane world, Stalking Cat is a forty-six-year-old self-employed electronics technician and gun-toting Republican known as Dennis Avner. He tells me he began surgically altering his body in 1980, driven to do so by a deep, almost instinctual need to follow an ancient tribal tradition.

"I'm a Native American, a Huron and Lakota," he explains. His voice is rough and guttural and sounds like a sandpaper tongue is scraping the roof of his mouth. "I'm following an ancient tradition of my tribe that involves changing my appearance to be closer to my totem, which in my case is cats. I associate most with tigers. Modifying my body allows me to be closer to them in both appearance and spirituality."

To date, Cat has had bridge and eyebrow implants; silicone injections in his cheeks, chin, and upper lip; and piercings that hold stainless steel studs into which he can insert whiskers. Plastic surgeons have also pointed his ears, elongated his earlobes, and split his lip. Amazingly, he also found a dentist willing to extract all of his human teeth and create a special set of dentures patterned after real tiger teeth.

I ask how difficult it was finding a dentist willing to do this.

"It was very hard."

"How many dentists did you contact?"

"Lots."

"Like how many?"

"Lots."

"What would they do when you called?"

"Generally, they wouldn't even talk to me."

"So how did the tiger teeth feel when you put them in? Did they take getting used to?"

"Nah. It's the tiger thing. They just seemed to fit. They felt right. Natural."

Stalking Cat has also been extensively tattooed—he's got more stripes on his face than Tigger—and he maintains two wholly functional tails. One is animatronic; the other, bionic. It works off of muscle impulses.

"They are very advanced tails," he assures me.

As Cat talks, a pale young man—a boy, really—wearing a studded dog collar and white T-shirt kneels down next to Cat, who begins to scratch the boy's scalp with his long orange-and-black striped fingernails.

"Feel good?" I ask.

"Purr," he says, his eyes rolling upward.

I take that as a yes.

Cat continues to talk, and I think about how it seems that furries come into their furryness in different ways. Mark was influenced by Disney, whereas Cat's path appears to be more spiritual, more related to heritage and tradition. I ask him about this.

"Oh, yes," he says, "Everybody comes to furry fandom from a different place. I come from the shamanistic angle."

"Shamanistic?" I glance at the boy on the floor. "So you're somewhat of a tribal leader?"

"Absolutely. Young furs come up to me all the time. They don't understand why they have such strong animal connections. That's because the American culture is not American. It's a mishmash of other cultures, and a lot of people who live here have animal connections that come from elsewhere. I don't know where the connections come from. They can come from the animals themselves. From Native Americans. From the Celtic tradition. The animal journey is part of many cultures. There are many earth-based religions that revere rocks, trees, and animals, and anybody with roots in those religions have animal connections. But it confuses many people, because it's not something accepted by mainstream American culture. People who start to feel those animal connections end up here."

"And they come to you?"

"Yep."

"And what do you tell them?"

"Generally, people come to me when they feel a strong animal connection but they don't know what animal it is. It doesn't make sense to them. I mean, these are white kids from Irvine. But I can intuitively sense their animal. I tell them 'you're probably a coyote or wolf or squirrel or whatever, and you haven't been able to accept it yet.' My role is to help people be comfortable with their animal connections. Once they accept that everything happens for a reason, they can learn to accept themselves."

The furries around the table all begin nodding, all in seeming agreement with Cat's words. One woman in particular wants to talk. She's dressed from scalp to stilettos in black leather, and is clutching a leash attached to a collar on a tall man standing beside her. To me, she looks more S&M than Chip and Dale.

"You want to know what brings furries together?" she asks. "Furs are here because they don't fit in anywhere else. For real furs, this is the only place they feel comfortable." She points to her leashed companion. "See, we're Goths. We like coming to furry cons because furs are accepting and tolerant of others outside of mainstream society. Most societies have social restraints and those restraints don't always work for everyone. But here, the social restraints outside don't apply. We can be ourselves."

Her comments remind me of those expressed by the Christians and the filkers and the science-fiction fans in Chicago. "Seems like everyone's just looking for a place to belong," I say.

"That's exactly it!" she says. "We're not the only people who feel restricted by so-called normal society. We're a utopian society that accepts people for who they are."

Cat looks up at her and slowly scratches his cheek with his long nails. "Yeah," he says, "but a lot of people don't accept our vision of utopia."

The young man sitting on the floor next to Cat stands to leave. "You should let Cat scratch your head before you go," he says. "It's really awesome."

"Really?" I ask.

"Really," he says.

And without giving more than ten or twenty seconds' thought to what the bartender behind me might think, I bend my head toward Cat for a courtesy scratch. The tips of his long tiger nails point into my scalp and he begins to move them back and forth. It sounds a bit like paper crinkling. The boy was right. It *does* feel good. And I'm not sure what to make of it other than it seems a fitting end to a perplexing day.

• • •

Back in my hotel room, I call Angela and do my best to describe the day's events.

"You okay?" she asks, after several minutes. "You don't sound so good."

I tell her I'm fine, but confused. This group is not as overtly joyous as the others I've been with. Their sense of community is strong. Their *need* for community is strong. But I find myself reacting to that community from a position of disbelief, as if I've wandered into some carnival freak show. And the fact that I even use the word freak to describe the furries kinda freaks me out. How will I ever feel free to freely express my own individuality when I don't allow the same of others?

Angela gently suggests I not be so hard on myself. She tells me it's normal to react like this to people you're unfamiliar with. That she felt the same way when I told her about the Grobanites and she's not beating herself up for not buying a Josh Groban quilt.

But *still*. I sense that vibrating below the surface of all this is a lesson about acceptance and understanding. A lesson about how you—and by you, of course, I mean me—can't possibly begin to embrace your own weird sense of self if you don't allow others to do the same. I mean, just because *I* would never wear tails or tiger dentures does that mean *they* shouldn't either? And how do they do that anyway? How do they overcome the self-consciousness, the fear of what people like me might say about people like them?

Angela listens quietly as I grapple with all this. Finally she says, "Don't overthink all this, honey. Just try to have a good time."

When we hang up, I get into bed and think about Stalking Cat and the inner strength it must take to walk around like a tiger twenty-four/seven. Me, I worry about broccoli in my teeth.

• • •

The next morning, I wake determined to understand if not

embrace the furries. Angela was right. I need to try and have a good time. My first stop: the Fursuit Performance Workshop.

I walk into the seminar and sit down in a row of seats where I'm surrounded by several life-size animal characters. There's a black-and-white Dalmatian wearing a grass hula skirt; a sand-colored kangaroo with a heavy curved tail; and a large brown bear sporting a colorful Hawaiian shirt. The bear is sitting in the back row with his fuzzy arms crossed in front of his chest.

The presenter, who's wearing a gray pony costume and looks like the mascot of a college football team, walks to the front of the room. He takes off his head and holds it under his arm.

"Hi, I'm Horsey," he says.

Horsey explains that he worked for many years as a character at Disneyland, but now he's a full-time freelance furry doing gigs as Tony the Tiger, Astro Boy, and Broadway Bear at Wal-Mart openings and kids' birthday parties. No one says as much, but I suspect audience members are deeply envious of his employment situation.

"There are three primary rules to fursuiting," he begins. First rule. In a fursuit, you don't have a face, so you don't need to smile. Second rule. Subtle movements don't work. Don't tap your toe or wiggle your fingers. Third rule. There are no limits. In a fursuit, you can dance, you can somersault, you can get away with a ton of stuff. You can rub people's bellies, pat their butts, give them hugs, rub them on the head. It's totally addictive.

"Think of it this way," he says. "If the Three Stooges did it, you can do it in a fursuit." The animals gathered around me nod their heads vigorously.

For the next hour, Horsey shares thirty years of fursuiting experience with us. We learn the dangers of fursuiting, chief among them excessive heat. "In some suits, you spend fifteen minutes outside in the summer and you're dead," Horsey says.

We learn of the rewards. "People will treat you like a

celebrity. You'll draw a crowd. Johnny Depp, Madonna, Tony the Tiger—it's all the same."

We also learn, sadly, that some people have it in for fursuits. "People will whack on fursuits," Horsey cautions us. "They'll punch your stomach, pull your tail, kick you in the shins, hit you in the head with a baseball bat. Really. I've experienced it all. Parents will tell their kids, 'Honey, there's Tigger! Go kick him!' I don't know why they do this. To make them less afraid, I guess."

When his talk ends, Horsey gives the fursuiters present a chance to practice performing. The smiling, wide-eyed Dalmation in the hula skirt scampers to the front of the room and immediately stands in front of a large fan that has been set up to keep the fursuiters cool. The Dalmation bends over in front of it and allows the fan blast to swirl the hula skirt in the air around him. He looks coy, or at least as coy as an ever-happy dog face can look, and it slowly dawns on me what he's doing. He's vogueing the famous photo of Marilyn Monroe standing over the subway grate.

Now *that's* adorable.

• • •

Yesterday, I learned that only about 10 percent of furries are drawn to fursuiting; most are content with much simpler tails and safety pins. But those who do choose full body fur, complete with hooves and manes, are hams at heart—a fact that becomes evident at the Fursuit Show and Tell that immediately follows the workshop.

A small stage and klieg lights have been set up in an adjoining conference room and the suited furries begin dashing back and forth in preparation for their two o'clock performance. They scurry as if auditioning for a part in a movie—or searching for a really good smell. They hand little slips of paper to the emcee. They consult with the sound technicians. They fluff and flutter, their nerves apparent. Finally, twenty-five minutes after the show was scheduled to begin, the fursuiters take the stage.

A puppy named Puppy does the Macarena until he's drug off by his leash. A unicorn named Zachariah recites poetry—which is eerie, because his mouth doesn't move; only his horn does. My favorite is Sunshine, a black-and-white skunk with oversized yellow glasses, white go-go boots, and a miniskirt patterned after the British flag. Sunshine walks to center stage and camps, "I like my skunks shaken, not stirred."

• • •

Cheered by the charms of the fursuits, I head back to the lobby to wait for the fursuit parade to begin. Because of the heat—it's close to ninety degrees outside—and because the suits can be so hellishly hot even on a cool day, there's been talk of moving the parade inside.

I sit in a stuffed arm chair next to a tall pink-cheeked young man, one of the few I've seen this weekend who's not wearing ears or a tail or on a leash. We begin chatting and I learn his name is Ben Frame. Furry name: BenCoon. He's twenty-one years old, works graveyard as a hospital switchboard operator in San Diego, and has been into furry fandom for about six years.

"Fandom helped me learn how to deal with all the crazy, unstable people who call the hospital in the middle of the night," he says, laughing.

Sensing that he might have a healthy perspective on all of this, that Ben Frame might be to the furries what Linda Omalia was to the Grobanites, I ask him how he got into furry fandom.

"Like many people here, I was that kid in high school who was always picked last for the sports team. I was a high-level autistic and had Attention Deficit Disorder. I would constantly retreat into my own little world. I would scribble. Or read books. I wasn't interested in the world of adult things at all." As he talks, Ben rubs both of his arms as if trying to warm up. "Then I discovered Multi-User Dungeon games online—these are sophisticated chat rooms wherein you create a character to interact with other people in a virtual world. One of the MUDs I got into was called TigerMUCK. I'd play TigerMUCK for hours every day. I guess you could say I'm your total generic outcast."

Ben says this without any shame or apology or defensiveness. Like he's telling me a basic fact about himself. Like his hair is brown. Or he wears glasses.

It was through TigerMUCK that Ben learned of furry fandom. Six years ago he started drawing cartoon animals (most furries eventually learn to draw, he says), went to his first furry convention, and has been a regular ever since. "I walked into that conference and felt immediately comfortable," he says. "They were people like me—fringe, nonstandard, outcasts."

Ben looks up as the line of fursuiters conga their way through the glass patio doors into the lobby. Being a furry veteran, he seems unimpressed. He ignores them and continues his story. "Fandom gave me perspective on how to deal with people. For you, talking to strangers is a common occurrence. Not for me. I had to learn how to be comfortable in social situations. And being with other outcasts helped me do just that."

Ben is so direct and articulate I have a hard time believing he ever had trouble talking to people. "But you seem so confident," I say.

"Hmmm. Confident? Indeed. You should've seen me a few years ago."

Ben takes a deep breath and runs his hands through his hair, then crosses one long leg over the other and begins to roll and unroll the hem of his blue jeans.

"You know, most furries typically had unhappy childhoods. They didn't fit in. They felt like freaks. And they did anything they could to escape mundane reality. There's a saying that by and large furries are bi and large. And I think that's true. I wouldn't say the majority of fans are gay, but a large percentage is. Tell you the truth, I think many are gay for a lack of options."

"And you?"

Roll. Unroll. "I have a boyfriend, but I consider myself bisexual. Actually, there's a full cross-section of fans here. Furry fans are smart, fat, gay, straight, and there are lots of alternative sexualities. Bondage. Domination. Sado-masochism. These groups are integrated in furry fandom because we're a welcoming place for all kinds of outsiders. But sexuality is not the focus." Ben stops and grins at me. "This would be an excellent study for a psychologist, don't you think? There's so much written here in big bright colors."

For the next half hour, Ben and I chat like two people waiting for a bus. He tells me about his parents. I tell him about Denver. We talk about computers, which are Ben's other passion. He has fourteen of them at home, five of which are always doing something. I decide I like Ben. A lot. But when he starts rubbing his arms again, I sense it's time for me to go. I stand and thank him for helping me to better understand the furries.

"Sure," he says. "With all that the furries have done for me, I'd like to communicate a positive message. That this is a place for social acceptance and interaction, neither of which I had before."

As I start walking away, Ben calls me back. "Know who you should talk to?" he says. "Brenda DiAntonis. She'll give you another perspective."

"How so?"

"She's an artist," he says, "and a born-again Christian."

• • •

I find Brenda in the art show sitting behind a long conference table covered with binders and a display board with magnets of her illustrations. The illustrations are of unicorns and horses and tigers and zebras, many of them wearing colorful bikini tops and cut-off shorts and jewelry. They look like the kind of drawings you'd see in a little girl's story book. A sign says, "The Art of Xian Jaguar."

"Shee-an?" I ask, using the Chinese pronunciation of the word.

Brenda laughs. "No, it's pronounced *Christ*ian. Just like X-mas is used for Christmas, I use X-ian, for Christian. It's easier to spell on AOL."

"And Jaguar?" I ask. "Is that your animal character?"

"That's what my personality is like. Jaguars are lazy. Like me. They like to sleep. And I *love* to sleep. Also, they are loners. And I like the pattern on their fur. It's fun to draw."

Brenda tells me all of this quickly, nervously, as if fearful that taking a moment to breathe might cause me to lose interest and walk away. Not a chance. As with Ben, I like her immediately and sense she's just the person I need right now. If a born-again Christian can find herself at home here, certainly I can too.

We walk out to the pool. It smells like coconut and chlorine and the surface of the pool reflects the bright sun with a chromelike intensity. Brenda and I sit underneath a round umbrella, and I ask her how long she's been a furry.

She laughs. "Actually, I don't like to use the term furry," she says. "I think it's silly. People think we're hairy or something."

"Then what do you call yourself?"

"I just say that I'm an artist."

We begin speaking, and I learn that Brenda's interest in art began early, when she was a young girl living in the high desert of Southern California.

"We weren't allowed to watch much television. There weren't any other kids around. The only thing we could do was read books—and there weren't very many of those. Out of desperation, I would create fantasy worlds and retreat into them for fun."

At some point during her long lonely childhood, Brenda started to draw Disney-like cartoon animals, and liked illustration so much she eventually pursued and obtained a bachelor of fine arts degree from Cal State Fullerton. Today, she works as an illustrator for a children's book publishing company. All the while, she continued to draw animal characters on the side. "I thought I was the only one who did this until I stumbled onto a furry website in 1998," she says. Once she realized just how many people out there liked cute animal characters, she became an eager, enthusiastic participant in furry fandom.

I ask her what it's like to be a Christian in this environment. "I mean sure, there is an emphasis on animals and artwork," I say. "But there's also a sexual aspect to all of this. You okay with that?"

She nods her head rapidly, to let me know she knows exactly what I'm getting at. "I don't pretend it doesn't exist. I'm pretty clean, but I'm not prudish. I don't go, 'Oh, no! I saw a boob!' I just don't go looking for the bad stuff." Sure, in her own art she'll draw nudes, but she draws them in the anatomically correct classical style.

"You know, it's a huge misperception that everyone here is out for sex," she adds. "That this is one big pervy community. The sexual element? It's a lot of talk, if you ask me. Ninety-eight percent of people here had a bad childhood. Like me, these people were teased and isolated. What do you do when isolated? You do what I did. You retreat into fantasy. You don't socialize. You don't date. You don't engage in normal social or sexual practices. Then, when you grow up and find that there *are* people like you, people who are shy and backwards, all those years of repression come out. You tend to overdo it. But while people here might be *drawing* sexually explicit scenes, or *acting* overly affectionate in public, they are not all going upstairs and having sex. Believe me, they're still waaaay too repressed."

I press her. "But even if it is all talk," I say, "doesn't it push your buttons just a little?"

Brenda sits back in her chair and crosses her legs. Her large, dark-brown eyes look thoughtfully at mine. "You know," she says, "I want to change fandom for the better. I mean this is *so* cool. The art and the characters are great. I want to make my light shine and be a positive influence on others. That's better than condemning others or turning away from them. If anything, being a furry has strengthened my faith. I've learned how to turn down temptation. I've learned how to accept people who are different than me. I've learned how to help them. How to love them."

I smile at Brenda, thinking how *some* people—and I'm not naming names—could learn a thing or two from her.

Brenda and I walk back inside to the art show and she hands me a three-ring binder full of her illustrations. I flip through the book and its colorful collection of playful and charming animal characters. Most of the characters are female, they're expertly rendered, and they're all—in a word—cute.

Midway through the binder, I come to an illustration that so thoroughly captures what I've learned about furry fandom that I decide to buy it from her. It's an 8x10 color illustration of a dragon. But instead of green scales, the dragon has brown fur. Instead of breathing fire, he's wearing a colorful beaded necklace. And where most dragons look menacing, this one looks like the happy visitor at a children's birthday party.

Its title? Misfit Dragon.

Brenda normally charges eight dollars for copies of her illustrations, but she wants me to have this one for five.

I take Misfit Dragon upstairs to my room. In the elevator, I think about how I came here on a mission to understand shared joy. But the joy here has not been plainly evident. At least not at first. And part of the reason could be my own selective perception. I'd read about the seamier side of furry fandom and let my prurient dopamine receptors lead me toward the pack of furries that had not been appropriately spayed and neutered.

But what I'm discovering is that there *is* joy here; it simply resides on a lower plane. And what I conclude is that the things which cause us to jump out of bed in the morning aren't always those wacky, over-the-top, get-a-look-at-my-cool-autograph-collection interests that we absotively, posolutely, have to share with others. Sometimes we have to satisfy needs lower on the survival scale first. Sometimes we have to learn to communicate, join, trust, and find ways of feeling comfortable in our own skins before we can fully express who we are. Sometimes we have to let the indomitable human spirit push us forward before we can relax and be happy in exactly the right manner.

And I use the word "we" deliberately.

For what I'm coming to realize is that the furries I've met are all, in one way or another, in the process of unfolding.

As am I.

• • •

In a hotel suite off the main lobby, about twenty furries—most of them middle-aged white guys in T-shirts; a few with tails, most without—are gathered around a television that's playing a mix of Saturday morning cartoons and music video clips featuring animated animals. The presentation has been billed as "Furry Music Videos." I squeeze into the last open seat and begin to watch, instantly recognizing many of the clips from my own childhood.

There's Atom Ant—"*Up and at 'em Atom Ant!*"—and the Cattanooga Cats and Secret Squirrel and Huckleberry Hound and Woody Woodpecker and my personal favorite, Josie and the Pussycats. All around me the furries are chuckling and elbowing their neighbors and alerting each other when an especially good video comes on.

"This is a great one!"

"Be quiet—I *love* this one!"

"It's the Hampster Dance with Hampton and the Hampsters!!!"

The giggling men in the room remind me of my nephew when he was ten. Any minute now, I expect them to launch into a round of armpit farts.

I find their childish spirit strangely infections and before I know it, I, too, am chuckling and tapping my feet and allowing myself to enjoy the videos along with everyone else. And why not? And when a music video with Elton John singing a song from *The Lion King* comes on, and when Nala and Simba start romping across the screen, and when the furries around me all start singing, I join in.

Of course, I don't sing loudly. In fact, I don't really *sing* at all. What I do sounds more like Dustin Hoffman in *Rainman*. But I don't care. Because Nala and Simba are nuzzling on the screen, and because I'm finally having a good time with the furries, and because yes, Elton, in response to your question, I *can* feel the love tonight. Thanks for asking. Especially since it took this wide-eyed wanderer a while to get here.

CHAPTER ELEVEN

How Did We Get Here and Where are We Anyway?

"America is a vast conspiracy to make you happy."
—John Updike

NEVER GIVE UP ANYTHING YOU'RE GOOD AT, I ALWAYS say. Actually, I never say that. But it seems appropriate to say right now while sitting at a table inside the Browne Popular Culture Library at Bowling Green State University in Ohio surrounded by a set of encyclopedias, each one the approximate size and weight of a cinder block.

After the perplexing foray into furry fandom, I felt I needed a break. I needed a break from all the costumes and shared histories and insider language that surround passionate fanatics. So instead of looking at American passion from the ground level, I've decided there might be something to learn by taking a thirty-thousand-foot view. And I like research. Hence, the library.

The Browne Popular Culture Library was established in 1968 on the belief that what people do in their spare time—what they collect, read or buy—can tell just as much, if not more, about a society than a dusty collection of farm tools or the crumbling edifice of a church. Elvis posters, comic books, *Life* magazines, mail-order catalogs—according to pop culture scholars, these are the artifacts that reveal the true heart of a culture. And Bowling Green State is the only place in the country devoted to archiving such artifacts.

(The university also has the peculiar distinction of having a cemetery in the middle of campus, but that's another story.)

When I arrived here this morning, the library director gave me a tour of the archives, housed in a large, labyrinthine room that reeks of decomposing paper. Wandering through the gunmetal gray shelving was like traveling through several decades' worth of America's fanatical passions. We passed shelves laden with trading cards, travel postcards, paperback novels, and pulp magazines devoted to every imaginable interest, including needlework, famous monsters, shortwave radio, and popular religion. One aisle was stacked floor to ceiling with nothing but zines, those little magazines produced in big cities, small towns, and back bedrooms by enthusiasts of everything from werewolves and female jazz to Dracula and Horatio Alger. There were at least seven zines devoted to *The Wizard of Oz* alone, including *The Emerald City Mirror*, *The Oz Collector*, *The Oz Gazette*, *The Oz Observer*, *Ozmopolitan*, *Oziana*, and *The Baum Bugle*.

Bowling Green also boasts one of the most comprehensive *Star Trek* collections ever gathered in one place. Archived in long, light-blue cardboard boxes are *Star Trek* action figures, Christmas ornaments, Taco Bell glasses, Happy Meal boxes, a Mr. Spock liquor decanter, a zippered briefcase from the Vulcan Science Academy, and the entire, magnificent, wonder-to-behold Starship Enterprise painted on one teeny tiny grain of rice. The complete collection—some 1,950 items— was the decades-long work of Marie Wakefield, a U.S. Army librarian who had to part with her possessions when transferred overseas.

Looking at her treasures, I had to wonder if Marie might have had a bit too much time on her hands. Which is exactly why I'm here. Did a growth in leisure time contribute to Marie's obsession with *Star Trek*? To the boardgamers' immersion in a World at War? To the Lady in Red's fascination with Mayberry minutiae? Or was it something else? What is it about American society today that is allowing or encouraging or facilitating the growth of so much fanatical devotion?

I've been searching for clues inside various pop culture encyclopedias for the last two hours under the watchful eye of a black-masked Batman who's staring at me from the end of the table. It's a life-size promotional advertisement for the *Batman* movie starring Michael Keaton and Jack Nicholson, and somehow strikes me as the perfect mascot for my search.

Hoisting one giant volume after another, I begin to discover that we Americans have been hurtling toward the valley of fanatical excess for almost a century. Bit by bit, decade by decade, we've grown and morphed and expanded from a nation of solitary hobbyists, a nation where interests were indulged by individuals on a small scale in their spare time, into a nation where a *Star Wars* convention in Indianapolis will attract more than 30,000 light-saber-wielding fans.

The first evidence of this inclination toward excess appeared in the 1920s, when the rise of industrial society and the accompanying growth of leisure time gave Americans more hours in which to play — and play they did. In the roaring twenties, thrift, sobriety, and restraint were politely shown the back door, as post-World War I America welcomed the ability to be truly zany. But their chosen entertainment was cheap. People sat on flagpoles, gulped goldfish, and participated in days-long dance marathons. People like thirty-two-year-old dance teacher Alma Cummings, who once danced for fifty hours straight, exhausting several male partners in the process.

The 1920s gave Americans their first addictive dose of passionate fanaticism. But just as it was revving up, the fun whiplashed to a stop. The Great Depression, followed by World War II, made it once again unseemly and impractical for Americans to have too much fun. Whereas quiet, self-esteem-building hobbies like stamp collecting and needlework were encouraged as a way for people to survive the stress of hard times, unchecked exuberance was a definite no-no. The country was in crisis, after all, and everyone had to band together.

When the war ended, and the country eased out of its depression, years of pent-up playfulness were released like a nuclear blast. Enter the 1950s. Cash was relatively plentiful. Companies were growing. Babies were booming. And Americans were ready to pick up where they'd left off. They went seeking fun and found it on that newfangled television, where all those newfangled companies sold all sorts of newfangled, fun-giving products. People bought propeller beanies, Slinkies, and over 100 million Hula Hoops that decade. Americans also wore Davy Crockett coonskin hats, writhed like the dancers on American Bandstand, and would probably have gone utterly, berserkly, over the top, if not for one thing: the 1950s was also a decade of conformity. Of the Organization Man. Of hewing to established traditions. Sure, you could be a kid and wear that coonskin cap—every other kid was—but try to wear that hat to the office and look out. In the fifties, the manifesto was fitting in. And furries? Forget about it.

In the 1960s, the country turned a corner once again. Of course, you already know all about the sixties. Tune in. Turn on. Drop out. *Rebel.* To hell with the artificial social constraints of post-war America. You want to have a good time? You go right ahead and rip that gray flannel suit to shreds. Hey, man, it's your right as an American. But remember: we need to band together. We're here for women. For blacks. For the environment. For getting the boys back from 'Nam. Buy all the bongs and Beatles albums you want, but don't forget we're on a mission here, a mission to change the world. Selfish is out. Social change is in.

And it stayed in until the 1970s, the decade of black lights and Afros and Farrah Fawcett's nipples on that poster. Worn out from a screaming decade of riots and political protest, Americans turned quietly, narcotically inward. They searched for their erroneous zones and became their own best friends, as it gradually became acceptable, once again, for people to pursue their own individual groove things. They no longer had to worry about social conformity or social change. Personal happiness became the goal to strive for. But sadly, while there were no doubt some Barbie collectors lying low in the seventies, they and other budding fanatics were kept tethered by one thing: the lack of lucre. In the 1970s, unemployment was high, the national debt soared, and there just wasn't enough money to spend frivolously.

But all that fiscal restraint ended in 1980, when a Hollywood cowboy was elected president, the country's wealth exploded, and the consumer culture shifted into credit-card-driven overdrive. In the eighties, shopping became the national pastime. The Material Girl ruled. And now that people had the money *and* social support *and* personal inclination to pursue whatever pleasures they pleased, national spending on recreation nearly doubled—from $149 billion in 1980 to $250 billion in 1989. Sporting goods. Tickets to Broadway plays. Season tickets for the Broncos. Don't worry, be happy. And while there was plenty of talk about the Overworked American, when compared with their pre-industrial, dead-before-you're-fifty counterparts, people in the eighties seemed to be bursting with play-time energy.

Then, as if all this weren't enough, the Internet came along and hyperlinked one person's passions to another. Whatever obscure bit of fun you pursued—collecting Hallmark ornaments or talking about the philosophical values of *The Simpsons* or perfecting fixed-axle yo-yo tricks—you could find others to share it with. From Yahoo to AOL, online communities sprouted like Beanie Babies. Suddenly, once-solitary hobbies like drawing furry art or playing Legos became robust shared enthusiasms. And with all that social support and camaraderie, there was no longer a need to feel ashamed of an unusual hobby.

No doubt about it, Americans were unapologetically jubilant as they rounded the corner into the new millennium. But then we were immediately felled by the twin towers of 9/11, the growing worldwide threat of terrorism, corporate greed and wrongdoing, and the anxious, gnawing fear that we don't know who we can trust—a fear politicians have capitalized on. But has that fear pushed Americans off of their flagpoles and back into their basements? Not hardly. Americans haven't stopped having a good time, but they do seem more selective about who they hang with. We might not trust the couple next door or the co-worker one cubicle over or that creepy guy sitting next to us on the train. But we are willing to trust people who share our pro-clivities, be it Josh Groban's snack preferences, Christian sci-ence-fiction, or *Batman* movies starring Michael Keaton, as opposed to the ones with Val Kilmer or George Clooney or Christian Bale. Membership in organizations like the Rotary Club and the League of Women Voters may be on the decline, but it's not because community is dying. It's because people have found other, more inherently satisfying and presumably safer ways to express their social sides.

I push the encyclopedias away and lean back in my chair.

Fifty years of socially approved fun combined with thirty years of self-absorbed self-interest, twenty years of wealth, ten years of online connectivity, five years of social trepidation, and a few bunny hops later you've got the ideal climate for hundreds of furries to gather proudly at a Holiday Inn in Costa Mesa, California. Viewed through this historical lens, the furries and their ilk aren't idiosyncratic fringe groups at all. But rather, the sign of an affluent, technologically adept society that values indi-vidualism, personal happiness, and the right of diverse others to live, be, and express themselves openly.

CHAPTER TWELVE
Running From G.I. Joe

"Take the Jeep and get some ammo!"
—*Talking G.I.Joe*

AN HOUR LATER, I CHECK MY THEORIES ABOUT THE RISE OF fanaticism with Dan Shoemaker, an instructor of popular culture at Bowling Green. Dan is a short, chubby redhead with a playful, pointy red beard that makes him look like Santa's head elf.

"I would be careful of oversimplification," he says. "But generally, yes, I think you are on the right track."

Dan and I are sitting just off the kitchen in a small house he recently rented near campus. Boxes are plunked along the floor in various states of unpacking, giving the place a look of semi-organized chaos—it's a look that mirrors my own feelings in this late-in-the-third-quarter stage of my journey. It's a look that says, I know what I've got, and I've got a lot, I just don't know where to put it all. Which is why I've come to talk with Dan. Perhaps he can help me sort through the confusion.

After he confirms my own cultural impressions, Dan, being the dedicated teacher he is, tries to help me understand his scholarly view of popular culture and its influence on American pastimes. He speaks slowly. He uses words like "message construction" and "homology" and "cultural logic." He tells me he's not so much interested in looking at the *causes* of cultural fanaticism as he is in looking at the *symptoms*. Which is all very fine and interesting. But homology and cultural logic—unless I'm widely mistaken—aren't going to help me understand why some people chase passions like cheetahs, whereas others, like me, don't. So I change the subject. I ask Dan about his own passions. He rolls his eyes. He knew this was coming.

Dan gets up and walks over to a built-in credenza on top of which he's arranged an impressive display of plastic action heroes. He spreads his arms and tilts his elfin eyebrows. "This is me," he says, "and these are my toys."

Dan begins looking through his collection for an action hero to share with me, and as I watch him, that nagging uncertainty returns. Why don't I have a thing, a thing that excites me so much I want to raise my palms, tilt my eyebrows, and share it with others? Dan has a thing. So do millions of other Americans. And based on my research, the technological and economic and social climates are right for every last one of us to find our own interest, passion, obsession, call-it-what-you-will *thing*. And here I sit, thing-less, in the middle of Ohio, talking to an obviously intelligent man who also happens to have an unfettered affection for Spiderman, Captain Action, The Green Hornet, and other miniature comic-book heroes.

Dan finally settles on a G.I. Joe Action Figure. He brings it over to the table and launches into a fevered monologue about the plastic doll. The one we are looking at, he says, is known as the Land Adventurer model. It has a Kung Fu grip, Brillo Pad hair, and a beard, and like all G.I. Joes, a rugged cheek scar to denote toughness.

"Originally, G.I. Joe's hands were shaped to hold a rifle," Dan says, pointing to the doll's tiny molded hand, "but when Vietnam became less popular, the rifle grip was replaced by the Kung Fu grip."

I look at the Kung Fu grip and the cheek scar and do my best to feign fascination with Dan's fascination of the doll. But I get nowhere. Instead, I experience the same nonreaction I did when Malibu Barbie was first presented to me. But since Dan has been so nice and has taken so much time with me I feel duty-bound to show an interest in his collection.

"So why do you like G.I. Joe?" I ask, thinking how many times I've asked some version of this question over the last several months.

"Oh, *God*," Dan says. "Like I know."

He looks down and turns the Land Adventurer G.I. Joe over and over in his hands. "In some ways, I'm hesitant to say that I am a collector. But look," he points to the action hero display. "I have them." Then he narrows his eyes. "But I'm *not* fanatic about it."

I say nothing. What is there to say? Few of the enthusiasts I've spoken with would characterize themselves as fanatical or even overly passionate. Those are descriptions we reserve for other people, which may explain why none of my friends were willing to own up to a fanatical passion when I originally asked. Fanaticism, no matter what side of the line you're on, is something other, *stranger* people do. And that line is something we control for ourselves.

Several months ago, I sat transfixed as a friend unraveled two hour's worth of details about *The Sound of Music* and all its stars, and where it was filmed and how and why the movie had affected her so much. This woman, who's highly educated, speaks several languages, and grew up abroad, was so over-the-top in love with *The Sound of Music* that she'd attend *Sound of Music* sing-alongs. The event attracts fans dressed in lederhosen and nun habits and Nazi uniforms, who watch the movie on a big screen and, as the name suggests, sing along.

"But I'm *not* a fanatic," she assured me. "I'm not like most of the people who go to the sing-along."

"Why's that?" I asked.

"*They* dress up," she said. "I would never do that."

For her, costumes were the line that separated mere interest from unmitigated insanity.

I'm not sure where Dan's line is, and why he doesn't consider himself a fanatic, but we spend the next hour talking about G.I. Joe's illustrious history. We talk about Nazi G.I. Joe, French Resistance G.I. Joe, and Australian Bush G.I. Joe. He shows me the Nostalgia Pack he recently bought, a new release from Hasbro's Timeless Collection that is aimed at older collectors. The pack includes a face mask, binoculars, portable light, shoulder holster, pistol, facemask, searchlight, walkie-talkie, Morse code kit, gun, gun case, field radio and dog tags. Dan bought the Nostalgia Pack at Meijer's, a Midwest department store chain.

"Like I said, I'm not a fanatic, but what would happen is that I would go to Meijer's looking for stuff to use in my classes, and then I'd find stuff that *I* liked."

I continue to ask Dan questions, and he continues to oblige. We move out of the G.I. Joe trenches and into the territory of Johnny West, Captain Action, and Big Jim, and then we soar into the action hero universe of DC and Marvel Comics. We circle around Batman, Captain America, the Lone Ranger, Kato, and Aquaman. And for some reason, the more Dan talks, the more molded action heroes we discuss, the more irritated I become. I find that I'm growing weary of little dolls and happy eyebrows and the arcane minutiae of hand grips. And although I continue to act interested, I find I don't really want to learn about Dan's other collections—his Big Little books or his refrigerator magnets or his six-thousand plastic-encased comic books. I... just... don't... care. And it's not his fault. When Dan pulls the lid off the first of twenty comic-book storage boxes, something inside of me snaps, and I make up an excuse about having a phone meeting in twenty minutes.

I drive to Bowling Green's four-block downtown, find a restaurant, and order a glass of cabernet. The waitress brings me a small airplane bottle of wine, cracks the metal lid, and pours it into my glass. Great. Not quite what I was looking for, but we'll make it work. The wine is terrible. I order a second glass/bottle. Then some dinner.

After dinner, still needing something I can't quite identify, I drive to Dairy Queen and order a chocolate cone. The cone arrives. This being the Midwest, the glistening thick chocolate swirl is enormous, reaching from the bottom of my chin to the top of my forehead. I finish it on the way back to my hotel where, once inside my room, I call the airlines to see if I can get an earlier flight out tomorrow.

CHAPTER THIRTEEN
On the Couch

"Always remember you're unique, just like everyone else."
—Bumper sticker

AT NINE THE NEXT MORNING, I GET INTO MY RENTED RED Dodge Neon and drive back to the Bowling Green campus.

For months now, I've been collecting academic journal articles in an effort to unravel the psychology behind fanatical passion. I went through these files the other day. Several articles were more than forty pages long. One had seventeen pages of references alone. All of them used impressive and illuminating academic terms like "symbolic interactionism," "psychological phenomenology," and "leisure-identity salience," which meant, of course, that I understood little between the words "Introduction" and "Summary." (Which for no good reason reminds me of a joke: *Q: How many Freudian analysts does it take to change a lightbulb? A: Two—one to change the bulb and one to hold the penis, er, I mean, ladder.*)

But I digress.

Knowing I'd be at the university, I found a flesh-and-blood academic that I hope can help me understand the psychology of fanatical passion without resorting to academic code words. Her name is Anne Gordon, and she's a well-published professor of social psychology. Since I'd arranged to meet with Anne three weeks ago, and since I'm nothing if not responsible, and since booking an earlier flight last night would have cost me at least one hundred dollars, and since I realized after a good night's sleep that fleeing town because of G.I. Joe was probably not the mark of an especially well-balanced person, I decided to keep my appointment with her.

Holding a Styrofoam cup of coffee in my left hand, I drive through campus. Bowling Green is your quintessential state college with clumps of square brick buildings, some grassy areas, and a large athletic field. But the most attractive feature, in my mind, is the shady on-campus cemetery known as Oak Grove. Although my-end-of-life preference is for cremation followed by a worldwide ash-scattering by a coterie of devoted friends and family members, interment on the grounds of a college campus would merit a close second. I drive past the cemetery, park outside the psychology building, and walk inside to find Anne. Because the university is in summer session, few students are around.

I find her working on a computer inside a cool, well-lit second-floor office. She's got auburn hair, an alert, healthy gaze, and is wearing flip-flop sandals and a shiny new coat of toenail polish. She looks like the type of person who gets up early to take a few invigorating laps around the pool. I sit down beside her desk.

"I'm fascinated by your project," she says, wheeling her chair closer to mine. "Tell me about the people you've been spending time with."

I briefly recount my travels and the people I've met and the observations I've made. I tell her about how these fanatical subcultures seem to be thriving. I tell her about the pride of the ice fishermen, the bonds between pigeon racers, the need of science-fiction fans to find other smart people, and the amazing acceptance and species variety of the furries. I tell her how quick people have been to judge others who have passions they don't understand, how the Grobanites were ready to Grobangle me for even suggesting they might have something in common with Barbie collectors, and how I recoiled at being falsely categorized myself. I tell her all of this in a rush, excited to have finally found someone who seems interested in the details of my experiences.

Anne smiles and nods as I talk. I can tell she gets it. Like me, she's an observer of human nature, a seeker of answers, a person whose career is fueled by the simple question, "What's up with that?" Anne sits up in her chair and points to a yellow legal pad on which she's written a list of points to cover with me.

"What you're talking about are all normal psychological processes," she says, and launches into a crash course on social behavior.

To understand why people do the things they do you have to look at their situation, she says. That's a core tenet of social psychology—that situational forces are often what cause people to act the way they do. Although we'd like to think we act based on a deep-seated set of internal values or personality traits, we're also strongly influenced by external forces. You might insist that stealing is wrong, but what if you've been flooded from your house, are starving, and no aid is on the way? See, given the right environment, many people would steal or lie or attend a furry convention in order to feel less lonely. From the outside, though, it's hard to see what those situational forces are. We can only see a person's behavior, thus we judge based on actions alone. Someone who rescues a child from a well is a hero, whereas a fur-suited furry is merely nuts. That's because we can't always see the situation that would cause someone to don a smiling rabbit costume. And situations, Anne stresses, are often deeply psychological. We can't see the loneliness. We can't see the love of cartoon animals. We can't see the juicy, self-esteem-building feelings that come from finally being regarded as an insider as opposed to an outcast.

Plus, the psychological situations that cause people to act a certain way often develop over a long period of time. People aren't fanatics from day one. Their interests typically start small and grow more intense as their situations change. A Barbie collector, for instance, may start out with one or two or six dolls on a shelf in her bedroom. One day, perhaps on a whim, she attends her first Barbie convention, and collecting the dolls moves from a solitary sport to a social activity. She starts shopping for dolls with friends, her collection grows, and gradually she begins to sense there might be some value in her collection—perhaps as an investment, or for posterity, or as an inheritance for her grand-kids. Suddenly, her collection has *meaning*, and collecting in and of itself becomes a worthwhile activity. Then, one fall afternoon, let's say her only son is murdered in a church, and Barbie and the supportive Barbie community are the only things that get her through. Any doubts she may have harbored about the value or importance of Barbie collecting disappear at that point, and she becomes an unapologetic life-long devotee. But to the casual observer who can't see that history or those psychological forces, the Barbie collector with several hundred dolls is considered to be utterly off her trolley.

"See, fanaticism is not caused by just one situation," Anne says, "but a longer string of situations invisible to the observer."

Anne pauses to explain that she's an *evolutionary* social psy-chologist, which means she looks at how psychological needs have developed and evolved over thousands of years. And one of the strongest evolutionary needs, she says, is the need to belong. When we lived in groups of thirty or fifty people, we depended so strongly on one another that to be excluded by the group lit-erally meant death. That's why so many of us are terrified of not fitting in, of not finding our tribe, of wearing the wrong clothes to the cocktail party. In fact, when people experience social exclusion, the pain center in the brain lights up on an MRI the same as it does when people experience deep physical pain. Rejection, in short, can feel just as painful as a broken ankle. But broken ankles can be mended, whereas rejection must be endured. The fear and pain of exclusion is why people will trav-el across deserts to find places of acceptance. It's why the furries travel to Costa Mesa, California. Why the TIE fighter pilots travel to Schaumburg, Illinois. And when you think about it, those travels are healthy ways of dealing with rejection.

"Think of Columbine," Anne says. "There, you had two smart kids who felt excluded and massacred their classmates. A science-fiction convention, by comparison, is a pretty healthy coping mechanism."

The importance of fitting into a tribe cannot be overstated, she stresses. That's why we tend to show such favoritism to our own group, and will stick by it come hell or high water. After all, you'd never support and defend a group that wasn't *worthy* of such support and defense would you? Of course not. Nobody would. And this can't help but lead to feelings of superiority.

Anne tells me about an experiment in which people were asked to estimate the number of dots on a slide, and were then divided into groups of "overestimators" and "underestimators." The researchers didn't really know how many dots were on the slide, and people were assigned to the overestimator and under-estimator groups on a random basis. Later, each group was given the opportunity to allocate points in a game and the overestima-tors consistently allocated more of their points to *other* overesti-mators, whereas underestimators gave theirs to, you guessed it, other underestimators. Even though the group classifications were meaningless, and people in each group had no contact with one another, they still showed a preference for their "own kind."

The point, she says, is that it doesn't take much to activate this in-group bias. Grobanites will claim that Grobanites aren't crazy because Josh Groban is a living, breathing, talented human being. But *Barbie* collectors? Anne facetiously rolls her eyes. Grobanites think *they're* crazy because Barbie is just a plastic doll.

I smile at Anne, thinking how much I'm enjoying this con-versation. I feel like I'm talking to someone who's energized by the mysteries of human nature in the same way I am. If I'm an overestimator, so is Anne. If I'm foraging for berries on a sunny hillside, she is just a few paces away.

"I love this stuff," I tell her.

"I can tell," she says. "I do, too."

The upshot of all this social comparison, she continues, is that how you feel about yourself is based largely on who you compare yourself to. Grobanite to Grobanite? That feels good. Grobanite to Barbie? Not so good. Researchers have tested this idea through research on Olympic medalists, and what they've continually found is that bronze medalists are more satisfied with their lives and accomplishments than are silver medalists, even though they came in third. Why? Because bronze medalists compare themselves to all the people who didn't get a medal, whereas silver medalists compare themselves only to the winner. Consequently, silver medalists go through life ruminating about what might have been, what they could have done differently. And in some cases, that sense of disappointment lasts a long time. The research suggests that how satisfied people feel with their circumstances is greatly affected by who they compare themselves to and how they stack up.

Upon hearing this, my neurons begin to spark and flicker with recognition. I don't tell Anne this, but I fear I've been a silver-to-gold person much of my life, forever comparing myself to those who have what I lack. When my first book was published, I obsessively tracked the sales ranking on Amazon—not against other first-time essayists (translated: those writers nobody reads), but against Pulitzer Prize winners, say, or J.K. Rowling. I've compared the lines forming around my eyes not with other fair-skinned middle-aged women, but with, oh, Halle Berry. I've always believed this tendency to be my own unique form of self-flagellation. But if what Anne is saying is true, social comparison is something we all do, which naturally leads me to wonder how *my* ability to compare socially stacks up against others'. I make a mental note to obsess about this more later. But right now, Anne has moved on. She's now talking about how people join groups because group membership is meaningful.

Human beings are the only species aware of their own deaths and that can be terrifying, she explains. As a result, people have to make their life mean something somehow. They have to find value and worth in their activities—and often, a lot of that value and worth comes from the groups they choose to belong to. If I find playing board games an enjoyable way to spend my time, and all these *other* people find playing board games with me an enjoyable way to spend time, well, that must mean that playing board games is worthwhile, and that my participation is valuable. Thus, my life has merit.

This gets me to thinking about reverence, and so I tell Anne how often God or faith or a hands-spread-wide appreciation for life has come up in my conversations with fanatics.

"The people I've met seem to find something deeply significant about their activities," I say. "They talk as if they've been blessed by God to have found ice fishing or pigeon racing or Josh Groban."

Anne smiles her knowing smile again. "That sense of rapture you talk about? That's related to connectedness, to meaning. It's important for people to feel connected, to feel they're not alone in life. Whether that sense of connectedness comes from God or spirituality or their ice-fishing buddies almost doesn't matter. People can find meaning in a myriad of ways. What does matter is that they're not alone, that they're part of a tribe, and that they're doing something that's deeply satisfying."

Anne crosses the last item off her list and sits back in her chair looking very much like a satisfied teacher who's found an appreciative student—which she has.

"Just look at you," she says. "You've obviously found meaning in what you do and in the people you've chosen to spend time with. You seem to be quite fulfilled by your life."

I stare at Anne, not quite sure what to say. How can I tell

her that I've felt anything but fulfilled, that it was, in fact, a lack of fulfillment that launched me on this journey? I want to disagree with her. I want to tell her that I'm really like a teenager—forever bored and disaffected and picking at my cuticles. But even as this thought forms, I realize it's not true. I *have* been fulfilled, and fulfilled by the quest itself. The travel. The newness. The education. The eyes-wide-open conversations I've had with people so unlike me who've taught me about the humanity we share. But I haven't been focusing on those things. I've been the silver medalist focused solely on my deficiencies. And where does *that* come from anyway?

I could blame a WASP upbringing that taught me how impolite it was to boast about one's self, and how I somehow internalized that to mean that I must not have a self worth boasting about.

I could blame an evolutionary drive to be better and stronger and taller than all the ooze-bound generations that came before me. Doesn't the drive to be better than you are automatically carry with it a focus on that which needs bettering, a focus on how you're less than?

I could blame being an American and how there's something about living in this goofily optimistic, ad-driven country that continually reminds you there's always a way to become healthier, happier, and capable of longer, more luminous eyelashes than you ever thought possible.

I could blame a host of things for my insistent, almost defiant focus on my deficiencies. But regardless of where it comes from, it's clear to me now that this focus has been all wrong. I've been comparing myself to people who have what I *don't*, as opposed to embracing that which I *do*. I haven't been missing passion at all.

I've been missing perspective.

A breeze rustles the bright green leaves on the shade tree outside Anne's window. It's a brilliant, blue-sky summer morning, and I'm inside talking to a fellow tribe member, to someone who's as interested in the great wonder of it all in the same way I am. Someone walking by the office would see the two of us leaning forward, knees on elbows, like little girls sharing a back-yard secret.

I grin stupidly at Anne. "You're right," I say to her, trying not to sound like this is the first time this thought has occurred to me—which it is. "I *am* fulfilled."

PART THREE : Emerge

CHAPTER FOURTEEN

Hep cat

"Hot funk, cold punk, even if it's old junk,
it's still rock and roll to me."

—Billy Joel

THE MUSIC LIBRARY AND SOUND RECORDING ARCHIVES AT
Bowling Green State University houses more than three-quarters of a million popular music recordings, everything from 78s of Glenn Miller to twelve-inch disco singles of the Bee Gees, and digital recordings of Nirvana to boxed sets of old-time radio shows. Let's conservatively assume that each recording runs an average of fifteen minutes, albums being longer, singles much shorter. If you were to play the archive's recordings eight hours a day, seven days a week, you would be able to listen to music for more than seventy-two years—through eighteen presidential administrations—without ever hearing a song repeated. Bill Schurk, the archive's director, is the man responsible for amassing that collection and although he hasn't actually sat down and listened to all 72 years' worth of music, he's probably come closer than anyone.

When I first called the good people at Bowling Green and explained my research involving passionate fanatics, Bill's name kept popping up in conversation.

"Have you talked to Bill Schurk?"

"Bill Schurk's your man."

"You want passion? You want *fanatical?* Bill Schurk's the biggest music-lover-collector-fanatic I've ever seen."

I was told that Bill manages the library's record collection, and that he also has a suffocating record collection of his own at home. So I arranged to meet with him to see if the epiphany experienced in Anne Gordon's office was legitimate. Can I be a silver medalist admiring Bill's gold without being enveloped by envy? Can I view him simply as a fellow tribe member without wishing that I too had the genetic ability to remember the flip side of every 45 ever owned?

I arrive at the third-floor library, give the receptionist my name, and seconds later a tall smiling man with silver hair and glasses rounds the corner. He's wearing a T-shirt that says *High Times Presents Potzilla* and a yellow Homer Simpson watch. He points to the watch. "Right on time," he says. "I like that."

Bill leads me down the hall into his office, a jumbled space in which every niche and cranny is jammed with music. Albums and eight tracks and cassette tapes and compact discs are shoved into bookcases, piled on the desks, and heaped, thigh-deep, onto the floor. I walk through a narrow channel to an empty chair and wedge myself into a tiny space underneath a poster for the Smoking Popes. In front of me a footrest of albums is capped by one called Music for Twirling. Elvis and Paul McCartney and Joe Cocker and the Hip Swinging Santa and hundreds of other pop music images, surround us. I've landed in the den of Doo Wop.

"So, Bill," I say, trying to gain some focus. "How did you get into music?"

And that's all it takes.

"Music? That's my *life.* I never *got* into it. My grandfather had an old wind-up record player. It was a Silver Tone brand, not a Victrola—even though everyone called it a Victrola, because it was a wind-up. You know. It's just like Band-Aids. Everyone thinks they're all Band-Aids even though they aren't. So my grandfather had this old wind-up and I listened to that. But my parents also had a wind-up. This one really *was* a Victrola. The earliest music I can remember listening to were pop singers of the 1920s. People like Billy Murray and Harry Lauder—he was a very famous Scottish singer, and Billy Jones and Ernest Hare and the Happiness Boys. The *songs*, not just the artists. But the *songs* were so ingrained in our minds. Like the famous 'Wreck of the Old '97.' *Everybody* in the United States had that record. That was by Vernon Dalhart. That was not his real name. He never sang under his real name. Hold on, let me get the date of that Dalhart thing because that was just soooo famous. Everybody and his grandmother listened to it. Let's see… here it is… twenty-five! Yep, 1925. That's when it was recorded. See, I was very influenced by my dad's music. He liked silly songs, silly pop songs, you know. Like Phil Harris's 'The Thing,' where a guy finds a thing on the beach, and you never know what that thing is. I also liked Dennis Day doing 'Clancy Lowered the Boom.' Boy was that a silly song! Apparently, Clancy would lose his temper. That's what it meant for Clancy to lower the boom. Get it? But those were my dad's songs. The first record that was mine was a three-record pocket set of Woody Guthrie doing *Songs to Grow On*. I mean back then, how many people bought Woody Guthrie? I would assume my brother would claim it was his album, but my mom and dad really bought it for everybody. I can still remember the picture on the original cover. They never had a picture of Woody on the cover, 'cause, you know, his image wasn't conducive to selling records to kids. So the cover was a bunch of kids playing on the floor.

"You know, I come from a musical family. My mom was a piano player and had a very nice voice. My dad would sorta sing, as a guy who can't carry a tune would sing. Dick played the clarinet, Kathy played the viola, Sandra tried to play the piano, and I played the record player, you know, the old wind-up. I learned early on that with a wind-up you could *do* things to records. You could make them go faster or slower. You could put a hamster on the record and gradually speed it up until the hamster would shoot off. Boy, that was fun! We'd also play disc jockey. We'd put on a record, and you'd have to guess the name of the artist and the name of the song, and whoever got the most right got to be the next disc jockey. Poor old Oleg Fedoroff. He could never remember the name of 'The Anvil Chorus.' 'The Anvil Chorus,' you know, it's a classical piece. I can't remember from what. Wait a sec, let me see if I can look it up. Oh, yeah, here it is. It's from the opera *Il Trovatore* by Verdi. Course, we could have cared less it was from an opera. We didn't play the flip side very much. That was called 'The Forge in the Forest.' It wasn't as much of a fun song as 'The Anvil Chorus,' which went dum, dum, de, dum-dum-dum-dum-dum. You would know 'The Anvil Chorus' if you heard it. You'd say, "Oh yeah. I remember that. That's famous.

"When did I start buying records on my own? Probably when I had a paper route. At first, I just bought more of the same stuff. You know, more of the same old 78s by Henry Burr and Billy Jones and Ernie Hare; you know, I mean, whatever artist I knew, I just found more of those in the junk shops. But by high school, I had friends to share current music with. I was into rock and roll and Muddy Waters and Bo Diddly and Fats Domino. I wasn't one of those weenie people who listened to Perry Como or Doris Day. I was more diversified. Once I started going to Giant Tiger, the bargain discount store, and Gray Drugs, I found you could get 45s real cheap, like for twenty-nine or thirty-five cents each. Then you could take a chance and get a lot more cool stuff. What was nice was that at Giant Tiger, they had a little bitty record player. You could cue up records on it and see what you wanted to buy. Usually, I'd go with my buddy Bob, and he'd be on one side of the rack and I'd be on the other, and we'd throw records to each other to cue up and consider. We could tell if it

was a cool record like within two seconds. You know. *Two* seconds. We didn't want to waste time listening to music there,
when we knew we had to go searching for more records.

"I'm not sure where all this comes from. I'm the only one in
the family that really collects. My brothers and sisters can't collect because they've moved. You can't collect and move. You really can't, unless, I don't know, you collect miniature books or salt
shakers. I've been in my house since 1970, and my wife says that
the only way to clean this house up is to move. You know, I get
this a lot. Not that she doesn't like my collecting. It's the clutter,
and the stuff in the house that everybody is responsible for that
nobody seems to be cleaning up.

"I keep all my records in a record room that is twenty-five
by twenty-five. I have probably about thirty thousand records in
my collection. They are more or less in order, by genre and by
artist. I've got rock and roll, and country, and traditional country,
and folk, jazz, pop vocal—all the different categories. Once the
shelves in the record room got full the records started piling up
on the floor. Then they made their way to an unused computer
desk on the back porch. All of a sudden, records appeared there.
I started getting the evil eye about what I was going to do with
those. I finally went to Meijer's and got another shelving unit
and you know what's scary? I filled it up, and you can't tell. You
can't tell that I put records on there because I still have so much
on the floor and everywhere else. You know what my granddaughter uses them for? She steps up on the records piled on the
floor to get to the dog biscuits.

"Now, I knew I was gonna be talking to you. And I got
something I want to tell you about what I'm doing. I got to start
to make some decisions about some things. My wife's been has-
sling me. Because, you know, we're not getting any younger. We
see a lot of people making the same kinds of decisions. About
what to do, you know, with the collection. So what I'm doing
now is I'm systematically starting to go through my 78s, and I'm

picking out the 78s the library doesn't have, and they're coming here. How does it feel to go through my collection? It makes me feel good, first of all, that the library's getting some records. But second of all, you don't notice it. You know. You don't notice a difference. Out of twelve albums, I'll only pull out one. Maybe two. I think I'm going to keep my rock and roll and R&B records for a while. But I don't know. You know. It's quite a decision.

"Besides, records aren't the only thing I collect. I have this huge collection of old *National Geographics*. They are like Ray Conniff albums; you can always get too many. I also have *Fortune* magazines and *Esquire* and weird, odd magazines. Magazines with strange titles. Old movie magazines. Picture magazines from World War I and propaganda from World War II. And I've got newspapers and cartoon arts and children's books. I've also got old license plates, which I don't really collect. I just have a lot of them. Maybe a couple hundred. I can't always get more if I need them, but, you know.

"Is my wife a collector? No. No she's not. She knows I have this thing. This thing for collecting. But I haven't let it control my life like many collectors. I know too many collectors who never got married, or if they did, their collection broke up their marriage because they were so obsessive. Me, I let myself stay in control. Plus, I have *two* places for things—at home and here in the library. And here, well, here there is something cool almost everywhere you look.

"Look! Like this—this is so cool. This is Hula Homer. It's a dancing Homer Simpson. When you turn it on, Homer sings 'Tiny Bubbles.' They had to get the rights to it of course. It says so on the side of the box. And here, here, look at this. It's a little action figure of the Honky Tonk man, you know, the wrestler—the Honky Tonk Man? He carried a guitar that he'd whack people over the head with. See, he looks like an overweight Elvis. And I've got… what else? Oh, look! This is cool! I have a whole box of 45 centers, those little plastic discs people would put in their 45s, so they could play them on a turntable. And look at these cool things. These are little records, little two-inch discs with athletes talking about something. Here's OJ Simpson. I've never played 'em, cause I don't have the special record player, but they sure are cool. I get these things as presents from people. I get things that are dorky, stupid, weird, cool, neat, special—all kinds of things really. They don't give me records, though. I don't need those. But I did get a metal record with a painted picture of Ricky Nelson on it. That was cool! Hey—lemme give you one of my cool cards. Now, where did they run off to? I don't like regular business cards because they're so boring. But my cool cards, they're neat. Shoot. Where are they? I coulda of sworn I put them in—oh, here's one. See, it says 'Hep Cat' on it, from Hep Cat Perfume. That's much cooler than a regular business card. Here, you can have it.

"You want to know the best triumph I've had in collecting? It's hard to say. I mean, it's because I *see* so much and I *want* so much. There's almost nothing that I don't want. There's so little I'm not happy with. You follow me? It's what I discover. It's not that I'm *looking* for something. It's that I have *found* something I never knew existed. On Saturday, my wife and I went to a couple junk shops we hadn't been to for a while, and I found an LP from 1973 of Navy recruiting songs done by Lou Rawls and Dottie West and the rock group Ten Wheel Drive. You remember Ten Wheel Drive? No? Okay. Anyway. This was a recruiting record for the U.S. Navy done in 1973, and here I found it in a junk shop on a Saturday afternoon in Napoleon, Ohio. It's doesn't get much cooler than that.

"I guess what I'm saying is, that I like pretty much everything."

• • •

Dazed, I leave Bill's office, take the elevator downstairs, and step into the bright afternoon sun. I stand there blinking and trying to reorient myself, and as I do, as I watch students walk by with their overstuffed backpacks, I realize that progress has been made. Throughout Bill's entire monologue, cool as it was, I did not feel a single twinge of envy, not one molecule of desire for any part of his passion to become my own.

Well, except for maybe that Hula Homer.

That's *was* kinda cool.

CHAPTER FIFTEEN

The National Weather Service Has Issued a Warning

*"When you used to tell me you chase tornadoes,
deep down I thought it was a metaphor"*
—Melissa, in the movie Twister

I'M BOUNCING ALONG INSIDE A VAN IN WESTERN KANSAS with eight storm chasers who are desperately seeking that angry, roof-ripping freak of nature known as a tornado. It's sunny outside, the sky is a pale watercolor blue, and it's easily eighty-five June degrees. But far, far off to our left, a small band of cumulus clouds—"cu fields," in chaser lingo—is forming. Cumulus clouds are those white popcorn-shaped puffs that form innocently in the early afternoon. You've seen cumulus clouds thousands of times drifting above a silver water tower or behind a giant red barn, or in landscape paintings at amateur art sales. If clouds had personalities, these would be the friendly ones, the ones that would bring your daughter mint chocolate-chip ice cream when her tonsils were removed. But when conditions are right—that is, when the warm moist air from the plains rises up and meets unstable air in the upper atmosphere—these innocent little cumulus clouds take a Jekyll-like turn for the worst. They bubble and froth and grow, and push up giant soufflé-like towers packed with wind, rain, and hail and thunderstorms. And, if my fellow travelers are lucky, tornadoes.

Oh, how they want to be lucky.

It's two o' clock, and we've been looking at nothing but endless blue sky and undulating wheat fields and tidy bundles of rolled hay for hours. The storm chasers, who've come to Kansas from San Francisco and Chicago and Holland and other depressingly tornado-deficient points on the globe, are slumped in their seats. The van rises and falls on a black ribbon of concrete heading west on I-70 toward Colorado. We pass a KOA Campground promoting "Good Clean Fun."

Ten minutes pass. Then twenty. Then thirty. Then the weather radio inside the van breaks the silence and announces that the Storm Prediction Center estimates thunderstorms will be developing in the next one to three hours in southwestern Kansas. Predictions are for three-inch hail, meaning hail the size of baseballs or oranges or newborn kittens is likely to pound the Kansas plains later today. Inside the van, you can feel the pulses quicken. It's the first promising sign in six hours.

The leader of our expedition, Roger Hill, makes a quick decision to exit the interstate and head south on State Highway 27. He slows down, points the van toward Oklahoma, and accelerates again, growing more confident with each new mile.

"Ah, this is great chase country," he says. "You can't beat the visibility." He squints at the cu fields in the distance. "There'll be a tornado watch today for sure."

Behind me one of the storm chasers intones, "If Roger says it, it will be."

Roger Hill is the Grand Master and Gold Medalist of storm chasers, having seen, by his own account, more tornadoes than anyone alive today. In the last twenty years, he's spotted more than 270 twisters and caught 175 of them on videotape. The current record is a paltry 117. He's now in the process of documenting his sightings for the Guinness Book of World Records. What's his secret? Trial and error. Perseverance. Experience. And being willing to chase on those high-sky summer days when others aren't.

Newly re-energized, Roger starts a running commentary of what he's seeing.

"Look! At eleven o'clock! There's a large tower going up."

"See this spot? On August 23, 2003, a nice tornado touched down and destroyed a train depot."

"Whoa, didja see that bird? It used to be, if you hit a bird, you'd see a tornado."

The chasers sit upright and begin pulling out their cameras, and as they do the twenty four-hour weather station inside the van grabs their attention with one long emergency tone. Beeeeeeeeeeeeeeeeeeeeeeeeeeeeeeep.

"Ahhh, that's music to the ears," Roger says. He turns up the volume. We wait for the announcement. Seconds pass. Cameras are held suspended. Finally, it comes.

The National Weather Service has issued a tornado watch warning until 10 p.m. tonight.

"They used the T-word!" Roger screams. "We are a-heading to the promised land!" He leans toward the dashboard, turns on his radar detector, and guns the accelerator. The needle on the speedometer rises from seventy to seventy-five to eighty "Let's haul ass!"

• • •

I returned from Ohio feeling both calm and triumphant, like I'd finally come to some kind of understanding about my alignment in the earth's orbit. I even spent a morning shopping on the Internet for a Kung Fu-grip G.I. Joe to commemorate my time with Dan Shoemaker. (After twenty minutes of comparison shopping, however, I realized I was only searching for the doll to assuage my guilt in fleeing Dan's house without fully appreciating the treasures he'd pulled together for me.) But even though I returned home with a greater awareness of my own peculiar passions, my search didn't feel complete.

When I started this trek, I made a list of different kinds of people I wanted to study. The list included collectors, competitors, outdoor enthusiasts, music lovers, animal lovers, and pop culture fans. The list also included the adrenalin-fed category of thrill seekers, but I hadn't yet found a group of thrill seekers I'd feel comfortable spending time with. Rock climbing was out, for there's a limit to how high I'll climb for an interview. (Hint: two feet.) I also eliminated sky divers, spelunkers, and people like this guy I once met who, after wind surfing in the pre-hurricane surf in Florida, ran into a bar all wet and wild-eyed and wrote down a list of thirteen activities which he titled, "Shit That Can Kill You." The list included daredevil feats such as running through Death Valley and swimming from Alcatraz, all of which he went on to pursue and write about in a book called *Over the Edge*. In short, I eliminated all thrill-seeking activities that offered more thrill than my claustrophobic, acrophobic, fair-skinned self could take. But still, I was intrigued. Was it only an adrenalin hit thrill seekers were after? Or something more?

This on my mind, I was sitting in my chilly basement one dark summer afternoon, driven there by a tornado siren in my southeast Denver neighborhood. With Shadow, our malamute, at my side, I watched news reports about highway flooding and road closures while hail clattered through the basement's plastic window-well covers. Larry Green, the local weatherman, was reporting from the Channel Four Storm Center about the progress of a supercell moving slowly across the metro area.

Now, Larry's normally a pretty calm guy, his voice well-modulated and reassuring; the kind of voice you'd want to soothe you to safety in the midst of a natural calamity. But on this particular afternoon, Larry was talking like a used car salesman who's crammed sixty seconds worth of commercial time into one thirty-second slot. He was pointing to green and yellow and red splotches of color on the radar screen and warning Denver residents of the size and power and *danger* of the storm. Get away from the windows, Larry said. Get down to the basement, Larry said. Tornados *have* been spotted, Larry said. And as he said all this, and as I watched him from my warm, dry overstuffed recliner, and as Shadow stared at me in wonderment—I mean, we *never* get to watch television in the middle of the afternoon— it dawned on me: Larry digs this! I used to wonder how weather forecasters could get up and report on the same narrow subject every day. Warm fronts. Cold fronts. Chances of rain. Given the same job, I fear I would suffer a desperate boredom so all-encompassing I'd start tearing the couch apart with my teeth. But watching Larry, I could see he loved this. The lightning bolt flashed. Storm chasers!

So I searched the Internet and came across a Denver-based company called Silver Lining Tours, which offered the "atmospheric adventure of a lifetime." I called and arranged to join them.

• • •

My storm-chasing day started this morning at eight thirty outside the Crystal Inn, an airport hotel near Denver International. Roger gathered our group of sixteen chasers together for a report on where atmospheric conditions were most favorable in the nearby eight-state region. That's the thing with storm chasing— you go where conditions are good, and if that happens to be several hundred miles away, so be it. Earlier this week, Roger had roused the group at 6 a.m. and zigzagged 650 miles from the cloudless blue skies of the Rocky Mountains into a nest of six black tornadoes in the heart of Kent County, Texas. There were nine tornadoes reported in the country that day. Roger vectored his van to the precise location of six of them. At six o'clock that morning, mind you, no one was predicting tornadoes in Kent County, Texas. But Roger sniffed them out. In the process, several chasers lost their tornado virginity, and Roger won the everlasting devotion of the people on his tour. As one explained to me upon my arrival, "Roger is *God*."

Blending the precision of an accountant with the enthusiasm of a children's talk show host, Roger explained that the dew point and temperature and wind sheer and wind speed made southwestern Kansas and the Oklahoma panhandle the most promising today in terms of tornadic activity.

"And if conditions hold," he said, "we'll be looking at baseball-sized hail."

On that bit of cheering-clapping-high-fiving news, we climbed into two vans and headed east toward Kansas on Interstate 70. As the Denver suburbs gave way to open fields, Roger shared with me years of accumulated knowledge about tornado chasing.

• • •

What beginners must understand about storm chasing is that it's not a simple matter of looking at the sky and pursuing seductive little clouds. That's for amateurs. True chasers like Roger rely heavily on technology to help them find that spinning needle in the atmospheric haystack.

Roger's van is equipped with satellite radio, through which he subscribes to Baron's Mobile Threat Net, an onscreen service that provides up-to-the-minute access to radar and storm spotting data. He's also got a computer hooked up to the Internet in order to obtain updates from the National Oceanic and Atmospheric Administration; a CB radio for communicating with the other van; a satellite dish and television to view the Weather Channel; a ham radio for talking with the National Weather Service; a weather station with instruments for measuring temperature, humidity, dew point, and barometric pressure; a twenty-four-hour weather band radio; a global positioning system; a video camera with professional microphone; and, of course, the radar detector for ferreting out over-zealous highway patrol officers. All of this equipment—including the laptop, television and computer tower—is located just inches from the driver's seat, allowing Roger to drive, navigate, and continually monitor the ever-changing atmosphere.

"All of this helps you determine where to chase?" I asked.

"Yeah," he said, "and where *not* to chase. I haven't replaced my windshield in three weeks."

"*Replaced?*"

"Oh, indeed. I've had all the windows in the van knocked out by hail at one time or another. It's quite spectacular when that happens."

Roger Hill has been a storm junkie all his life but he's only recently been able to indulge his passion the way his passion was meant to be indulged. For many, many years, instead of chasing storms, he raised a family, paid the mortgage, and earned a steady paycheck—first in the Air Force as a contracting officer and then as a purchasing manager for the city of Aurora, a position that carried with it few atmospheric adrenalin charges.

Although he didn't know it at the time, the winds of Roger's fortune started to shift back in 1996, the year *Twister* touched down on the big screen. Suddenly, thanks to Hollywood and Helen Hunt, people all over the country were interested in big, bad-ass weather in a way they never had been before. Lacking satellite uplinks and inexpensive laptops and cheap cell phone service, these amateurs would scuttle around the Great Plains stopping at regional offices of the National Weather Service to gather data. As you might expect, the process was tedious and their success haphazard.

Recognizing the pent-up demand, Silver Lining Tours went into business in 1998 to offer more organized, technologically sophisticated storm chasing jaunts. Word got out, the company grew, and Roger joined them as a part-time tour leader in 2000. A year later, business booming, he resigned from the city of Aurora, bought a five-thousand-dollar monthly insurance policy for his van—"People are supposed to drive *away* from an act of God," he said, "not toward it"—and began to chase full-time. And full-time, in twister-tracking terms, means the humid spring and summer months.

In March and April, Roger chases down south through

Arkansas, Oklahoma, and Texas. In May and June, he crisscrosses the center of the country—Missouri, Kansas, Iowa, Nebraska, and Eastern Colorado. In June and July, he heads north to Minnesota, the Dakotas, Montana, and the Southern Canadian Prairie Provinces. And in August and early fall, when the activity on the Great Plains dies down, he heads to the Gulf States to spot water spouts and welcome hurricanes.

"Water spouts are neat," he said, "but it's not like seeing roofs ripped off of houses."

I asked Roger how he felt about winter weather.

"Winter? You mean like snow storms and blizzards? Naaa, they just don't do it for me." He paused. "Well, a snow-nado—those little twirls of snow on the prairie—those are better'n nothing."

"So what do you do during the winter time?"

"Oooh, storm chasers go through withdrawal in the winter months. It's called SDS, for Supercell Deprivation Syndrome. It's as real as anything can be. I find myself buying videotapes of tornadoes just to fill the void. I get reeeeal depressed. Some chasers will even watch water draining down the toilet just to see a cyclone."

Roger relayed all of this while driving and checking his computer and radioing updates to the driver of the other van and clicking through Baron's Mobile Threat Net, and turning around to face me every once in a while so as not to appear rude. Every shift of his attention was accompanied by a lurching swerve of the vehicle. Why does he do this?

"A complete and total obsession with the weather," he said, which he went on to demonstrate with a twenty-minute dissertation on the science behind tornadoes. As the wheat fields whizzed by, Roger talked about cool air and wind sheer and squall lines and skirts and updrafts and billows and how a shot of tequila, when added to the dry line, can create an unparalleled convective concoction. Actually, Roger didn't say anything about tequila. But he spoke so rapidly, and I understood such a small percentage, that he might as well have been talking about blender drinks.

What I did understand was that between 5 and 7 p.m. the atmosphere flips a switch and thunderstorms start to form. "Actually, six o'clock is the magic hour," he said, "the time when you go from puffy white clouds to explosive thunderstorm development. At least that's true here on the Great Plains. It's the best place for the biggest, baddest, most violent storms on earth. Bangladesh comes in second. In April, they have extremely violent storms, but I don't know how you'd chase them. Rickshaw, maybe? Elephants? I don't know how you'd do it. It sure would be cool, though."

At ten thirty, we stopped at a gas station just off the highway. As Roger gassed the van, the storm chasing tourists dashed into the attached mini-mart and packed their pockets with licorice, doughnuts, potato chips, and little yellow cellophane-wrapped cakes. I bought a plastic bottle of water. We started down the highway, and one of the chasers informed me in a nice-but-concerned tone that, really, I should've gotten some food. Chasers, you see, never know where they will end up or if there will be food when they get there. You just can't take the chance.

Back in the van, we settled in for the long ride to who knew where. To pass the time, I began chatting with my fellow travelers. Rob Darby, an amiable insurance company president from San Francisco, explained that he once studied to become a weatherman but became an insurance actuary instead.

"Actually, they have more in common than you think," he said. "Both use data in their work, and both can be wrong and nothing happens."

Bob Siefert, a mortgage broker from Marin, believes he likes storms because he was born during bad weather.

"I would sit outside for hours and wait for the storms to come," he said. "There was no Weather Channel back in those days. Only the weatherman writing on a Plexiglas board—remember? He'd draw a little smiley face for sunny weather."

Hans Muelder, an audiologist from Holland, confessed he's a bonafide tornado geek, but that tornadoes are just one item on a long list of physical phenomena he enjoys. He's also keen on the Northern Lights, hurricanes, volcanoes, tsunamis, and earthquakes. "Really," he said, his Dutch accent strong. "I love all of this stuff."

As Rob listened to Hans, his eyes widened. "You sure we weren't separated at birth?"

A few miles later, Roger turned on the Weather Channel inside the van. I watched the color monitor on the console between the driver's and passengers' seats, and the chasers behind me watched two drop-down monitors attached to the ceiling.

"You know what's great about this group?" Rob asked. "We're the only people we know who can gossip about the VJs on the Weather Channel. Have you ever noticed how Kristina Abernathy always seems pregnant?"

No, I confessed. I hadn't.

• • •

As the morning progressed, the movement in the upper atmosphere slowed and Roger couldn't tell where—or if—a storm might break.

"It's going to be a hang-tough kind of day," he said. "Dodge City is contaminated, and Amarillo has fizzled." Late morning, he decided to wait it out in Colby, Kansas, at his favorite restaurant, Twister's Bar & Grill.

Walking inside, it took a minute for our eyes to adjust from the bright Kansas sun to the dark bar interior. A dance floor lined one side of the room. A pool table nestled in the corner. And an outdated wall-sized television was broadcasting a NASCAR race in faded colors. It smelled like fried food and stale beer. There were just three other customers.

The waitress, overwhelmed at suddenly being presented

with eighteen patrons, scuffled around the tables taking our orders. Although it had only been two hours since the mini-mart, the storm chasers, uncertain as to where and when the next stop might be, hungrily requested burgers and grilled cheese sandwiches and potato chips and extra fries. Following their lead, I ordered a cheeseburger. The waitress asked what kind of fries I'd like.

"What kind do you have?"

She took a deep breath and tucked a loose brown strip of hair behind her ear. "We got straight fries, curly fries, onion rings, potato wedges, German fries—those have onions—American fries—those're without onions—hash browns, and potato chips. And if you don't want any a those, you can have a side salad." She stared at me. "What'll it be?"

"American," I said, feeling vaguely ashamed for making such an unadventurous choice.

While waiting for the food, Roger and the other guide monitored the ever-changing weather conditions on their laptops. They couldn't tell whether it made sense to head north to Nebraska or south to Oklahoma or east toward Missouri or back west toward Colorado. They just couldn't tell, couldn't tell at all. Not now anyway. It was too early, and the upper atmosphere was just sitting there like a child pouting on the front stoop.

The food arrived, the clock ticked on, and I struck up a conversation with Mary Wilk, a fifty-six-year-old retiree from North Bangor, Pennsylvania. Mary is an unabashed tornado addict who completed two back-to-back, ten-day storm-chasing tours last year, and when this tour ends on Saturday, she'll head out on another one Sunday morning. But you'd never know it to look at her. She's short, slightly overweight, and looks like the kind of woman who knits Christmas ornaments and bottle covers in her spare time. But in fact, Mary's a long-time member of SKY WARN, a nationwide network of weather spotters. She's got a weather radio in her kitchen and when bad weather is forecast, she hops in her car, speeds toward that badness and telephones in her impressions. Mary's one of thousands of weather watchers around the country who do this on their own time, on their own dollar, simply because it's a charge that can't be beat.

"A lot of people think we don't have storms in the Poconos, but we do," she explained. "Why do I like 'em? I like the beauty of 'em. The power. They're just irresistible." Mary paused and gulped from a large red plastic tumbler. "I don't like it when people get hurt, though. That's not good."

Over the years, Mary's been blessed to see an average of about ten tornadoes a year, but the ones she remembers most are the ones that got away.

"I once won eighty-thousand-dollars in a sweepstakes and took a trip to Dollywood to celebrate. A week after I came home, a tornado went right through the middle of Dollywood." She shakes her head, still pained by the memory. "I just didn't time it right." Her face brightens. "But you know, I do have another passion."

"What's that?"

"Bingo. I play bingo every week. With a four-thousand-dollar payout, what, are you crazy? Of course I'm going to play."

I asked Mary what would happen if she got a weatherspotting call during a bingo game. "Is it a tough choice—bingo or chasing?"

"It's no choice at all. My friends watch my cards so I don't have to decide."

Having seen eight tornadoes in the last four days, Mary's feeling quite sated and happy at this point—especially since before coming on this trip, she'd been unable to access any weather-related news on her computer for weeks. "I need to get an updraft for my computer," she said.

I looked at her, puzzled. "Do you mean an up*grade*?"

"Oh… yeah. See, that tells you where I'm at."

After paying eighteen separate tabs at Twisters, an activity that seemed to thoroughly disable the waitress, and after killing time at Wal-Mart for an hour, Roger decided it was time to get a move on. Something was starting to happen up there, and while he still didn't know if the storm would break in Nebraska or Kansas or Oklahoma, he was fairly sure it wasn't going to break in Colby.

• • •

Just an hour later, and here we are hauling ass to the promised land of three-inch hail.

The weather observations, or "obs" as Roger calls them, are looking good. We've got a temperature of 86 sitting over a dew point of 62. Tornados, stubborn as they are, typically won't arrive at the party until the dew point is at least 60 degrees, and the spread between it and the temperature is less than 20 degrees. While 86 over 64 is a bit wide, the obs are headed in the right direction. And based on the National Weather Service forecast, so are we.

We bounce over railroad crossings, whiz past electrical lines lined up like crucifixes, and speed past rumbling combine tractors. And even though it seems like we just had lunch, the chasers are munching again on Necco wafers and trail mix and licorice nibs and bubble gum. It's as if we're at a drive-in movie and have to finish eating before the feature presentation begins.

In Sharon Springs, we encounter a line of orange cones that leads to a construction delay, and the momentum that's been building inside the van comes to a depressing, decisive stop. We wait. Cellophane crinkles. Roger drums the steering wheel. "People in these towns don't like to see us coming," he says. "They know we bring bad weather." Minutes later, the flagman rotates his sign from "Stop" to "Slow," and we're once again zooming through one-intersection towns lined with Farm Bureau offices and Baptist churches and laundromats that have ingeniously been combined with liquor stores.

Kansas has fifty million acres of farmland and produces

more wheat and slaughters more cows than any state in the union. We see evidence of these feats all around in the yellow fields and white grain towers and enormous brown cattle pens packed haunch to hoof with Angus and Herefords and Charolais. We smell their dense warm manure before we actually see them. The unmistakable Kansas backdrop registers, but what we—and I do mean "we," for I'm starting to get into this— really care about is that growing cu field sitting at eleven o'clock in the distance. The clouds are starting to join forces and obliterate the blue sky. And while they're looking less friendly than they did earlier, Roger is not impressed.

"Those cloud towers have a high base," he says. "That means not enough moisture. We're going to have to get further south—and fast—if we have any chance at all." The speedometer needle inches to the right once again.

As the miles fly by, the dew point creeps up, the temperature slides down, and the cloud formation spreads lengthwise over the plains. Roger checks his GPS against the storm data and makes a quick decision to head east. He pulls a hard left, and the supercell shifts. It's now looming directly in front of us, all white and winsome on top; dark and disapproving on the bottom. Roger describes it as a mushroom cloud with a nice crispy convention.

"That's goooooood," he says, the sound coming from low in his throat. The closer we get to the storm cell, the deeper Roger's voice becomes.

At 4:08, the first rain splots the windshield. The wipers click on and the bug-splattered glass becomes a gooey, yellow mess. The inside of the van smells like wet soil and damp pavement, and the cars coming toward us now have on their headlights. Roger notices this and looks again at the menacing cloud formation.

"Oh… my… God," he says, his voice rumbling. "We have a *monster* core in front of us."

The core, Rob quickly explains, is the center of the storm

cell, the point at which hail is the largest, wind the strongest, the potential for ground-level damage most severe.

"We do *not* want to get cored," he says.

The weather station crackles to life.

Urrrk, urrrk, urrrk...

We fall silent, waiting.

The National Weather Service has issued a tornado warning until 10 p.m. If you are outside, lie in a ditch and cover your head with your hands. If you are in a mobile home, evacuate immediately. If you are indoors, stay away from windows.

Now, most people upon hearing this warning would turn away from the lumbering storm cell. But storm chasers are a class unto themselves. Instead of instilling fear, the warning serves to electrify them. Snack packs are crinkled and put away, camera settings adjusted, and seatbelts unbuckled to make it possible to quickly position one's self for prime viewing. Being the greenhorn in the group, I follow their lead. It's not that I'm new to severe weather—Colorado has plenty of that—but I've only seen one thin tornado, and that was seventeen years ago in Denver, from a distance of thirty miles. Due to the limited sight distance in the city, the experience was unremarkable and over rather quickly.

But here on the plains, you can see the flat horizon and wide sky stretching over several counties, the only obstructions being an occasional barn or bail of hay. You can watch, minute by minute, as tiny cu fields band together and shove their towers skyward, darkening and spreading until eventually you're not looking at clouds but rather at a hulking, monolithic, law-breaking *thing* that hangs heavily over the fields. We're hurtling toward that thing right now and it's got an eerie, Halloweeny, greenish cast to it.

"That's from hail," Roger says. "It reflects the light differently."

Watching that thing, I feel the first burble of anticipation. Earlier, I was more interested in the storm chasers than the storm. But now, with the dark supercell moving ever closer, I drop all pretense of cool detachment. I confess: I *want* to see a twister today.

But first, we must fill the tank with gasoline. We stop at a gas station just outside of Garden City, and Roger yells at us to go fast-fast-*fast*! As the two vans unload, some tractor-hat locals notice us.

"Y'all better hurrah," they say. "It's comin'."

We run around puddles into the mini-mart to collect the next phase of snacks. Caving under the pressure, I buy cashews and gummy dinosaurs. Bob buys pizza. Nobody, however, buys any water, because at this point in the chase game we can't be stopping for anyone to pee. We run back to the van, and as I circle around behind it, I notice a sticker on the back window: "Get in, sit down, shut up and hold on!" Which is exactly what we do. The van caroms through the parking lot, an empty green soda bottle flies across the floor and slams into the door, and within six minutes of stopping we're on the hunt again. Things are moving quickly now.

At 4:32, small bits of hail begin to ping the van, indicating that we're inching into the supercell, something we don't want to do. See, the trick with tornado chasing is to stay on the perimeter of the cell, away from the hail, and watch from a distance as the tornadoes twist downward from the base of the storm. In an effort to outsmart the cell, Roger shifts direction onto a narrow packed-dirt country road, and the hail gradually lets up.

At 4:52, the first "meso"—for mesocyclone—appears on the radar screen. A meso is a spinning red circle indicating the presence of strong wind sheer. Roger clicks on it. It's showing 80 mph winds. At 115 mph, chances are good it will spawn a tornado. Minutes later, the screen goes completely red, indicating the presence of severe thunderstorms across several counties in southwestern Kansas. They're the counties we're driving toward. The grasses lining the roadbed are bent at a 45-degree angle. The worst of the hail is again right in front of us.

Ten minutes later three more mesos jump onto the radar screen. Dust devils—or "gustnados," as Roger calls them—are kicking up in the fields. The wind and the darkness and the heaviness of the wall cloud in front of us make him think this might be the cloud to watch. He stops the van, and we scramble outside, cameras in hand. It's not enough, you see, to merely witness a tornado. It also must be recorded, preferably on movie film, to provide proof of the adventure.

We line the edge of the field, faces tilted skyward, hair flying crazily around our heads. The cloud—or *clouds*, it's hard to tell what this thing is made of—is churning end over end. It's roiling and boiling and marching directly toward us as if someone just opened the door on a gigantic steam shower. The wheat in front of us is bowing in submission, and there's a faint coppery smell of electricity in the air.

We wait, expectantly, for several minutes, but nothing happens. No pinpoint twister forms at the cloud's base. The core, however, is closing in, and Roger is nervous.

"Get-in-get-in-get-in," he screams. "HAIL IS COMING AND I DON'T WANT TO BE IN THE MIDDLE OF IT!"

Back in the van, Roger punches the accelerator, and the tires spin on gravel before lurching forward. As we rocket away from the hail, someone at the back of the van yells, "Look! A tornado on the left!"

Time stops for the briefest of seconds.

"A *tornado?!*" Roger shouts. He brakes and pulls to the side of the road just barely missing the bar ditch. I peer through the left window and see a gray spiral coming up from the field toward the sky. It's narrow, not at all like the black, block-wide behemoths I've seen on television and this confuses me.

"It's a land spout tornado," Roger explains. "It's weak, but it's legitimate."

• • •

A tornado is not something that is technically supposed to

happen, and they don't in very many places. Although torna-does have been spotted on every continent, 75 percent of them occur in the U.S., and more than a third of those in Tornado Alley, the vertical strip of geography running through Nebraska, Kansas, Oklahoma, and Texas. But even in Tornado Alley, tornadoes are a rare phenomenon. Less than one in one thousand thunderstorms produce tornadoes, and any particular spot can expect to wait, on average, 4,000 to 10,000 years between roof-lifting twisters. Given these odds, I'm happy with the little land spout.

And so, it seems, are the rest of the chasers. They're already viewing their photos on the backs of their digital cameras and promising to e-mail images to one another once they return home. But far from satisfying their craving, the land spout has fueled it. On the radar, Roger sees another cell forming toward the south. But it's not just any cell. As he puts it, "There's a *bomb* going off down there."

We zigzag through the fields on narrow country roads, eas-ing out of one storm cell and sliding underneath another. According to the radar, the cell we're now chasing is seven miles wide. Four mesos are spinning, one of them clocking an impres-sive 138 miles per hour. The wheat fields on the left side of the van are leaning in one direction; the corn fields on the right are blowing the exact opposite. It's after five o'clock now, prime time in tornado terms, and the atmospheric action is at its peak.

Roger peers up through the windshield. "This thing is an absolute monster," he says. "Look behind us for power trans-formers blowing up and power lines snapping. This is a very dangerous storm, *very* dangerous."

Prior to coming on this trip, friends asked me if I was at all nervous, at all scared about getting sucked skyward to Oz.

No, I replied, I wasn't nervous.

And I'm not now, even given the potential for popping power lines. In fact, if I had a riding crop, I fear I'd be crawling onto Roger's back and slapping his fanny in an effort to get him to giddyup even faster. And I don't mean this is any sort of weird sexual way. (Shame on you.) Although the electrical thrill I'm feeling *does* seem like something I should go to confession for.

As if sensing my thoughts, Roger turns to face me. "I *told* you this was addictive," he says.

Although our plan was to stay along the perimeter of the storm cell, our route has been hampered by the lack of roads. As a result, the cell has moved in all around us and the National Weather Service warnings are now being repeated over and over in a continuous loop.

If you can hear thunder, you are close enough to be struck by lightning.

Do not use your car to try and outrun a tornado.

This is a dangerous storm situation. Act quickly. Abandon cars and mobile homes.

But we're not abandoning our car because we're no longer chasing the cell; it's chasing us. And even with the GPS navigation system, Roger is running out of escape routes. We turn onto a rutted dirt road, and the van bounces up and down. The sky is black and yellow and green all at once. A clear, bright white lightning bolt reaches down from the sky and connects with the ground to our immediate left. "Jesus!" someone behind me yells, and then, "Look-look-look, there's a tornado directly behind us!"

Roger brakes and we turn and kneel on our seats searching for it. I can't see the tornado but the three chasers at the back of the van vouch for it. Roger doesn't want to wait for the possibility of another one. He accelerates just as the weather station emits a loud crackle. The warnings immediately stop and are replaced with static.

"Jeez," Roger says. "This is the jaws of death."

A few miles down the road, thinking we may have few—if any—chances left to photograph the supercell's structure before getting cored, Rogers stops the van. We stumble outside to the edge of a creek teaming with frogs. The frogs are bellowing loudly, their throaty croaks mingling with the thunder that's growling all around us. Two minutes after stepping out of the van, we feel the first icy pricks of hail. This time, we don't need to be told.

Immediately, we're back in the van trying to outrun the core that has enveloped us. It's now hailing as if the skies are settling some long overdue score. We're surrounded by a gray and silver miasma, and the headlights struggle to lift the darkness. Inside the van, no one is speaking. No one is even *eating*. Instead, we're all no doubt wondering if we're gonna get out of this thing before the windows explode inward blasting shards of glass toward unprotected skin. Of course, I could be projecting my own thoughts on the others. But still. Tumbleweeds race across the roadway as if they too want the hell outta here. Five miles up the road, we pass a blocky modular home being towed slowly in the opposite direction.

He's gonna be sorry.

Roger drives as fast as he can—perhaps even faster—and gradually we edge out of the core, the hail turns to rain, darkness recedes, and within thirty minutes we're on dry pavement once again. We're now heading west, away from the weather and toward a thin band of evening sunlight.

Except for the click of the windshield wipers, all is quiet inside the van. But it's not a tense quiet. It's a contented quiet. The kind of quiet you might feel after a hard workout or day on the slopes, when all you want is a taco and a cold mug of beer.

With the chase day now over, Roger gets on his cell phone and arranges for us to spend the night at a Super 8 Motel in the oxymoron known as Liberal, Kansas. At seven o'clock we pull into the small town and learn, in a delightfully unexpected coincidence, that Liberal is home to a replica of Dorothy's house and the Land of Oz museum.

"You know," Roger says, "a tornado once touched down in Liberal and missed Dorothy's house by a block."

I don't know about you, but to me, this is the kind of fac-
tual coincidence that makes life worth living.

• • •

Here's a confession I'm not proud to make. My older sister has
lived in Kansas since the 1970s, and I've never visited her despite
living just one state away for the last twenty years. Sure, I've had
my excuses. But were I a better, bigger person, I would have
overlooked those excuses and done the right, sisterly thing years
ago. But I'm not better and bigger. I'm a tiny speck of humanity
spinning on a vast blue planet, with billions of other specks who
are all trying not to burn the toast each morning.

Forgive me for indulging in a moment of insignificance.
But I can't help it. It's now ten at night, and I'm leaning against
Roger's van and watching the most singularly impressive display
of lightning I've ever seen. All around us, in a heart-filling 360-
degree span, the India ink sky is showing us just how majestic
nature can be when left to her own devices. I know that sounds
cliché. But it's true. When crawler lightning reaches its long
white tentacles across the sky, and lightning bolts command your
attention like circus whips, and sheet lightning illuminates whole
stretches of the heavens as if God just popped a flashbulb, and
when all of this is going on at the same time accompanied by the
deep, ongoing roar of thunder from some unknown place far, far
away, well, you can't help but trot out a few superlatives. It *is*
majestic here in the nighttime flatlands of Kansas. And when
you spend a day traveling from peaceful blue sky into an angry
black supercell, you begin to realize how irrelevant, in the atmospheric, interplanetary, metaphysical scheme of things you really
are. And this, I realize, can be an enormous blessing.

Today, the vast unbroken openness of the Kansas landscape
made it impossible for me to do what I've always done and that
is compare myself to other people, other things, other ways of
living. And that's because there's not much out here. There's
nothing to bump up against, nothing to compare myself to,

nothing that demands any reaction on my part at all. So instead of analyzing and comparing and composing an identity for myself based on what I saw or didn't see reflected around me, I was forced—or maybe allowed—to be just me.

And right now, that me is quite satisfied to be leaning against the hard cool metal of a van, watching the fields brighten underneath the most magnificent show of sky-born electricity I've ever seen. And if that smacks of some kind of New Age, what-the-bleep-do-we-know spiritual reverence, then so be it.

• • •

Roger Hill's success as a storm chaser may very well depend on his willingness to chase when others are not, but that doesn't mean things always work out the way he wants. And today is one of those not-working-out kind of days. It's early Friday afternoon, and we've been traveling north through Kansas for hours, and the data feed Roger relies on is not giving him a fix. Best chances for a tornado today reside three states north, in Montana, and there's no way to make it there and back to Denver in time for the out-of-town chasers to catch their flights home. But I'm not disappointed. Traveling inside the sunny van gives me a chance to visit with Rob and Bob and Hans and the other storm chasers.

Curiously, we don't talk much about chasing at all. We do, however, talk about aliens and agriculture and the Zodiac sign and the human genome. They, too, believe that passions must somehow be genetic. We talk about how Americans are the Donald Trumps of fanatical passion, a claim that the storm chasers from England and Holland heartily endorse. And when they ask if I'm planning to spend time with any other Trumpian fanatics, I tell them about the upcoming pigeon race in the Bronx. Even though months have passed since I first met with the flyers, I'm still not sure I'm ready for another rendezvous.

In between conversations, the storm chasers stop at Wendy's for fries and burgers and shakes. We amble into the

Burlington Snack Mart for beef jerky and Chick O Sticks. We waddle into a Dairy Queen for Blizzards and soft-serve cones. Standing outside of DQ, licking my chocolate twist, I explain my theory that storm chasing is really just a cover for something less socially acceptable but far more seductive: snack chasing.

No one disagrees.

• • •

Entering Colorado mid-afternoon, the road rises and falls and twists its way through old farming towns with one-room post offices, and new communities with treeless golf courses, and closed-in suburbs with strip malls and bus stops, and finally ends back at the Mile High City.

There's a tradition in storm chasing that insists those who've seen a tornado must celebrate with a steak dinner. Our group makes plans to rendezvous at Black Angus at seven o'clock. Even though I've only been with the group for two out of six days, and even though I'm not really a storm chaser, they ask me to join them.

"You *did* see a tornado," Rob says.

I don't commit right away. As a writer, as an observer, I've always worked to keep a comfortable distance between myself and the people I'm curious about. But this trip has been different. I didn't merely watch what was going on, I participated. I didn't envy the storm chaser's joy. I embraced it. I didn't hide behind a notebook, safe in my separateness. This time, for the first time on this journey, I allowed myself to cross the divide that separates "me" from "them" and enjoy the experience of being a "we."

"Well?" Rob asks again.

And without over-thinking it, I tell him that, yes, I would indeed like to join the storm chasers for dinner. And when I do, I join them in raising a glass in celebration of the unexpected and transformative power of nature.

CHAPTER SIXTEEN

Flying Home

*"Good instinct usually tells you what to do long before
your head has figured it out"*

–Michael Burke

THE AVERAGE PIGEON RACER HAS HAD 2.5 WIVES. IT'S A
number they all agree on, a number in which they actually use
the decimal. Two. Point. Five. Like they've conducted a scientific study or something—and maybe they have. Because pigeon
racing is not exactly a spectator sport, they do have a lot of time
to kill during races. Maybe while waiting for their birds to come
home, they call each other on cell phones.

"Yo! Joe! How many women ya been with since joining the
club? Six? Oh—I'd only counted five. Oh, yeah. Steph. Forgot
her. But ya didn't marry her didja? What's that? Only married
three of 'em? Okay. Got it. I'll put you down for three." And so
it goes.

Or so I imagine. I don't really know what goes on during a
pigeon race and that's why I'm on the subway returning to the
Bronx to fulfill a promise I'd made to the members of the Bronx
Pigeon Club several long months ago.

It's a Thursday evening in late September and the club is
hosting its annual World Trade Center Memorial Race this
weekend. Tonight, flyers will be bringing their birds to the
Morris Yacht Club on City Island, where the pigeons will be
entered into the race and packed for shipment in long silver
metal trailers. Sometime tomorrow, those trailers and their avian

cargo will head several hours south to Weston, West Virginia. Come Saturday morning, the birds will be released and clocked on their way back home.

All of which sounds interesting enough in the abstract. But I've already been on the subway for an hour—and yes, to answer your question, the express line *would* have been quicker, but that presumes one would know how and where to get on the express line, which I didn't. After getting off the subway, I'll have to find a bus to City Island and then find my way to the yacht club, and already it's close to eight o'clock and dark outside. If you haven't guessed already, I'm a little cranky, because meeting with the pigeon racers is proving to be just as taxing as it was the last time around. And I haven't even arrived yet.

• • •

Sometimes you can't comprehend why you've done something until well after that thing has been done. And so it goes with this journey, which is now nearing its end.

When I was a child, I envisioned myself living many different ent lives. An artist in Paris. An executive in San Francisco. An heiress in Greece. And I imagined I would somehow live all of these lives simultaneously. I'd raise Nubian goats in the country and attend theater downtown. I'd make movie deals during the week and sing in a punk band on the weekends. I'd launch IPOs, volunteer at Indian orphanages, import silks from China, and perform surgery in my spare time.

Then I grew up. And I realized that without the ability to clone myself several times over, I'd be stuck with just one life. My life. So I'd better make the best of it. Thus I became a journalist, reasoning if I couldn't physically experience all those other lives, I could vicariously do so by writing about them.

Then I grew up a little more. I bought a house. I acquired bills. I met Angela. We settled in together. And in my search for stability and a decent income, I became, not a globe-trotting travel writer, but a stay-at-home business journalist. I wasn't interviewing saffron-robed monks in Tibet or skinny little rock stars in London. But the work was satisfying in its own right, for a while. For a while I truly believed my work was helping corporate executives learn how to make the American workplace a happier, more humane place for employees. But I gradually realized—and this may come as a bit of a shock—that business executives didn't really care about their employees. At least not the same way I did. And, well, you can't be the kind of person who dreams of living thirty-two different glamorous lives and then spend twelve years writing fruitlessly about business without it beginning to wear on you. It just doesn't work. And the point at which it wasn't working the most was the point at which I wanted, needed, an all-encompassing passion to release me from the daily drudge. That was the point at which I wandered into a Barbie convention and entered an ice-fishing tournament and began to fall slowly and irreversibly in love with all the passionate fanatics who welcomed me into their worlds. What I didn't realize at the time, but I do now, is that although I thought I was searching for passion, what I really needed was to regain access to the youthful, many-lives-to-live adventurer I'd somehow left behind.

And I have.

Which is why I feel so compelled to complete this trek at a pigeon race. I didn't know what this journey had in store for me at the beginning and I don't know what a pigeon race holds for me at the end. But I trust something beneficial will result.

At the very least, I'll get to say I've been to a pigeon race.

• • •

After more than an hour and a half of travel, the subway doors open at Pelham Bay Park, the last stop on the green line. Somehow, I manage to find the right bus to City Island, and somehow I manage to get off at the right stop, and somehow I manage to find my way through the dark, chill streets to the Morris Yacht Club.

Inside, the club is a swirl of noise and activity and not at all what I'd envisioned. When I heard the words "yacht club," I pictured leather club chairs and potted palms and stiff waiters silently carrying silver trays of vodka gimlets. But the Morris Yacht Club, with its clackety wooden floors, shiny white walls and warm-lasagna smell, is more like a community rec center. And tonight, it seems, every flyer in the community is here. They're talking, eating at large round tables, and adding their caged birds to the ceiling-high stack of wooden cages that lines the right side of the large room.

I stand at the doorway and immediately spot several flyers I recognize, including Reno and Joe and Vinny. They appear to recognize me, too, probably because I'm the only woman in the room. Reno walks over to me.

"Hey, I remember yous," he says. "You were, what, writin' a book or somethin'."

Yes, I tell him. Still am. That's why I'm here. I want to see how a pigeon race works up close.

A few of the flyers sitting nearby overhear this and migrate their way into our conversation. Soon I'm surrounded by men named Tom and Rico and Nick and Jimmy and they're all telling me about some aspect of the race. They tell me approximately 1,800 birds have been entered by two hundred different lofts. It costs a minimum of one hundred dollars per bird to enter the race, but then there are the added costs of shipping and betting—and betting alone can add thousands of dollars to the cost of entry. But really, they would prefer I not mention betting because betting is illegal.

"Hey, you're not with the IRS are ya?"

No, I tell them. I am not with the IRS.

Reassured, they continue. They explain that pigeon racing is just like horse racing. That the big money is made on the side by betting for or against certain lofts, or for or against certain birds. But even without those big side bets, the fastest bird on Saturday will land a whopping fifty-thousand-dollar top prize, and the top 150 birds will each earn at least one thousand dollars. In fact, the stakes are so high in this race, the club has had to resort to randomly drug testing the birds.

I look at the testing station set up along one side of the room. The testers, two young men in backwards ball caps, are taking pigeons out of their cages, lining them up on squares of wax paper, and waiting for them to do what it is pigeons do best. Once their business is complete, that business is scooped into little baggies and shipped off to a lab.

I ask the flyers what they're testing for.

Steroids, caffeine, any kind of drug enhancement, they say. See, anytime there's money to be made, and a man's ego is at stake, you're going find guys trying to beat the odds. You wanna know why, they ask? They'll tell me why. Because winning a race, no matter how much you've trained the birds, ain't easy. This race is especially tough because the route the birds take from West Virginia to New York is an unnatural one. The pigeons have to fly over mountains, and pigeons, they say, don't like mountains.

Trying to absorb all this, I look up and see Cecil Coston walk into the room. Cecil is the young, retired NYPD officer whose loft sits on top of the Bronx Pigeon Club, the flyer who introduced me to his birds two years ago. Because I have a passing acquaintance with his birds, I called and asked if I could join him on race day this Saturday. At first, he was hesitant. He hadn't been in a race all year, hadn't been training his birds, wasn't sure he was going to do so well, didn't want to be embarrassed, and on and on. But then his racer's ego kicked in.

"Oh, what the heck," he said. "Sure, sure, you come on up. We'll have fun."

Cecil is a tall, light-skinned black man with a shaved head and charismatic smile. He leans over and gives me a kiss on the cheek while lightly holding my hand. We make plans to rendezvous at the club Saturday afternoon.

Two hours later, I arrive back at my Times Square hotel

tired, incredibly thirsty, and craving a beer—which is unusual, because I don't like beer that much. But I don't want to go to a bar, and the hotel I'm in is too low-budget for a mini-bar. So I walk to a small corner grocery store, pick up a green bottle of Heineken, and ask to purchase a bottle opener.

A man sitting next to the counter speaks up. "You don't need to buy no opener. There's one outside next to the door."

The clerk disagrees. "She can't do that. New York don't allow open containers."

"Sure she can. She don't look like no bum."

The man grabs my bottle and heads outside where I hear the crack-whoosh of the top being opened. He comes back in and places the bottle in a brown paper sack.

"There you go, ma'am. Just don't let the cops see ya."

I pay for the beer and walk outside clutching the sack close to my chest. One night with pigeon racers and already I'm drinking from a brown paper bag.

• • •

I've been culling through my notes from this journey and have come to realize that spending time with passionate fanatics rearranges the way you look at the world.

I first noticed this while at the furry convention in California. Needing a break from the lions and tigers and bears, I'd gone across the street to the Hilton for dinner. Sitting inside the hushed lobby restaurant, I watched cliques of white, middle-aged professionals gather for dinner; the women dressed in Nordstrom's finest with matching shoes and purses; the men relaxed and confident in clothes selected by their wives. Or so I assumed. Unlike the furries, none of the diners wore bob tails or barked, and watching them, I was quite astounded to discover how thoroughly boring they seemed. Especially since they were my people, or at least the people I'd always assumed to be my people. Middle-class. Tidy. They did nothing to call attention to themselves and I couldn't believe how much I wanted to run away from their tameness and back toward the colorful, foot-stomping den of furry fandom across the street.

Now the psychologically astute observer will recognize this as the defensive reaction of a subject (me) running from that which she fears she's become (them). And to a point, the psychologically astute observer would be right. In college, one of my chief goals was to never be middle-aged and middle class at the same time, fearing such a combination would doom me to that big beige sinkhole called "average."

Yet here we are.

But my preference for the furries—on that night anyway—was eye-opening in another way. It helped me see how subtly yet swiftly perceptions can change. Reading through my notes, I came to see just how many times my preconceptions about fanatics have been imploded through real-life experience.

Before setting out on this trek, I assumed these subcultures were nothing more than narrow bands of like-minded humanity. I've since learned that people who come together around the same passion do so with an openness and eagerness to share it with others regardless of who those others might be. As a result, these subcultures can be amazingly diverse. When born-again Christians and leather-leashed Goths come together at the same party, when middle-aged women and gum-snapping teenagers gossip online about the same celebrities, when retired auto workers and international money managers play the same board games, well, to me, that can't help but breed the kind of understanding, acceptance, and community that's always been the promise, if not reality, of America.

Another notion that's crumbled is that computers and the Internet do nothing more than isolate us in our homes. Maybe this was true, early on. But community-building sites like Meetup and Yahoo and Mayberry.com are pulling like-minded people together in ways never before envisioned. Solitary Lego users are crawling out of their basements in record numbers to create regional face-to-face clubs. Attendance at furry conventions and boardgaming conventions and fill-in-the-blank conventions is growing rapidly. Shy people and smart people and people with ADD are finding a voice and acceptance online that gives them the courage to venture into supportive offline communities. And they *are* venturing out. Whereas previously, misfits and outcasts and Poindexters struggling to find a tribe may have stayed home, safe in their separateness, now they are finding passionate connections that allow them to feel safe in their togetherness.

Perhaps the most delightful, life-affirming discovery of all is how willing Americans are to embrace their passions and broadcast them to the world, regardless of what that world might think. Geeks, in a word, have become chic. But it's not just computer nerds or chess dweebs who have found a voice for their interests. If you define a geek as a person with any oddball proclivity, then geeks are flourishing in every stratum of American society. There are wine geeks, weather geeks, movie geeks, bird geeks, car geeks, and geeks who do nothing more than follow others geeks around the country in order to study their geekiness—not that I'm at all defensive about this. Geekiness has become an acceptable, proud badge of honor in America, the mark of someone who's actively engaged in some facet of the world around them. If this isn't something to celebrate, I don't know what is.

• • •

On Saturday afternoon I arrive at the Bronx Pigeon Club and follow Cecil up the rickety wooden stairs to the flat tar-paper roof of the garage. He opens the thin plywood door to his coop and we step inside into a gust of fluttering pigeons.

"Hi boys and girls," he says. "Havin' a good day?"

After showing me the improvements he's made to the coop since I was last here, Cecil gets me a chair, places it on the roof, and goes back inside to find another one. I settle in to wait.

In front of the clubhouse, the traffic on White Plains Road rumbles with the sound of buses and heavy bass of hip-hop. The greasy smell of McDonald's French fries floats on the breeze. It's gritty and urban, but also quite pleasant. It must be seventy-five degrees outside and the sky is a dense autumn blue. In a nearby backyard, a woman and two small children rock lazily on a porch swing. Though I'd been dreading my return, I feel my heart filling with the unexpected pleasure of sitting here on this gorgeous fall afternoon.

Cecil comes back outside and begins pacing back and forth. "Wait. Wait. Now's a waiting game," he says. He looks at the sky and starts jingling something in the pocket of his baggy blue jeans.

I look at him and try to decide if it's okay to talk, or if Cecil is one of those racers who'd prefer that unsophisticated visitors keep their thoughts to themselves. I take the chance.

"So Cecil," I say. "When do you expect the first birds to come in?"

He shrugs. On a good day pigeons fly fifty miles per hour. It's 389 miles from West Virginia to this roof, and the birds were released just after 8 a.m. It's now almost four o'clock, which means the birds should be coming in by now, but there's no word on any arrivals from any of the other lofts. Cecil points up at an airplane that's descending toward La Guardia Airport.

"See, planes land into the wind and that plane is going directly southwest, which is the direction the birds are coming from," he says. "That's good because you want the wind going in the same direction as the birds. But it's not *that* good because if it *was* that good some birds would be home by now."

Watching the airplane, I ask Cecil how many birds he has in the race.

"Fourteen," he says. "Seven boys and seven girls."

I think about all the pigeons left in the coop behind me. "How many do you have overall?"

"Me?" Cecil points to his chest. "About ninety."

"*Ninety?*"

"Phhht." He waves a hand in front of his face as if swatting a gnat. "That's *nothing*. Most guys got twice that many."

"How much do you spend a year on the birds?"

"I spent three thousand dollars on this race alone if that gives you an idea."

"But how much do you think you spend in a *year?*"

Cecil eyes me as if trying to decide how trustworthy I am. "I spend four thousand dollars a year," he says, laughing. "No. That's not true. I'm gonna give you a figure, but I'm gonna give you a lowball figure. I'm gonna say five thousand dollars. I'm gonna say that I spend five thousand dollars a year on the birds." He smiles. "But I'd still be lying, if you know what I mean."

I nod. I know what he means. "So does your wife have any hobbies?"

"Oh yeah. She got hobbies. Goin' to the mall. Shoppin'. Comin' home and saying 'Here, you gotta pay for this.' That's her hobby."

He looks at the sky again and then at his watch. He's right. Waiting. That's what pigeon racing is all about.

Cecil's comment about his wife gets me to thinking about the flyers and their 2.5 wives. I ask him if this figure is accurate. "Yep, that's about right," he says.

"And you?"

"I got three kids by three women, which sounds bad, but it's not that bad. You wanna know why it's not that bad? It's not that bad because they were all spaced out and because I pay for 'em all. I can't stand it when I read about guys who don't support their kids. I pay for mine. Just the other day, my oldest daughter called me. '*Daddy,*' she said. That's when I know I'm in trouble, when she says daddy. '*Daddy,* I want a new car. Can you pay the first six months' car insurance?' How can I say no to that? I mean, I do say no, but it don't mean nothin'."

He looks at the sky and continues to jiggle his keys. "Yeah, it's true a lot of guys have trouble with women. But that's what's so great about the club. If you get in a fight with your wife or your girlfriend, you can come sleep here. There's always beer in the fridge, and look…" Cecil walks to the edge of the roof and starts pointing to the restaurants below. "Here you got Chinese, you got pizza, you got Mexican. You can eat anything you want here. Yep. Many a guy has spent many a night sleeping on that table in the club."

As he talks, I notice some pigeons fluttering around the brick apartment building across the street. "Are those homers?" I ask.

"Naaa, they're clinkers, park birds. I can tell because their necks are shorter than homing pigeons." He starts cracking his knuckles. "Hey, you want a Coke? I'll go get us something to drink."

Sure, I tell him. "I'll holler if something comes in."

"No, no, don't do that!" he says. "You'll scare 'em away."

Cecil walks downstairs and I return my attention to the cloudless blue sky realizing how rarely, if at all, I look at the sky in the city. Above me, a pair of orange and black Monarch butterflies are rocking southward on their annual migration toward Mexico.

I think of the journey that's brought me here and the question that fueled my travels: who *are* you people? Over the last three years, I've logged more than twenty-five thousand miles, talked with hundreds of people, and collected an eclectic array of souvenirs, including a glow-in-the-dark Josh Groban pen, a Lego sculpture titled *Emerge,* and a set of cat ears and a tail that I bought—but never wore—in preparation for my visit with the furries. (When I bought the ensemble, the clerk asked if I'd like a safety pin in order to attach the tail and wear it out of the store. I assured him that wouldn't be necessary.)

The people I spoke with were young and old and rich and poor and highly educated and not. They were God fearing and atheist, Democrat and Republican, outgoing and introverted. In short, they were just like you and me and everyone else we know except for that thing. That interest, passion, obsession, call-it-what-you-will *thing* that grabbed their attention one day and didn't let go.

Reflecting back, I still don't understand the mystery of where these things come from. It seems that passions choose us, not the other way around.

But having said that, people's passions do seem to be greatly influenced by popular culture—by what they see on television or in the movies, by what they read in books, by what they hear on the radio, by what they buy at the mall. Most of the fanatics I spent time with were influenced in some way by the American media–and–marketing machine, including the Barbie collectors, Grobanites, boardgamers, furries, TIE Fighter pilots, Lego users, and Mayberry fans. Even the storm chasers were able to chase storms thanks, in part, to the demand generated by the movie *Twister*. Is this good or bad? I don't know that it matters.

Passionate fanatics also seem to share a universal human struggle and that is balancing the need for individuality with the pressure to conform; the need to be unique with the need to be belong. The people I met with were proud of their passions, proud that those passions weren't shared by everyone in human society, proud that dressing up like Otis the Drunk or fishing on a frozen lake wasn't something "most" people do. But still they seemed driven to do these things within a supportive community wherein they *were* accepted. No wonder these subcultures are growing so rapidly; they are one of the few places in American society where people are allowed to be comfortably different.

Perhaps the most delightful characteristic shared by the fanatics I met was their ability to tap into their unbridled, enthusiastic, inner ten-year-old selves. Yes, ten. That's the age when we're allowed to be fully absorbed in something totally meaningless. The age before we care what others think. The age when it's still okay to be silly, dress up, laugh at dumb cartoons, build stuff we think is cool, collect stuff we find fascinating, and play outside until it's dark and cold and still whine about having to come in so early. It's the age before the twin social pressures of restraint and conformity take over and squeeze the silliness out of us.

And it's the age I most needed to reclaim.

• • •

Cecil returns and hands me a cold can of Coke. It's now five o'clock and he's moved from jingling his keys to chewing his cuticles. Vinny Musto, the Great Musto's son, maintains a loft of pigeons on top of the apartment building next to us, and he's been monitoring the race on his cell phone. He whistles to Cecil.

Cecil walks to the edge of the roof. "Yeah! What is it?"

Vinny tells him three birds have clocked in on Staten Island. One at 4:40. One at 4:41. One at 4:45.

Cecil faces me and becomes visibly deflated by the news. "It's never our day in the Bronx. Never. The winds were supposed to be good. Phhht. Now, we're fighting for the thousand-dollar prize. Now, we're just hoping to get the birds home. It's over for the Bronx guys now."

I want to reassure him, but being a rank beginner, I'm not sure I'd have much effect.

"Of course, just cause they say they clocked at 4:41, that don't mean it's true. You never believe what you hear." He pauses. "Phhht. All the suspense is out of it now, now that you know you can't win."

Cecil and I sit quietly, and though I don't admit this to him, I selfishly think how disappointed I'll be if I don't see a pigeon come home.

Vinny calls back down from the roof with more news. Castellano's got 'em. Schaefer's got 'em. Jerome's got 'em.

Cecil shakes is head. "The race is over now," he says. "It was over fifteen minutes ago and I got nothin'."

I start to worry that Cecil will go into the clubhouse instead of waiting for his own birds. Technically, he doesn't have to be present because the birds are electronically timed. But after traveling all this way, I don't think I could accept not being able to see a pigeon land. Even though I've seen thousands of pigeons land thousands of times before, in parks and plazas and on the crumbling brick ledges of old churches, this is different. These birds knew exactly where they were going when they left this morning, and there's something about that I find impressive.

But Cecil's still shaking his head. "Once you know a guy's clocked and you haven't clocked… naaa. Phhht. That just takes all the wind outta me."

A gray and white pigeon lands in the tree above us. Cecil looks up and does a quick double-take. Immediately, he's on his feet.

"That one's mine!" he says. "That one's mine! They always land in this tree or that roof first! There's cats around here and the birds want to make sure it's safe."

Cecil throws back his head and starts whistling to the bird.

Thirty seconds later, the pigeon lifts off the branch, spreads its wings, and floats down to the small wooden entrance to the coop. An electric thrill zaps through me. He really *does* know where home is. The bird stops at the entrance, bobs his little pigeon head, and struts inside.

Instantly, Cecil is a changed man. "I feel much better!" he says. "We're definitely in the money now."

Although he won't know exactly how much money until all the times come in, he feels certain his bird has landed in at least the one-thousand-dollar category. Cecil walks over to the timer underneath the coop. The bird clocked in at exactly 17:26:06. It's pigeon number ten on his list. "I better go inside and get him some food and water."

Cecil returns carrying Number 10 in his hands. The bird has a gray head and a neck that sparkles with green and lavender iridescence. I ask him about the bird, and he tells me it is a son of Louis, who was his most winning pigeon. He's been breeding the bird for years to take advantage of his good genetics.

Recalling that Cecil said birds don't get named until they win a race, I ask him what he will name this pigeon. He looks down at the bird.

"Hmmm, he's a Son of Louis. Let's see… S-O-L. That's what I'll call him! Sol! Hello Sol." Cecil nuzzles the pigeon's head. "You know my friends who don't race birds think I'm strange for doing this. I tell them if I had the money, I'd be racing horses instead, 'cause nobody thinks that is strange." Cecil thinks about this for a moment and starts chuckling. "And you know what I'd name my first horse? I'd name it *I Got the Money Now!*"

He takes a deep breath and turns back toward the coop. "Well, I better call the wife and let her know I got a bird and earned our money back."

Cecil leaves and I'm alone on the roof once again, amazed to discover how content I am. It's as if my own bird has flown home. I gaze upward at the sky where planes continue to slowly descend on La Guardia, followed by flocks of Canadian geese headed in the same direction. South for the winter. Like the Monarch butterflies, like the homing pigeons, the geese are driven to travel based on some primal need to be where they belong. Instinct tells them where to go and when, and they happily follow those limbic urges without extensive planning or therapy or worry about what neighbors might think. They don't weigh their options or decide, what-the-heck, to stay in Maine for the winter. They just go. They just *are*.

I could learn a thing or two from geese.

Still staring upward, I notice a pigeon has landed on the point of the roof across the alley. The roof is one of those places Cecil says his birds often land before swooping into the coop. Ten seconds later, the bird takes off and lands on the tree above me. Uh—oh. I stand and start whistling to encourage the bird to come down. I start clicking my tongue. I start waving my arms above my head. In the back of my mind, I see myself as I am: a crazy middle-aged woman on a roof talking to a pigeon. But I don't care. I don't feel crazy. I feel determined. Come on, little guy. Come *on*.

But the bird is not budging. Perhaps he's afraid of me. Perhaps he thinks I'm a giant calico or something. So I change tactics. I sit down. I shrink into myself. But I continue to whistle and click because I don't want Cecil to be disappointed in me.

Four minutes pass.

Four long minutes.

Horns honk. Sirens blare. The Bronx goes about its business without any sense of the drama unfolding above me.

And then finally, slowly, the bird pushes off the branch, arcs downward, lands on the edge of the coop, and strides inside.

I want to break out cheering. Since I'm alone on the roof, this feels like my victory. Like I did this. Sure, Cecil *helped*. But where was he during the vital clicking, whistling, come—on—baby phase? I feel the same way I did when I caught a fish during the ice—fishing tournament. Cocky. Self-assured. Triumphant.

Cecil returns, and I deliver the news like a child presenting a straight-A report card. "Another pigeon came home!"

He checks the time clock, determines which pigeon it is, and begins to tell me about the bird's pedigree. Which is interesting, but not what I care about. What I care about is what Cecil is going to name this bird. I feel it's my responsibility to make sure the little guy or gal goes forth in life with more than a number.

"So what'll it be?"

"I'm not sure," Cecil says. "Let me get the bird."

He returns holding a pigeon that looks an awful lot like the first one that came in.

"*Well?*" I ask impatiently.

Cecil looks at the pigeon. Then at me. Then back at the bird again. He bites his lower lip. Finally, he speaks. "I know what the name will be!" He swivels and points his index finger at my sternum. "From now on this pigeon will be known as... *Shari.*"

I blink several times in disbelief. I feel humbled and elated and goofy all at once. *"Shari?"* I ask, brows tilted upward.

"Yep. Miss Shari."

I grin stupidly at the bird. Some people have comets named after them, or airports, or scientific theories. In our culture, the naming of something after someone is a privilege, a show of respect and admiration and immortality. Because I'll never be the kind of person who has a comet or airport or theory named after her, I'm delighted to accept the honor.

Cecil hands me the pigeon, shows me how to hold it, and grabs my camera for a photo.

As he adjusts the camera, I look at the bird and suspect she holds a lesson for me. A lesson to follow my own instinctual drive for happiness. A lesson to not let self-consciousnesses or social constraint hold me back from my own magnetic true north. A lesson to act ten and run around flapping my wings every once in a while.

Cecil looks up and tells Shari and me to smile. He doesn't have to. I'm already smiling so hard it feels like my cheeks will pop off.

The pigeon has landed, and me along with it.

• • •

I'll be flying home myself tomorrow driven by my own instinctual need to be where I belong, with the people I love, following my own lily-pad jumps from one interest to another.

Looking forward, I'm not likely to take up photography again, or Tarot cards or running or belly dancing or tennis. I've already done those things, and there are so many more lives to be explored for me to limit myself to just one. Maybe I'll collect rocks. Maybe I'll strike it rich and gather diamonds. Maybe, probably, I'll go with Angela on an Arctic dog–sledding tour. Anything is possible. And that's the beauty of it. For even though I won't be flying home with a single fanatical passion tucked inside my suitcase, I'll be packing something far more important. Something I didn't have when I started this journey. Something that passionate fanatics have had to teach me, by example, over and over again.

You see, in the process of learning and understanding who these crazy misunderstood fanatics were, I also came to learn and understand who I was. More important, I liked what I saw.

In short, three years ago I headed out seeking passion.

But what I found was self-acceptance.

Where Are You People?

"The less things change, the more they remain the same."
—Sicilian proverb

EVERYBODY HAS AT LEAST ONE FANATIC IN THEIR LIFE. THE uncle who loves Bruce Springsteen. The neighbor with hundreds of trolls in her yard. The co-worker who collects Coors beer cans and is still mystified by his divorce. Thanks to this project, I'm now happy to have many passionate fanatics in my life. As this book was going to press, I called several of them for an update on their lives.

Judy Stegner, the Barbie collector whose son was murdered, recently got married and moved into a new three-bedroom house in Irving, Texas, where her husband graciously allowed her to convert the 11 x 17-foot living room into her Barbie display area. "In spite of everything that's happened to us," she said, "we're incredibly blessed in our lives."

• • •

Ice fisherman Jeff Oliver still lives in the Rocky Mountains without a computer, cell phone, garbage disposal, oven, or his wife. He also continues to fish almost daily. The morning I spoke with him he'd just come off an unprecedented 10-day streak without fishing. "The lake had frozen over too much to get a line in, but not enough to drill a hole through," he said. "Man, I was practically shaking from withdrawal."

• • •

Mayberry's Lady in Red, Pat Bullins, went on to grab her fifth straight victory in the Mayberry Days Trivia Contest, but lost her crown by coming in second last year. "I don't know what happened, honey. It was weird. It was awful. I didn't cry 'cause you can't let something like that get you down. You have to go forward."

I asked if she was planning to compete next year.

"Oh, honey, are you outta your *gourd*? You know better'n that. Winners don't quit and quitters don't win. I'm still watching *The Andy Griffith Show* almost every day. Yeah. I'll be back."

• • •

Kenneth Junkin/Otis the Drunk also remains immersed in the Mayberry community. Since we were at Mayberry Days together, he's met Andy Griffith ("I don't know if I really *met* him 'cause I only said 'How ya doin'?' But if that's meeting someone, I guess I did. I wasn't dressed as Otis, though. I was in my civvies."). He also continues to manage the Mayberry Squad Car Nationals and is planning the first-ever Mayberry Cruise. As far as the Trivia Contest, he, too, is at work preparing for next year's battle. "You bet I am," he said. "It's a year-long thing to come up with good questions."

• • •

Grobanite Linda Story Omalia has been keeping busy with her family in the long quiet months since the last Josh Groban tour ended. What are the other Grobanites doing while Josh is on sabbatical? "They're bored, and because they're bored, they're fighting on the forum," she said. "They got into this huge fight about how Josh's hair looked in a photo of him with his girlfriend. It got so bad, Josh's managers went to him and said, 'You gotta do something! They're fightin' about your hair!'"

"Did he?" I asked.

"Yeah, he made a special appearance at a Grobanite Meet 'n' Greet and told the Grobanites they really should work to be nicer to one another."

· · ·

Furry Sylys Sable, aka Mark Merlino—he of the many-splendored partnership—admitted that he'd finally come across something in the furry community that surprised even him. "I went to Oklacon, a furry convention in Oklahoma, and couldn't believe how many good ole boys had gotten into furry fandom. It was like, 'Hi. I'm Clem. This is my truck. This is my dog. I'm a furry.' It was *weird*."

· · ·

Record collector Bill Schurk continues to slowly go through his record collection in an attempt to downsize it to a more manageable level. But, he confessed, "the culling hasn't made that much of an impact."

· · ·

Storm chaser Roger Hill has begun offering organized hurricane-chasing tours. His first big hurricane was Katrina, which he witnessed from inside a parking garage in Slidell, Louisiana. I asked what the experience was like.

"Uh… intense," he said.

But although Roger is deeply impressed by the savage fury of hurricanes, tornados—and the intellectual challenge involved in finding them—remain his first love.

· · ·

Finally, when I called pigeon racer Cecil Coston, he gave me an update of a much more personal nature.

"Remember Shari?" he asked. Of course. How could I forget my namesake pigeon? "Well," he said, "it turns out that Miss Shari is a *Mister* Shari."

Sadly, I neglected to get the details of how he could tell the difference.

Acknowledgments

A BOOK ABOUT PASSIONATE FANATICS WOULD NOT BE possible without the full cooperation and ardent support of, well, passionate fanatics. Hearty thanks go out to everyone in this book who helped me understand their world a little better, especially Judy Stegner, Jeff Oliver (I may still take you up on that summer fishing trip), Kenneth Junkin, Pat Bullins, Linda Story Omalia, Denise Hampton, Robert Spencer, Felix Greco, (whose Lego sculpture, *Emerge*, sits on my desk and reminds me daily what life is all about), Mark Merlino, Ben Frame, Brenda DiAntonis, Dan Shoemaker, Anne Gordon (especially Anne Gordon), Bill Schurk, Roger Hill, Rob Darby and Cecil Coston. In sharing their passions with me, these people were sharing the best parts of themselves—and helping me get in touch with mine—which are gifts I'll always treasure.

For being there at the conception of this idea, for sharing my passion in fanatical subcultures, for trying to Grobanize me and failing, and for providing the crucial last-minute manuscript review, a million hosannas to my forever friend, Allan Halcrow.

I would also like to thank my extraordinary Goucher tag team for helping this book come to fruition through close reading and wise input. The team includes Philip Gerard, Leslie Rubinkowski, Thomas French, Suzannah Lessard, and the Master Gopher who orchestrates it all, Patsy Sims. Robert Root also deserves an honorable mention for keeping me on track with the Introduction.

Two people, perhaps more than any other, are responsible for making this book more than just a groovy idea: Kristen Auclair, my diligent agent (and humble Christmas tree farmer); and Jeff Nordstedt from Barricade Books, whose tail-wagging enthusiasm for crazy American enthusiasts matched—and perhaps exceeded—my own.

I am also indebted to my Bounce Group—Pamela Kramer, Pete Lewis, Olivia Mayer and Doug McPherson—for allowing me to tell stories about my journey before they hit the page (and in the process, helped me to learn what the journey was all about); and to my Lighthouse students for reminding me each week what a privilege it is to tell real-life stories.

Finally, most importantly, my deepest lasting gratitude goes to the incomparable Angela Ekker for her unwavering support and constant encouragement, and for enduring many long weekends alone as I went galloping around the country. Thanks for celebrating every step of this journey with me, usually with a glass of good champagne. This book wouldn't have happened without you.